Two Kings of Uganda; or, life by the shores of Victoria Nyanza, etc.

Robert Ashe

The BiblioLife Network

This project was made possible in part by the BiblioLife Network (BLN), a project aimed at addressing some of the huge challenges facing book preservationists around the world. The BLN includes libraries, library networks, archives, subject matter experts, online communities and library service providers. We believe every book ever published should be available as a high-quality print reproduction; printed on- demand anywhere in the world. This insures the ongoing accessibility of the content and helps generate sustainable revenue for the libraries and organizations that work to preserve these important materials.

The following book is in the "public domain" and represents an authentic reproduction of the text as printed by the original publisher. While we have attempted to accurately maintain the integrity of the original work, there are sometimes problems with the original book or micro-film from which the books were digitized. This can result in minor errors in reproduction. Possible imperfections include missing and blurred pages, poor pictures, markings and other reproduction issues beyond our control. Because this work is culturally important, we have made it available as part of our commitment to protecting, preserving, and promoting the world's literature.

GUIDE TO FOLD-OUTS, MAPS and OVERSIZED IMAGES

In an online database, page images do not need to conform to the size restrictions found in a printed book. When converting these images back into a printed bound book, the page sizes are standardized in ways that maintain the detail of the original. For large images, such as fold-out maps, the original page image is split into two or more pages.

Guidelines used to determine the split of oversize pages:

• Some images are split vertically; large images require vertical and horizontal splits.
• For horizontal splits, the content is split left to right.
• For vertical splits, the content is split from top to bottom.
• For both vertical and horizontal splits, the image is processed from top left to bottom right.

TWO KINGS OF UGANDA.

See p. 11.

CAMP IN UGOGO.

Frontispiece.

TWO KINGS OF UGANDA

OR,

LIFE BY THE SHORES OF VICTORIA NYANZA.

BEING AN ACCOUNT OF A RESIDENCE OF SIX YEARS IN
EASTERN EQUATORIAL AFRICA.

BY

ROBERT P. ASHE, M.A., F.R.G.S.

WITH MAP AND ILLUSTRATIONS.

LONDON:

SAMPSON LOW, MARSTON, SEARLE, & RIVINGTON
LIMITED,
St. Dunstan's House,
FETTER LANE, FLEET STREET, E.C.
1889.

LONDON :

PRINTED BY WILLIAM CLOWES AND SONS, LIMITED,

STAMFORD STREET AND CHARING CROSS.

To

MY FATHER,
GEORGE ALEXANDER HAMILTON ASHE.

PREFACE.

THE events of the last few years in Eastern Equatorial Africa have aroused so much interest in all quarters that a book which attempts to describe them at first hand ought not to need any apology, except on the score of the writer's deficiencies; and of these I am only too conscious. I should be sorry to deprecate criticism, but it is only fair to say that the following pages have of necessity been hastily written, amid many interruptions, and while engaged in other work. Indeed, they could hardly have been prepared for the press without the kind help and encouragement I have received on all sides.

I must first acknowledge the kindness of my old college friend, Mr. J. Spencer Hill, of the Clarendon Press, who has given me the greatest assistance in reading both the MS. and the proof sheets, and has always been ready with valuable suggestions, of which I have largely availed myself. For the three excellent illustrations of African scenery, I have to thank the skill of Dr. B. Woodd Walker, who drew and re-drew them from my description, until I felt that the impression which I myself had carried away would be conveyed to the reader. I am indebted to the courtesy of Mr. Eugene Stock, editorial secretary of the Church Missionary Society, for so willingly placing at my disposal the publications of the Society; and I must acknowledge my obligations to Mr. Mackay and the Rev. R. H. Walker for the free use I have made of their correspondence. Mrs. Hannington has kindly allowed me to reproduce a part of the Bishop's last diary; and the Hon. Roden Noel has permitted me to insert his lines on " Samweli " from ' A Modern Faust.' I must also thank other friends for their willing help in transcribing a portion of the MS. for the printers. Lastly but not least I must acknowledge the kindness and courtesy I have received from Mr. Marston while the work has been in progress.

In conclusion, it may be well to explain some of the native names which constantly occur. In the title I have allowed the familiar word " Uganda " to remain, though the correct form is " Buganda," which becomes " *Uganda* " at the coast, owing to the phonetic interchange of " B " and " U." The root word is " -ganda; " *Bu*ganda is the country itself, " *Mu*ganda " a native of the country, " *Ba*ganda " the plural of

" *Mu*ganda," and " *Lu*ganda" is the language. The same remarks apply to the interchange of "B" and "W" so often met with—*e.g.* the "Wahuma," as Speke names them, call themselves "Bahuma;" and I have followed their own pronunciation, although the Baganda call them "Bayima."

R. P. ASHE.

May, 1889.

CONTENTS.

———◆———

CHAPTER	PAGE
I.—En Route to Mamboya .	3
II.—Through Ugogo to Uyui	12
III.—Uyui to the Nyanza .	21
IV.—Visit to Roma at Bzinja	29
V.—Musalala to Buganda .	37
VI.—King Mutesa	47
VII.—Interviews with Mutesa	58
VIII.—Mutesa's Death .	71
IX.—The Political Condition of Buganda .	84
X.—Accession of Mwanga	100
XI.—Causes of Suspicion	112
XII.—Lugalama .	122
XIII.—Death of Lugalama	136
XIV.—Interviews with Mwanga	148
XV.—News of Hannington	163
XVI.—Death of Hannington	181
XVII.—Baganda Converts	196
XVIII.—Baganda Converts and Martyrs	215
XIX.—Farewell to Buganda	232
XX.—First Journey Home	244
XXI.—Second Journey to the Nyanza	251
XXII.—Second Journey to the Coast	274
XXIII.—Manners and Customs of the Baganda	285
XXIV.—The Bahuma, Wahuma or Bayima	332
Appendix	343

LIST OF ILLUSTRATIONS.

———

CAMP IN UGOGO . . . . *Dr. B. W. Walker* . . . *Frontispiece*

MULESHI'S FERRY . . . . *Dr. B. W. Walker* . . *To face page* 35
　　　　(*From a Sketch by Rev. R. H. Walker.*)

SCENE OF LUGALAMA'S DEATH *Dr. B. W. Walker* . . . „ 　„ 206

NAKAYIMA . . . . „ 　„ 289

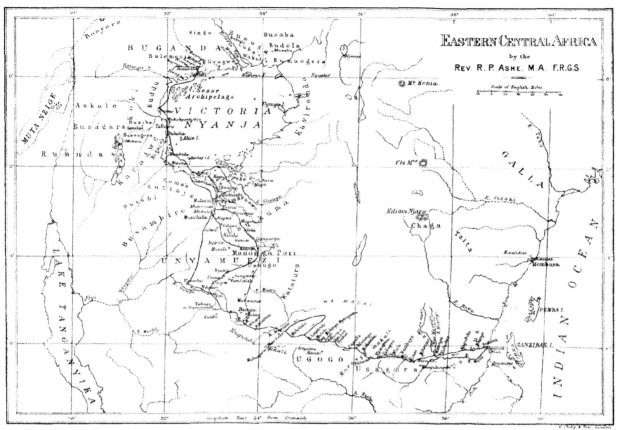

EASTERN CENTRAL AFRICA
by the
REV. R. P. ASHE. M.A. F.R.G.S.

Scale of English Miles

London, Sampson Low & Co, Limited.

TWO KINGS OF UGANDA.

PROLOGUE.

TWICE within the last six years it has been my lot to make my way to the shores of the Victoria Nyanza, and for a little while to turn over the pages of the book of African life as it is revealed in those regions where I sojourned, and through which I passed.

As I begin my narrative, the same feeling is uppermost in my mind as that expressed by the traveller Burton, in his book on Zanzibar, where he speaks of the sadness and solemnity of sitting down to write the story of past years.

How darkly for me the record is stained with blood —blood of the boys put to death in Uganda; of the murdered bishop who perished on the shores of the Nyanza; of the martyred natives who so nobly died and of yet another companion, killed at Mkange, a place within sight of the coast through which my fellow-travellers and myself had passed unscathed before him, only a few weeks since, on our way to Zanzibar.

But though death has been so busy among these pioneers of Christianity and civilisation, all who have fallen have bravely done their part, and have contributed much to the great work of opening up one of the finest portions of the globe to European influence and enterprise.

I hope in the following pages to show that Africans possess the seeds of solid character, which, when developed, will enable them to overcome the destructive elements in Western civilisation. If this be so, there is no reason to despair of the future of the dark races of Africa, nor to believe that the lives which have been laid down on their behalf have been sacrificed in vain.

CHAPTER I.

EN ROUTE TO MAMBOYA.

IN May of the year 1882, a party of missionaries was on its way to various stations in the interior of East Africa, by way of Zanzibar. The journey down from Aden as a first-class passenger in the SS. *Mecca* was one of the most trying and disagreeable experiences of travel which I have ever undergone. I have dragged myself wearily over plains in Ugogo, and through the forests of Unyamwezi; I have been tossing for days on the Nyanza in native-sewn canoes; I have even been a passenger on a slave dhow upon the great lake; and I have more than once made the journey in an Arab dhow between Zanzibar and the mainland. But for thorough misery and complete discomfort, that long twelve days' struggle against the monsoon in the *Mecca* surpasses them all. As one of our passengers remarked with grim humour, we were of the number of those who say in the morning, "Would God it were even," and at even, "Would God it were morning." Overhead eternal blue sky—all around us eternal blue sea. Flying-fish were so numerous, and appeared so constantly, as to make the sight of them quite intolerable. The monotony was broken once or twice by a glimpse of Africa—now Guardafui, standing out bold and

B 2

terrible in the burning sun, making one realise vividly the idea of

> "Wild heat—raging to torture the desert."

Again, in the distance, the vague outline of the coast at Lamu, and further to the south, Mombasa.

At length the island of Pemba came into view, and we beheld with delight the glorious greenery of its tropical vegetation and forgot in a moment the discomforts of the voyage. Shortly afterwards we were within sight of Zanzibar, where we saw in the distance the white and dazzling buildings of the mart and capital of East Africa. A few more hours and we were lying at anchor opposite the Sultan's palace.

Zanzibar, or Unguja, as the natives call it, has been so often and so admirably described that I need not enter into any details. Had any of our party, however, possessed the poet Coleridge's faculty for counting abominable odours, he might have spent a considerable part of his time daily in doing so without exhausting the number. In this particular Cologne would be left far behind.

The streets of the city are narrow and tortuous, and in the wet season are simply watercourses. A walk through Zanzibar in a shower of rain is quite an adventure; overhead water is pouring off the flat roofs in cataracts, while underfoot is a swiftly-flowing torrent ankle deep. In fine weather, however, the whole town is alive with bustle and business, and bright with the variegated costumes of many nations. Shops there are of all kinds and descriptions, kept by all manner of people. Fair-faced languid-looking Indian women sit and display their wares, waiting patiently for customers, as also men of the same nation, who, to judge by their appearance, have evidently grown fat upon their gains; their commodities include cotton-stuffs, spices, gold and silver thread, lamps, attar of roses, onions, and other miscellaneous articles of frequent barter. Fruit-shops too abound, kept by vivacious negroes; there are also not a few almost European establishments owned by Goanese, where anything in reason may be purchased, from a dress-suit to a packet of pins. Arabs are stalking along with an air of superb contempt—the Arab has certainly mastered the art of looking as if the place belongs to him. Here comes one of them riding a gaily-caparisoned donkey, his slaves running in front calling out, " simila, simila," " by your leave." Now we meet a big black man carrying two enormous bunches of bananas slung over his shoulder at each end of a stick, he also cries out " simila." At another place a bevy of women and girls, every one of them slaves, are at work carrying mortar and stones for the masons who are building a neighbouring house, all the while chanting some monotonous but not unmusical African melody. Further on a number of men chained together are at work. They are the Sultan's chain-gang undergoing penal servitude for offences against his Highness, or at the instance of some one of the European consuls. One day I encountered the Sultan's soldiers in a narrow

street; to my surprise they politely broke their ranks to
let me pass. The army is, on the whole, well-drilled,
and, could the men be depended upon to obey a
European, they would be formidable antagonists to any
opposing native force on the mainland.

It had been arranged that we should take up our
quarters at the French hotel. I was invited, however,
to be the guest of the Universities Mission at Mbweni,
a beautiful place some four miles out of the town, where
there is a large and flourishing training establishment for
freed slave-girls. There were many wonderful things
at Mbweni, including among others a steam-roller; but
what struck me most was a novel kind of razor in use
among the girls, which consisted of a piece of broken
glass with a chisel-shaped edge. I have never seen
this substitute for a razor anywhere, although shaving
the head is a universal custom among Africans.

After nine days of preparation, we found ourselves
on board an Arab dhow bound for the mainland, with a
fair breeze behind us. The dhow was a dirty and
dingy craft, some forty feet long by nine feet beam.
She had no deck, and so we were obliged to perch
ourselves unhappily here and there on the top of boxes.
When we neared Sadaani the tide was out and our
vessel stuck fast some quarter of a mile from the beach,
bumping heavily on the bottom as every wave rolled
under her. This must have been most damaging to
the dhow, it certainly was exceedingly unpleasant for
her passengers. We were not, however, long left in

this situation. A miserable dug-out canoe half-filled with water came alongside to take us ashore. And so at last, as the sun was going down, our little company stood safe and sound on African soil.

It is needless to dwell much upon the details of our outfit, but I may mention some of the mistakes which were made : we were provided with Epsom salts by the stone, but found ourselves short of common table salt. Our large supply of castor oil was but a poor compensation for the entire absence of such a necessary as butter, and for my part I would gladly have exchanged our elaborate distilling apparatus for another common tea-kettle. The ordinary equipment of an African traveller consists of tents, camp-beds, chairs, stools, buckets, pots, pans, cups and saucers, plates, blankets, guns, pistols, boxes of clothes and books, scientific instruments, provisions and medicines. He carries with him also goods for barter, consisting of bales of cloth made up into loads of from sixty to seventy pounds; beads of various kinds, copper, brass and iron wire, gunpowder, and soap, which is a very important article of commerce in the interior.

Our caravan was made up of nearly five hundred porters, or Wapagazi, as they are called—none too many for a large party of seven white men, a greater number of Europeans than is usually seen together in Central Africa. Our leader was Mr. Charles Stokes, who had already made the journey to Uganda; the others were the Revs. James Hannington (the future first Bishop of Eastern Equatorial Africa), Cyril Gordon, Joseph Blackburn, Walter Edmonds, Mr. Wise and myself.

Each of us had engaged one or more Zanzibar or Freretown mission boys as personal servants. My boy, Tom Tofiki, was quite above the average, and possessed, at any rate, the great virtue of honesty ; he was somewhat sluggish and by no means a good walker or worker —in fact he either would not or could not do anything very well except sing hymns, and that he did excellently. He never learnt to cook anything except "ugali," a thick coarse kind of porridge, and he used every morning to concoct a peculiar compound which he called coffee, but which rather exercised one's faith when it appeared at breakfast.

Our other porters were distributed in three camps : the Wangwana or Zanzibaris, who were all nominally Mahometans ; the Wanyamwezi, whose country stretches from the other side of Ugogo to the Nyanza, and the Wasukuma, or people of the north, who live on the shores of the lake. The Wangwana individually often display many fine and admirable qualities, though in large numbers they generally give infinite trouble. My experience with them on the whole has been fortunate, and I rarely found them insubordinate without some apparent reason for their disobedience. The Wanyamwezi belong to a sturdy and enterprising race ; they come in great numbers to the coast, conducting their own caravans. I have often seen four or five hundred of these people travelling entirely on their own account, bringing the ivory belonging to their principal chiefs to the coast for sale. It is curious that the Wagogo, whose country lies between the Wanyamwezi and the sea, rarely or never venture to Zanzibar themselves, but are content to make the Wanyamwezi pay toll for passing through their territory, both going and returning. The Wasu-kuma, or Northerners (which the name implies), who live on the south and south-east shore of the Nyanza, are in many respects similar to the Wanyamwezi, but are even less civilised. In their own country the men, at any rate, entirely dispense with clothing; but at the coast they give way somewhat to the prejudices of civilisation. All the porters, whether from Zanzibar or from the interior, are divided into small companies under head men, at the coast called "Wazee," or elders, by the Wanyamwezi, "Wanamhara" or "Wanyampara," which has the same meaning. It is an almost universal custom for people from the interior to take a new name when they reach Zanzibar. Mahometan names are often chosen, such as Hamisi, Omali, Tofiki, and the like.

After a couple of days at Sadaani we began our long march into the interior. Of this town I need say little: it is a mongrel and miserable place, partly Arabian, partly Indian, and wholly African. We were courteously received by Bwana Heri, its governor, who finds it to his interest to keep on good terms with Europeans. Soon after leaving the town we entered

on a beaten track or footpath some eighteen inches
or two feet wide.   Footpaths of this kind wind on
from village to village, and connect tribe with tribe,
so that the traveller finds the way clearly marked and
well defined throughout the whole of this wide region.

The first few marches were not examples of successful
African travelling; frequently we were up and off without anything to eat; often we had to wait for hours after
reaching our camp until our tents came up, and before
the cooks could prepare any kind of a dinner another
couple of hours had usually passed away.   On one
occasion we were twenty-four hours without a meal—a
specimen of the blunders which inexperienced travellers
make, and sometimes with fatal results, of which the
African climate is made to bear the blame, rather than
the travellers' carelessness.   Nor did matters seem
to improve as we advanced, the fact being that there
were far too many of us for comfortable travelling.
While making the first stage of our journey through
Useguha, we were fairly well supplied with native food
—unripe bananas boiled and mashed, beans, sweet
potatoes, rice, and the invariable fowls and goats.   One
day, while enjoying this fare in our dining-tent, we saw
to our consternation that the grass to leeward* of us had
been set alight by the natives, and soon a glorious line
of fire came sweeping up towards where we were

---

* I believe it to be a fact, that except in case of a very high
wind, an African prairie fire will come up against the breeze rather
than with it as might be expected.

encamped. Immediately our men rushed out pell-mell to meet it, armed with boughs and sticks, and after an exciting contest succeeded in beating it down. Soon afterwards, while we were finishing our dinner, we saw all the men rushing madly off in the direction of the villages, yelling and brandishing their spears and other weapons, intent on taking revenge upon the natives, who had twice this day fired the grass in the neighbourhood of our camp. Stokes dashed after them, calling out as he passed, "Gentlemen, my men are off, and I cannot stop them; you may write that in your books." Alas, how often has the African traveller to write in his journal that his men have bolted; he is only fortunate if they do not take some of his valuables with them. I think our porters reckoned on the support both moral and physical of the white men; but when they saw that we were determined to prevent their attacking the natives, they obeyed their head men and came quietly back, and so ended what to us had been a very exciting day. We travelled on slowly, passing by the hills of Enguru to the beautiful mountain region of Mamboya, which is the first English mission station on this route. It is situated on the side of a lofty hill, which rises far above it; and, standing on the verandah of the house, we looked sheer down into a circular valley enclosed by a glorious panorama of mountains, which tower one above another, and stretch away mountain beyond mountain until they lose themselves in the blue distance.

CHAPTER II.

THROUGH UGOGO TO UYUI.

RELUCTANTLY we left Mamboya and turned our faces westward once more; the road here winds along the rocky mountains which stretch for fifty miles up to Mpwapwa or Mhamva, on the borders of the Malenga Makali, the "wilderness of bitter waters." This road is proverbially dangerous, being infested by the Ruga-ruga, or fighting men of the Wahehe tribe. The danger is no imaginary one, as I know by experience, for in the year 1886 I sent one of my men this way with a message, when he was badly wounded, and a Munyamwezi man who was with him was shot dead. The last time that I passed through the same district I myself saw the naked body of a poor lad, doubtless some straggler from a passing caravan, lying dead at the side of the path, pierced by many spear wounds. It is not surprising, therefore, that our party should encounter these notable Ruga-ruga. About a dozen of them showed themselves to our advanced guard; but when they saw white men armed with guns, they made a precipitate retreat, their flight accelerated by a volley from the guns of the Europeans. I was behind at the time and did not share in this victory. One of our party, however, very nearly lost his life, for during the encounter, his neighbour's gun went off by accident and shot the sight off the rifle which he was holding, but fortunately did no further damage.

The Malenga Makali, or Wilderness of Chunyo, is so called from the strong saline water found at both sides of it, which is especially strong in Ugogo. We made our camp at the entrance of this waterless tract; but before undertaking the next stage of our journey, we visited the beautiful mission station of Kisokwe. There we stayed till late, talking with our hospitable hosts, Mr. and Mrs. Cole, for we knew that we should be able to make our way to our camp by moonlight. At midnight, when we reached the wind-swept plain in which our tents had been pitched, we found that they had been blown down. We shouted in vain for our boys. At last we began pulling the tent about, intending to set it up ourselves. A deep and sleepy groan issued from the tangled heap of canvas and ropes, and out crept our boys Tom and Robert, the youths whose duty it was to have had the tent ready for our reception. This little incident is an admirable illustration of African character. Sooner than take the very small amount of trouble involved in tightening the ropes and hammering in the pegs, they preferred to let the tent collapse entirely. The expression "Haithuru," the Irishman's "Och, it'll do," is the formula with which both Celt and Swahili leave undone, with an untroubled conscience, any necessary but distasteful duty.

The next afternoon we entered the wilderness and

kept on until nightfall, when we waited an hour or two for the appearing of the moon, by the light of which we intended to continue our journey. In a few minutes the prairie, which but an hour before had been loneliness itself, the silence only broken by the incessant chirping of the grass crickets, or the call of some night-bird, or the weird, dismal howling of the hyænas, was suddenly blazing with a hundred fires, and loud with the crackling of dry fuel, and the laughter and ceaseless chatter of our five hundred porters. A few hours later solitude again resumed her reign, and the scene relapsed into the silence from which it had been so strangely awakened. Wearied with our long night march, we were glad indeed as the dawn broke to find ourselves entering upon Ugogo.

Ugogo is a succession of great bare plains, enclosed by hills, rising abruptly from the level of the plain, which is studded here and there with the enormous baobab or "embuyu" trees, and at frequent intervals the small villages or "tembes" of the people. These are long, narrow, low, mud-roofed buildings forming an enclosed square, into the centre of which the cattle are driven at night. A "tembe" may contain from two to twenty families, according to its size. The architecture of Ugogo is the poorest attempt at house-building I have ever met with, except the grass huts of the handsome Watusi or Wahuma herdsmen.

The Wagogo, like the Masai have large herds of cattle, but they cultivate the ground extensively, while the latter do not. I imagine that they are very closely allied to the Masai tribe; for their weapons are much the same, and it is a moot point whether the Masai supply the Wagogo with the great broad-bladed spears they use, or *vice versâ.* The Wagogo warriors are a wild-looking set with their great spears and painted shields. Their dress consists of a bib of leather, not reaching quite to the waist; a small square of leather hangs behind, and serves as a mat to sit upon; a thong of hide round the waist, falling down at one side or behind, giving them the appearance of possessing a tail. They twist string of their own manufacture into their short woolly hair, and the ends hang down to their shoulders like long plaited hair. Both men and women frightfully distend the lobes of their ears, and the women insert a piece of wood which looks like a large-sized "draughtsman." The pear-shaped end of a bottle-gourd is also a usual ornament for the ears of both sexes, as well as other miscellaneous articles; I have seen, for instance, a husk of Indian corn, a snuff-box, the handle of a teacup, an empty cartridge-case, and a bishop belonging to a set of chessmen, fulfilling this duty of ear-distender. Our party was a source of continual wonder to these unsophisticated people. I recollect one day, when separated from my companions, being found by a group of Wagogo. I was evidently a new sort of man, and the first specimen of the kind which they had ever seen. Their astonishment knew no bounds. One old

man ventured to approach while I stood still for inspection; he cautiously advanced one finger till it touched
my beard, and then timidly withdrew it. The next
thing which attracted his attention was my ear; he
again put out his hand and very gently took hold of
it, feeling it to see what it was made of, but I had
no time to spare them for more minute examination.

Water was always a difficulty in Ugogo, and at one
camp it was so bad as to be, I should think, poisonous;
it did not lose its horrible stench even when made into
strong coffee. It was here that one of our companions,
Hannington, became so ill that we almost despaired of
his life. In fact he sent for us to say farewell. We
revived him, however, with stimulants, and in a day or
two more he was able to be carried forward.

We passed out of Ugogo into the great wilderness
called the " Mugunda Mukali," which separates Ugogo
and Unyamwezi. This Mugunda Mukali, "or terrible
garden," takes at least six days to pass through, and food
has to be carried to last during that time. Our porters
bought their meal, and, wrapping it in a piece of calico,
slung it round their waists; this, and the calabash for
water and the cooking-pot which every fifth or sixth man
carried, completed their outfit. The dreaded banditti,
or Ruga-ruga, also infest this wilderness, and it was
while journeying here that a young Englishman named
Penrose lost his life some years before. He had been
sent out by the Church Missionary Society, and was

bringing up a caravan from the coast. A chief named
Nyungu, whose villages lay at some distance from the
caravan route, had recently quarrelled with a French
traveller, the Abbé du Bayx. The Frenchman had a
powerful and well-armed caravan, and the chief was
afraid to attack him; but he vowed vengeance against
the next white man who passed that way, and this
happened to be young Penrose. He was deserted by
his men, who carried off his ammunition in their flight,
and, though he stood his ground, he fell at last
overpowered by numbers. This encounter took place
by the banks of a small lake called Chaya. Some
time afterwards, our leader Stokes passed the place, and
among the skulls which were lying about picked out
one which from its conformation seemed to be that of
a European, and buried it. We emerged from the
Mugunda Mukali with a great firing of guns and
rejoicing on the part of our porters at having come in
safety through the "terrible garden." We spent a day or
two at a place called Itura, and then once more entered
a wilderness, which stretches some sixty miles up to
Uyui, the second stage of our journey. Here, while
making a night march, we came suddenly upon a lion
at his supper. We had left our camp at midnight with
about twenty porters, as there was a glorious moon.
Stokes, with the main body, was to follow the next
day. Hannington and I were behind, and he was
propounding the question "who was the prophetess
Noadiah." However, the sudden crack of a rifle a few

C

hundred yards ahead, followed by a sustained fusillade, rudely dismissed Noadiah from our thoughts, and concluding that it must be an attack of the ubiquitous Ruga-ruga, we rushed to the front, where we found a scene of great confusion. Many of the party were scrambling up a tree, loads were lying about in all directions, some of the men were holding their emptied smoking guns, a fine retriever dog which we had with us was barking furiously; and all this commotion was caused by the royal diner-out, no doubt annoyed at being so unceremoniously disturbed. Hannington in a state of great excitement seized his fowling-piece; Tom handed me my pistol which he was carrying, and Gordon grasping his umbrella, we advanced to the attack. Hannington's guardian angel, in the shape of one of the porters, now rushed forward, imploring him not to imperil his life, and to emphasise his appeal he hung on to his master's coat-tails. Hannington sent his would-be deliverer reeling backwards; but during this little diversion, one of my tent-boys, Robert, rushed past us with a small rifle which he had borrowed from one of our companions, and wildly let fly, as quickly retreating again. The lion now drew off further into the jungle, where we could still hear his angry growling. Then came a struggle in Hannington's mind, between his passion for adventure and more prudential considerations; but I think we all felt that it was hardly worth while to run the risk for no particular purpose of receiving the attack of a wounded lion—we could not hope at the first shot to do more than disable him, since it was too dark to see anything, and besides we were insufficiently armed, and therefore we turned tail and left him master of the field. Our porters, seeing that the attack was abandoned, now descended from their tree, and once more we resumed our journey, but not till late the next day did we reach Uyui.

Here Hannington became so desperately ill, that we decided it was impossible for him to attempt the journey to the Nyanza in his present state. We could not keep our large caravan waiting indefinitely, and so, after remaining twelve days, in hopes some decided improvement might take place, we were obliged to resume our journey without him. This anxious time at Uyui I shall never forget. Until I left, I took it in turns with Gordon to watch by our sick friend. He was lying in a large, bare room without any door, the only furniture being a camp-bed and a few boxes. He was often delirious with fever, and as night drew on his brain would become full of the busy fancies which fever brings. In that dimly-lighted room the shadow of death seemed to be almost visibly hovering. Without, ever and anon, one could hear the dismal howling of the hyenas which were skulking round the house. Within, the sick man kept on uttering what seemed ever uppermost in his mind, the word "Uganda" constantly recurring. Suddenly he called out, "He has come!" "Who has come," I said. "Mackay has

come to meet me, and has brought it." "What has he
brought?" I soothingly asked. "A coffin," he replied,
and turned over in his troubled sleep only to dream
again of something terrible; and so the long night
wore away.

CHAPTER III.

UYUI TO THE NYANZA.

AT Uyui we bade our companions farewell, and, with our number now reduced by one-half, we struck due north along the route which Stanley had taken when he crossed the Continent. Passing by a very friendly chief called Mutinginya, we were stopped at a little village in his neighbourhood, where the people wished to levy " hongo," or the usual blackmail; and on our refusing to pay their demands, they forbade our men to draw water, and stationed an armed guard round the well during the night. Next day our people were determined to go and take the water by force, and it was with no little difficulty we prevented bloodshed. However, our friend Mutinginya, on being appealed to, sent over one of his Wanhamhara, " head men," who settled the matter satisfactorily; and we were allowed to go peaceably on our way.

At one of the villages in the neighbourhood I witnessed for the first time the extraordinary body-dance which prevails among so many African tribes. It consists of a rhythmical contortion of the whole of the body, the shoulders and breast and stomach being twisted and worked about in all directions. The first time you see it, it looks a most disgusting and degrading exhibition; but in time one gets used to the sight. On this occasion it was performed by a number of young girls, who worked themselves up into an extraordinary state of excitement, and looked as if they were under the influence of some magician's spell. They gradually approach a stranger nearer and nearer, advancing slowly till they touch him with their hands. In my case, I broke the charm by giving them some beads, which sent them away quite satisfied, and left me even more pleased at their departure.

We now entered the Manonga "pori," or desert. A long tramp of eighteen miles brought us to the Manonga River, which some of our men told me was "mto mkubwa sana," "a very big river." I saw a fringe of tall trees—the invariable sign of a river—but on reaching the bank and looking down no water was visible. To adapt Hood—

> "I saw instead but the river bed,
> For the faithless stream was dry."

However, by digging about a foot we came to fairly good water. It is a common circumstance with many African rivers in the dry season to sink beneath the sand, though it gives the inexperienced traveller considerable disappointment.

Our next adventure was with the hostile natives of Samwè—the nearest inhabited district—with whom we had a long four-days' palaver, or "shauri," about the payment of hongo. In fact, things came to such a

pass that the natives determined to fight. They brought
out their flag and defiantly planted it outside the
village. The women were ordered inside the stockade,
and soon the great war drum rolled out its summons to
the warriors of neighbouring villages to come to the
attack. Upon this we yielded, and paid their enormous demand of more than a thousand yards of white
cotton cloth; but we said, "We will not go further this
way, but will return straight back by the way we have
come." "You may go where you like," they insolently
replied, "now that you have paid." However, when we
actually did go back—which they did not believe we
should do—they sent messengers after us to beg us to
return, and offered to restore the cloth which they had
extorted from us; but we were firm. We had been
promised another road by the great chief Mirambo,
who wished to have Europeans in his country; so we
determined to go to him and claim his promise. I may
say that eventually, through Mutinginya's influence, we
regained most of the cloth which the people of Samwè
had made us pay, and six cows for the bale which
they had already cut up. The cows we presented to
Mutinginya as an acknowledgment of all the trouble
he had taken on our behalf.

The news of our return had preceded us to Uyui,
where we had left Hannington ill, with Gordon, who
was especially taking care of him. Such an unexpected
event electrified him into new life, and in spite of his
great weakness and the intense suffering which he had

already undergone, he formed the heroic resolution of pushing on to the Nyanza.

It is needless to enter into details of this troublesome journey, yet it must not be supposed that moving about in any part of East Africa is free from difficulty. It is a long series of worries, greater or less, and fever and fatigue are almost necessary accompaniments.

Five or six days' travelling brought us into the country of the great chief Mirambo, who has been called, not inaptly, the Napoleon of East Africa. In the beginning of his career he was only a small "Munhamhara," or head man; but by his genius and force of character he gradually consolidated his power, and made himself master of nearly the whole of Unyamwezi. Marvellous for the rapidity of his marches and the suddenness of his attacks, his name at this time was a terror to his enemies, and, as we had occasion to prove more than once, a tower of strength to his friends. I have read somewhere that the name "Mirambo" has an etymological connection with killing people: it may be something more than a coincidence that in the Luganda language the word "mirambo" means "corpses."

Some of us paid this redoubted chieftain a visit at his "Gwikuru," or capital, where I saw, to my astonishment, a large four-sided house, built after the manner of Zanzibar. It was by far the most solid structure I have ever seen in the interior of Africa. A number of Zanzibar masons and carpenters, "mafundi," were employed upon it. Mirambo received us courteously in a small circular hut which he used as a general reception-room for his guests, and where he transacted business. The walls were lined with quivers full of poisoned arrows. The chief was dressed in a short English-made coat and the customary native loin-cloth, but the material was richer than that usually worn. He was a tall, fine-looking man, with a good, clever face. After ordering his attendants to bring us stools to sit upon and a large calabash of fresh milk, the conversation began—through an interpreter, of course. He asked us where we were going, and when he understood it was to Uganda, he said, "Ah, truly your beards will have grown long e'er you return." What else we discoursed of I cannot recall; but after talking for about half an hour, and renewing his promise of protection and help, he bade us farewell.

The contrast between Mirambo and Mutesa—the two greatest chiefs whom I met with during my sojourn in Central Africa—was most striking in every particular. Mirambo, kindly and courteous to all, frank and friendly with strangers, living as a plain man among his fellows, although so much greater than they in all that makes men great. Mutesa, kindly too, but formal, fearful of his dignity, crafty, suspicious, and capable of acts so vile and foul that they may only be hinted at, surrounded by an abject court, an object of grovelling adoration to slavish thousands, but really great in nothing. This is the Mutesa of whom, later on, I have more to say.

The very name of Mirambo inspired so much fear in the breasts of our Moslem porters that they had deserted us by dozens. Mirambo had been carrying on a constant war with the Arabs at Unyanyembe, their important trading centre, which was in his country, and many Arabs and their black Mahometan slaves and retainers had fallen in the frequent encounters which had taken place. Hence the dislike of their co-religionists in our caravan to put themselves in the power of the chief. Their fear was altogether imaginary, for Mirambo never would have touched one of them, at any rate while with a European.

Another fortnight's journey through the picturesque district of Musalala brought us to the Nyanza, or at least to one of the swamps in which a small arm of the mighty lake terminates. Passing through the villages of this district, I saw for the first time a native loom at work. The spinning of the cotton is carried on in the spare moments of some of the youths. The apparatus is very simple: a stick with a hook at one end, and just below the hook a round disk through which the stick passes ; to get the twist the cotton is rubbed with the palm of the hand on the naked thigh of the spinner, just as the cobbler at home twists his wax end. The loom is of the roughest construction. The shuttle is slowly passed through the threads by the fingers of the weaver; and I think it takes fully three months to finish a piece of cloth two or three yards in length. When finished it is very strong, and has a dark-coloured border woven in; the yarn for the border is dyed in a peculiar manner. This cloth is largely worn by the women of Unyamwezi.

Here too I saw for the first time native Africans at work forging iron. Large quantities of wood are collected and burned into charcoal, but no oven of any kind is used. The smithies are grass huts erected over a convenient boulder or out-cropping rock. This forms the anvil, and for a hammer a large round stone is used; but in Buganda the people manufacture their hammers of iron. The ore is smelted in a charcoal furnace, the blast for which is supplied by bellows made out of goat-skin, tied on a piece of hollowed cup-shaped wood; there is no valve, but a space is left between the clay tube which conducts the blast to the furnace and the aperture in the wooden cup; the bellows are worked up and down by a vertical stick, round which the skin is gathered in the centre.

It was with the most eager anxiety that we awaited our first view of the great Nyanza, to reach which we had undergone so many toils and such utter weariness. We had visions of looking out upon a vast expanse of sparkling sapphire, and could already hear in imagination the breaking of the waves upon the beach. When the final march of twenty miles was over and we reached the last village before the lake, we felt sure that we should get a grand view of the water; but all we saw was a scrubby bit of forest. Before we rested we set off to seek for the Nyanza; after walking about three miles we came to a piece of rising ground, and following with our eyes the direction indicated by one of the elders of the village who had accompanied us, we saw in the valley below a long strip of vividly green grass and nothing more. "That," said our imperturbable guide, "is the Nyanza." It was with much disappointment that we retraced our steps, and it was not for another month that we really did see the never-to-be-forgotten sight of the illimitable expanse of that glorious inland ocean.

CHAPTER IV.

VISIT TO ROMA AT BUZINJA.

WHILE at the far end of the creek marked "Smith's Sound" on the map, we were in the territory of a young chief named Sonda, with whom we left most of our property. We pitched our tents in the forest some little distance apart, and about a mile from the village. We piled up thorn bushes to keep off wild beasts, and the first night that I spent in this forest I happened to be by myself. I had allowed my two boys to sleep in the village, as they had not finished building their huts near me. Before they left they had made a large fire in front of the tent, a welcome luxury on those chilly evenings. When their cheery "Kwa-heri, bwana," "Good-night, sir," died away, I was alone. A feeling of the utter strangeness of my position stole over me. Can it be true that I am in an African forest a thousand miles away from even the outskirts of civilisation? It is at such a time as this that the unanswerable problem of human life forces itself upon the mind, and the absorbing questions, What am I? Whence came I? Whither am I going? Why am I here? present themselves with over-whelming power. Those who know something of the "blank misgivings of a creature moving about in worlds not realised" will be able to sympathise with the feelings of one placed for the first time in the midst of this great unknown, unrealised world of strange, mysterious Africa. I was, however, startled from my musings by hearing the deep roar of a lion close at hand; but he moved off in another direction, and his voice became fainter and fainter, until at last it died away in the distance.

Our days while we sojourned here were spent in sickness and other employments, as one writer of African experiences has put it with unconscious humour. The other employments in our case were superintending the building of our temporary houses, buying, selling, cooking, writing letters. It was during this time that Hannington met with one of the most extraordinary lion adventures on record. He had gone out with his gun, followed by his servant boy Bakiti, when he saw a small animal at some distance moving in the long grass. He had no suspicion what it was; he raised his gun and fired, and the little creature rolled over dead. Instantly, with a terrific roar, there sprang out two great full-grown lions and came bounding towards him. His gun was empty, there was no time even to reload, so he turned and ran. The lions were almost upon. him, and as his pace grew slower and more uncertain, he heard the agonised cry of his faithful Bakiti, " Hapana, hapana, kimbia!" " No, no, run!" urging him to swifter flight. He, however, translated it " Don't, don't run," and immediately faced round. The lions then stood still, waving their tails and glaring at their strange opponent. It was an awful moment. At last the divinity which hedges the courageous conquered the lions, and they crept away abashed. Now it was Hannington's turn to be the pursuer, so waving his arms and shouting, he drove them away, and actually carried off the dead carcase of the fallen whelp.

Christmas was now drawing on, and although we were all of us more or less ill with fever and ague, we determined not to be done out of our Christmas dinner. Hannington has humorously described my pudding with its weevily flour and fermented raisins, but these drawbacks were in some degree counterbalanced by fresh eggs and good currants and suet and native meal. At any rate it was a great treat, and a Christmas feast of plum pudding is a national custom which every Englishman likes to observe.

While we were at Musalala, Roma, King of Buzinja, a country on the south-west of the Nyanza, sent messengers and presents inviting us to visit him and promising to provide canoes to take us on to Uganda. Hannington thought it best to accept his offer, and as we were dissatisfied with our present situation, it was arranged that I should go with him and Gordon to Roma's capital to look out for a suitable site near the lake for the new station at the south of the Nyanza: and that Wise should stay behind to look after the camp.

The journey to Roma's took us quite nine days, and

a very trying and disagreeable time it was. Our bill
of health was anything but satisfactory. Gordon was
so ill that he could not stand, and had to be carried;
Hannington was only just able to crawl, while I was
on the verge of a bad attack of fever, and altogether,
our experiences during this voyage, with drunken,
insubordinate and quarrelsome canoemen, in leaky
canoes, with insufficient provisions, and sometimes no
shelter, were not encouraging. One night we were
landed on a desolate shore in pouring rain and pitch
darkness, and after floundering miserably for about a
mile through grass dripping wet, and stumbling over
scattered rocks, we came to some human habitations,
and begged the owners for a night's lodging. They
said they were sorry, but they had nothing to offer
except a goat-house. We went to see it; but we
could not venture into such a filthy place. As the
rain had now ceased, we made our damp beds in the
little courtyard, and tried to sleep, but in vain; for
the rain came on again faster than ever. Here let me
record an act of rare kindness, one out of kindnesses
innumerable received from Africans. The good people
of the house, when they saw our sorry plight, took
compassion on us, and actually turned out of their
warm, snug dwelling to make room for us, while
they themselves spent the night huddled together under
a rough thatched shed outside.

We reached Roma's headquarters at last, all very
weak, and so ill that we had to stay in bed. Our beds

occupied the three sides of one not very large tent. Hannington, who found adventures in all places, beguiled the time in the intervals of fever with yachting recollections or reminiscences of cliff-climbing in Devonshire. We soon had a visit from the chief, a man of gigantic stature, partly sprung from the Bahuma race; but his good traits were sadly spoilt by cowardice, suspicion, and conceit; and no ancient Highland crone could be more superstitious than this representative of African royalty.

We had not been long, however, with Roma before we discovered that he had simply brought us into a trap. He made some paltry excuse for refusing us canoes, and extorted a large present; and to comply with his demands we had to encroach grievously upon our rapidly diminishing store of cloth. After much diplomatic intercourse the chief allowed Hannington to leave for Kageye, on the other side of Smith's Sound. We decided before he left that if he were successful in procuring canoes, he should send them for us, and that to induce Roma to let us go quickly, we would give him some of the small breech-loading guns which our porters were carrying. There are possibly some who may blame missionaries for giving a heathen chief fire-arms under any circumstances; but they belong to that select class who are given to fault-finding. But in our favour it should be remembered that we were short of cloth with which to buy even necessary food, and that as we had but little ammunition to give

D

with the guns, they were not likely to do much harm.
The question, however, is perhaps a fair one as to how
far the Christian Church is justified, in the first instance, in sending missionaries to countries which they
cannot reach without being armed.

Hannington succeeded in despatching canoes to take
us away, and while Gordon looked after the baggage, I
took the three little guns to give them to Roma. I
was invited into the straw-built house in which the
king received his chiefs and visitors, and duly presented our offering. In showing him how to load one of
the rifles, I happened, before inserting the cartridge,
to point the gun at my host. He nervously put it to
one side with his hand, and I could not help smiling
at his apprehension; this he evidently noticed, and so
he gravely took the carbine from me, and deliberately
loaded it and pointed it full at my breast. It was
my turn now to be dismayed, and I quickly put aside
the muzzle as he had done, saying at the same time,
"Poli, poli!" "Gently, gently!" This was just what
he wanted. "Poli, poli, is it?" he cried; "O ho! so the
Muzungu (white man) does not like a gun pointed at
him." And the old fellow shook with laughter,
repeating the words "poli," "poli," between his bursts
of merriment.

He and I had had a passage of arms some days
before this, when he had come to see us. On that
occasion he said very rudely to me that I was only a
child. "How then do you account for my beard?" I

MULESHI'S FERRY. SOUTH END OF VICTORIA NYANZA.

asked. "Very easily," he replied, "you were born with it." I could only make the rather weak and obvious retort that his not having a beard proved him to be a child—a retort which did not altogether please him.

Roma dismissed us kindly, and we managed to place all the baggage on board the canoes, and then Gordon and I took our seats. The canoemen, however, flatly refused to stir; they said that we should all be drowned, and that the canoes were overloaded. This latter statement was undoubtedly true; but what else could we do but make a start? However, when we urged them to go, they remained resolute in their refusal, and so I had to get out again with my eight men, and we decided that I should do the journey on foot back to Wise, whom we had left at Musalala, and that Gordon should join Hannington at Kageye.

Soon after I had made my way down to Musalala on the west of Smith's Sound, Hannington walked into our camp, having come down on the east side and crossed over at Muleshi's ferry. He was in a very serious condition. He had had so many repeated attacks of fever, and had suffered so much, that he at last felt that he was not justified in resisting our urgent advice that he should endeavour to reach the coast.

When all was ready for the start, I accompanied him for a mile or so of the way, and then sorrowfully we said farewell and clasped hands for the last time. I stood and my eyes followed the tall receding figure, now indeed bowed with the intense pain and suffering which he had undergone, and I wondered, as I watched him, whether he would ever accomplish the long eight hundred miles of swamp and wilderness, with its certain toils and unknown perils, which lay between him and Zanzibar.

CHAPTER V.

MUSALALA TO BUGANDA.

AFTER making the young chief Sonda an "appropriate" and suitable present of a pair of trousers, a tin box, and a surplice, Wise and I left Musalala, and started for Kageye. When we had reached the other side of the Urima creek, we received letters with the news that a small caravan of cloth was on its way to join us at Musalala. Wise very kindly offered to go back to meet it, while I hastened on to join Gordon at Kageye. The people of Urima are not unlike the Wanyamwezi, except that they do not chip the triangular gap in their two front teeth, and the men have even less idea of decency in the matter of clothing; the women, however, are dressed in skins. The curiosity we excited was unbounded. It was quite common for a bevy of women and girls to cluster thickly round our tent, making remarks and laughing at everything they saw. On one occasion I went to the door of the tent and offered some half-pence, hoping to propitiate these dark damsels. They, however, misunderstood my charitable intentions and there was a general stampede. I could not help laughing immoderately on seeing one huge creature fall heavily in her eager anxiety to make good her escape. A minute afterwards they were all back again as talkative as ever. This went on all day, except sometimes boys and youths took the places of the women and girls. Our male visitors were more bumptious, ignorant, and conceited than those of the other sex, and were some of the most objectionable persons I have ever met with.

We were now travelling in the rains, and our road lay chiefly through morass and swamp. We had to pass through a district called Usmawo, famous for the avarice and turbulence of its people. Usmawo lies midway between the districts of Urima and Usukuma, from which latter place we had engaged a number of naked savages as porters. Owing to the bad character of the people through whose country we were about to travel, we decided to make the attempt to slip past them in the night. Just as the sun went down we left our camp, and cautiously the thin line of dusky figures crept onwards through the darkness. Some of the long black trunks, carried by the unclad Wasukuma porters, looked like coffins in the dim light, and the moonbeams gleaming on the white paint of others gave them from a little distance the appearance of pale and flickering fires; and so in solemn silence this ghostly band of naked figures filed past the sleeping villages of Usmawo like a procession of the dead. To our great satisfaction we reached the border unobserved, but immediately we crossed over and stood in the territory of the Wasukuma the pent-up feelings of our porters broke forth and vented themselves in peals of laughter and shouts of triumph, together with the joyous blowing of horns, the beating of drums, and the firing off of guns.

A few days more and we arrived at Kageye, and were warmly welcomed by Gordon, who had been here for some weeks, and who, meantime, had made good progress with " Swahili," the language of Zanzibar He was being entertained by an Arab, or rather a half-bred Arab trader, named Said bin Saif; his African name is Kipanda Moto. Kageye is a wretched native village, which at that time was full of Arabs; it is a most dirty and most unhealthy place, chiefly memorable as being the spot where a young Scotch doctor, John Smith, of the Church Missionary Society, together with one of Stanley's companions, lies buried. It is near the island of Ukerewe, where Lieutenant Shergold Smith and Mr. O'Neil were murdered by the chief, Lukonge. At Kageye I spent more than six weeks, and during this time I paid a visit to Ukerewe. Gordon and Wise and myself had been strongly advised by our quondam leader Stokes, who had preceded Hannington to the coast, to fix our station on Ukerewe, and it was therefore decided that I should visit Lukonge and sound him upon the subject. Said bin Saif, the Arab mentioned before, lent me his canoe with some of his men who knew how to paddle. While it is only fair to mention this Arab's friendliness and kindness, it must not be forgotten he was paid at an exorbitant rate for all that he did; but it was quite worth while to pay well for the help which we received from him. We made the journey across in one day, and found the island of Ukerewe rich and fertile; food, comprising dried fish, bananas, fowls, goats, sweet potatoes, etc., is plentiful and cheap. Unlike the tribes from Zanzibar to the lake, the girls here are without the slightest apology for clothing, which is one out of many indications that ideas of propriety and modesty are perfectly arbitrary, and vary greatly among different peoples. In Usukuma, for instance, while the women are all most scrupulously clothed, the men are stark naked, while in Buganda the reverse is the case. There girls up to a marriageable age walk about unclad without a thought of shame; yet the men, and even the smallest boys, are carefully covered. It was not till the second day after my arrival on the island that I reached Lukonge's chief village. He received me kindly and appointed a house for me to sleep in, and sent me some milk. The next day I had an interview with him. I found him a very sedate and rather handsome man. He said that he was sorry that the first white men had been killed, and that he would warmly welcome others who would come and " build " * in his territory.

The death of Smith and O'Neil was a very sad affair, and is involved in some obscurity. It seems that an Arab trader, Sungura, had married one of Lukonge's

---

* "Build" is used in East Africa to denote settling down in a place.

daughters, and when trouble arose between the chief and the trader, the latter determined to remove his household to Kageye, and succeeded in prevailing upon the missionaries to lend him the *Daisy*, the mission-boat. He put his harem on board, and among the women was apparently the daughter of Lukonge. This action Lukonge naturally resented, as he looked upon it as an abduction, and consequently attacked the Arab, who took refuge with the missionaries, and they chivalrously defended him. Some of the natives said that while O'Neil fired on them, Smith was writing in a book all the time of the attack; they said that O'Neil succeeded in killing thirty of his assailants before he was finally overpowered. Another account says that when Smith saw he must be killed, he shot himself with his own pistol.

Mackay subsequently visited the scene of the murder, though he had great difficulty in inducing any of his followers to go with him, as they vehemently asserted that he would be killed. Lukonge, however, received him courteously, and actually restored a quantity of property which had belonged to the murdered Englishmen. During my visit I had a bad attack of fever, but I was able to present my gift to the chief. It was a piece of copper wire; and he was much pleased, and gave me in return a cow, which it was necessary to kill at once. I had therefore plenty of butcher's meat, but as I had run short of cloth, I could buy hardly sufficient food of other kinds to last us during the return journey to the mainland. One rather amusing incident occurred before I took my departure from the island. I was lying under a tree, lazily watching the blue waters of the Nyanza rippling in the sunlight while waiting for the canoe which was to take me back to Kageye. A few yards from me a woman was busily employed hoeing a plot of ground, when presently up came an inquisitive fellow. Perhaps he was merely of an inquiring and observant nature ; but he suddenly was attracted by the extraordinary sight of a white man lying under a tree, clothed from head to foot in garments such as he had never before even imagined. He hurried across the cultivated ground in order to make a closer inspection of such a curious phenomenon. But the unwritten law that trespassers will be prosecuted was put into swift and unexpected execution by the dusky daughter of Eve whose garden he was desecrating. Raising her hoe, she struck the unhappy intruder a heavy blow, which she repeated as quickly as she was able. At first he was utterly taken by surprise ; but as soon as he recovered himself, he promptly repaid the attention with interest. After a short scrimmage they parted in hot anger ; he, objurgating and spitting on the ground, made off to his own village, while she hastened to her home, which lay in the opposite direction, to gather her faction. Very soon I saw issuing from each village, an angry and excited crowd. I quite expected that it would end in a pitched battle ; but more peaceable counsels prevailed and the elders on both sides sat down to hold a long palaver and to discuss the whole question. At this juncture my canoe arrived and I not unwillingly left them to settle the matter by themselves. What the result was I never heard; but no doubt the danger of broken heads was averted when the contending parties had once sufficiently controlled themselves to sit down for what an African likes even better than a battle—a long "shauri," *i.e.* discussion.

I had arranged to take a passage in Said bin Saif's dhow, which arrived from Buganda laden with ivory and slaves a few days after my return from Ukerewe. She came into port hidden in a cloud of smoke from the guns of the Arabs and their retainers on board, who were firing a salute, which is the negroes' highest idea of expressing satisfaction. The dhow was lying at anchor opposite the house where I lived; but the morning after her arrival, when I looked out on the lake, she had disappeared. She had slipped her cable in the night and been dashed to pieces on the rocks which surround Kageye. The Arab bore his loss with even more equanimity than I did. It was Allah's will, and he would build another. However, it turned out well for me, for in a few more weeks thirty canoes arrived from Mutesa to bring on the new Muzungu (white man) and two Arab traders who were bound for Buganda. From one of these fellow-travellers I received no little kindness. I was very ill during nearly the whole of the twenty days' journey in the canoes, and old Said bin Hadj used often to help with his own hand in putting up my tent, and whenever he killed a goat he never omitted to send me a nice joint, though I had little except some tea to give him in return.

The canoes partly coasted along the west shores of the lake, and partly took advantage of the islands, making from one to another, but at sunset we always landed, whether on the coast or on an island, to pitch our tents and to sleep. While encamped on one of these islands, Kyakwogera,* the officer whom Mutesa had sent for me, took all his men off to raid a neighbouring island. He killed the few men whom he found there, slaughtered and cut up the cattle, and put the meat into his boats, and brought away alive the goats and sheep and women and children. When Kyakwogera and his men arrived, they set to work to devour the meat, and what they could not eat they dried over fires. It was pitiable to see how miserably ill they made themselves by sheer over-eating. Consequently, the next day, when we were once more on the lake, only a few of them were able to make any attempt at paddling the great canoe.

Among the prisoners was a little boy whom they called Kazinja. His real name was Kangire. He and his mother were seized and brought away together, and one of my followers purchased him with a coat which he had stolen. When both transactions came to light, we made him hand Kazinja over to the

---

* He was afterwards killed on the mainland near this very place.

mission as compensation for the theft of the coat. The child was eventually baptized, and went by the name of Bobby. He learned to read fluently and could sing hymns admirably and say prayers to perfection; but he belonged to a class which should be clearly distinguished from that of people who believe in Christ from deep personal conviction. If the existence of such a class were always recognised, it would do away with the slurs so often cast upon so-called converts. Bobby was a little liar born and bred; he could not keep his little fingers out of any tin or box or other receptacle for things pleasant to the sight and desirable for food. Though he could take the cover off a tin as well as any one, I caught him one day *flagrante delicto* owing to his inability to replace it properly, and on that occasion he got his deserts in the shape of a sound thrashing.

The poor little lad lost his mother on this voyage, and it was as well, for he was now separated from her for ever, as she would have been sold probably to one of the Arabs, and taken away never more to see her little Kangire in this world. The canoe in which she was travelling was upset by a hippopotamus, and she and two others were drowned.

We skirted the territories governed by Roma on the south up to those of Kigaju, his neighbour, and on past Kaitaba, pro-king of the Baziba; passing the important rivers the Katonga and Kagera we coasted along Budu, whose chief Pokino was one of the great Earls of

Buganda. Making our way along by the Archipelago of the Sesse Isles, we finally landed at a place called Entebe, about thirty miles from Mutesa's Lubiri, or capital.

A tremendous blowing off of gunpowder by my Arab companions announced our arrival, and directly we landed I made up the letters for Mackay and his companion, and sent two of my men off to the mission with them. The following day Mackay himself arrived, and gave me a warm and kindly welcome. I looked with intense interest upon the man with whom for the next few years I was to be so closely associated, and of whom I had heard so much; and who had remained at his post with such indomitable courage and patient perseverance. General Gordon had wished to secure him as one of his lieutenants in the Soudan; but Mackay preferred to do his self-denying work for Africa humbly as an English missionary rather than in the more pompous guise of an Egyptian pasha.*

As soon as Mackay met me my travelling troubles were at an end. He had brought a fine Muscat donkey down to the port to meet me. I gladly mounted and preceded him to the mission station, where I was kindly received by his fellow-missionary, Rev. P. O'Flaherty, who showed me my new quarters in the comfortable house which Mackay had built. How I first became acquainted with King Mutesa I must leave for another chapter.

* Mr. Mackay has been lately decorated by the Khedive with the order of the Osmanieh of the 4th class for his services to Emin Pasha

CHAPTER VI.

KING MUTESA.

I NOW come to the important figure of one of the two kings after whom I have named this book: Mutesa,* Kabaka † of Buganda, overlord of Buynoro, Busoga, Buzongora, Karagwe, Buzinja, and other peoples, nations, and languages—son of Suna, grandson of Kamanya, descendant of the Divine Kintu, who traces his descent for so many generations back as to put to shame the pedigrees of most of the inhabitants of these isles who boast the possession of a pedigree at all.

That he was of Bahuma descent there can be little doubt—the despised Bahuma,‡ or Wahuma, are the herdsmen in Buganda.

Mutesa succeeded to the kingdom on the death of Suna, a cruel, cold-blooded, and ferocious tyrant, who died miserably of small-pox while conducting one of the bloody raids for which the Baganda are infamously

---

* Mutesa, not Mtesa, which the Baganda could not say any more than the ordinary Englishman, who generally calls the name "teaser."

† Kabaka means "kaiser."

‡ The Bahuma or Wahuma in Buganda are called Bayima; the Baganda have no "h." Is it not curious that we change the Greek "u" into a "y" sound?

famous. He was feared and hated by his people, and it
is said that those who were deputed to bear the corpse
of the deceased Kabaka back to the capital for burial,
dashed it down to the ground with scornful fury, as if to
wreak an impotent vengeance upon the dead. The quiet-
looking, large-eyed lad Mutesa was chosen to succeed
his warrior father. He, however, soon earned and took
the significant name of " Causer of tears," "Mukaa-
bya," and by this name he was usually known ; but he
was still oftener styled simply "Kabaka," or the King.
Before officially "eating Buganda," as it is called, he
had to go and seat himself on the stone throne which
has been used for the purpose from time immemorial,
and which is some distance from Rubaga, where he
afterwards made his capital. When I knew him, only
one of his numerous brothers was left, the others
having, on various excuses, been put to death. The
survivor was a very meek-looking, insignificant man,
with a face scarred with small-pox, yet with a distinct
resemblance to the king; possibly his inoffensiveness
and insignificance accounts for the fact of his
lengthened existence.

Mutesa soon sent down to the mission-house to say
that he wished to see the newly-arrived "Muzungu,"'
" white man," and it was accordingly decided that though
I was far from well, I had better accede to his majesty's
commands. I therefore arrayed myself in my longest
black coat, in order to pay fitting respect to the great
monarch to whom I was about to have the high honour

of being introduced. And so I mounted upon the fine Muscat donkey aforesaid, which the king had presented to the missionaries, and, convoyed by Mr. O'Flaherty, I started for the palace. Turning off the magnificent sweep of road which led up to Rubaga, the now deserted capital, we passed along a beautiful lane, between lofty fences, "bisakati," formed of the tall tiger-grass which grows so abundantly in Buganda, and is used in making the enclosures which surround the houses and gardens of the upper classes. These fences are made by driving posts of some ten or twelve feet high into the ground at intervals of a few yards, to which are fastened horizontally long thick ropes of the reed-like grass-stalks. These form rails, of which there may be from four to nine, according to the height of the fence. To the rails are tied vertically stalks of the same grass in couples, thus making a smooth, close-fitting palisade. These fences look very neat, but constantly require to be repaired. Their erection is a regular craft, and forms part of the training of the youth of Buganda, and every feudal lord has the right to call upon his vassals for this service.

The way wound between groves of carefully cultivated bananas, "bitoki," where we saw women (who do all the gardening) carefully lop off the withered branches, and spread them along the ground to prevent the growth of weeds or grass.

We also passed by sweet potatoes planted in ridges, which were being weeded by some women, who, in the

E

interval of labour, were enjoying a quiet smoke. This curious habit, so common among men in Europe, prevails also all over East Africa, and is largely indulged in by women. The Wanyamwezi men, however, prefer snuff, leaving smoke to the female sex. The people of Ukerewe, Lukonge's island, mix powdered tobacco with water and then " snuffle " it up their noses.

We now came out on another magnificently wide road, which led in a straight line to Nabulagala, Mutesa's present palace—a road even wider than the widest street of the Irish capital. Presently we ascended a slight incline in front of us, from the top of which we obtained a splendid view of the surrounding country. Hills rose up on all sides, covered to their very summits with the rich and vivid green of banana groves. Away to the north-west were the purple hills of distant Bulemezi, one of the provinces, or earldoms, of Buganda. Behind us was the saddle-backed hill Mutundwe, with its solitary tree, a landmark for miles round; while before us, on its perfectly bare eminence, lay Nabulagala, the "lubire," or head-quarters, of Mutesa—a vast village of gigantic straw-built houses.

As my guide was pointing out to me the beauty of the view, a little page came panting up, his snowy cotton robe flowing behind him, to bid us make more haste. He wore the "luga," or necklet of bent cane, to show that he was one of the Kabaka's "baddu," slaves, or rather " bagalagala," pages. He made no salutation, but simply uttered the word "Jangu," "Come."

Soon another little fellow came running up, and he in his turn uttered the word "Yanguyako," "Be quick." These little pages have all the insolence of office, derived from the brief authority with which they are invested. Their names were probably Mukassa and Musoke, which in Buganda are as common as Duncan and Donald in the Highlands.

A succession of messengers met us until we reached the "Wankaki," or royal gateway. All the gateways which lead to "majesty" have names, and are kept by officers called "Bagazi," *i.e.* hall porters. If Swift had only been possessed of missionary proclivities, the world might have had a voyage to Buganda instead of a voyage to Lilliput. The heart would grow sick with scorn of all this beggarly pomp and paltry pride, were it not that here, as in Europe, in spite of it all, and across it all, there are found sterling qualities, generous impulses, and noble aspirations.

When the wide "Wankaki" was passed, we found ourselves in a spacious court, in which were one or two houses, the largest being the official residence of the king's head wife, or "Kadu lubarè." The houses of all the chiefs and upper classes in the country are exact models of the king's, only of course upon a much smaller scale.

The palisade which surrounds the "Kibuga," or royal enclosure, is different from the fence of all other persons in the country, with the exception of the priests of Lubarê and the king's eldest son. I have not seen the enclosures of the two queens in Buganda,

"Namasolè," mother of the king, and "Lubuga," sister of the king; but possibly they may possess the privilege of making their fences in the same style as the king. The difference between these sacred and royal palisades and the ordinary enclosure consists in the fact that the former are made with the reeds or tiger-grass crossed and wattled, while in the latter they are simply placed side by side.

Strange it seemed to find oneself, for the first time, in one of the great capitals of Africa. It was a bright and busy scene, and we were soon surrounded by a curious and noisy crowd. Here were people of all shades and complexions, from a light copper colour to jetty black. In front of us, going in the direction of the next gateway, towered the gigantic figure (nearly seven feet high) of Katorogo, the king's head "Muhuma," herdsman, though Sebalija is the Muganda chief who is responsible for the Kabaka's cattle. Katorogo was followed by a skin-clad company, whose dress presented a striking contrast to the brighter and more showy garments of the other courtiers. Among the ever-moving throng were musicians from Busoga, with their mud-coloured back-cloths easily distinguishable from the light brown or red cloths of the Baganda. Again, the "Bajona," or potters, are passing along, bearing on their heads enormous earthenware vessels, which they are about to present as tribute to the Kabaka. Behind us a great chief has just entered, clothed in a scarlet coat of fine English cloth richly embroidered with gold, all native work, and with bright pink trousers of the same material. This is Mukwenda, Earl of Singo; he is followed by a motley crowd of vassals—a wee slave boy bearing his pipe and shoes, other slaves carrying his gracefully decanter-shaped bottle gourd with its exquisitely worked " luseke," a long bent tube, on the outside of which is plaited beautiful fine-coloured grass. Mukwenda stalks along with the air of an emperor. But his peers do not forget that though he is an earl to-day, he is a mere mushroom nobleman, a parvenu, a peasant. Only a few years ago he was but a miserable " mugoma" or drummer—a harlequin on whom the royal favour had lighted. He carries in his hand a long curiously-shaped white staff, which has been polished with Nature's own glass-paper, the rough leaves of a certain tree which are called " luwawo." On his head he wears a red fez. He, like us, has come to " kika," that is to present himself at Mutesa's grand " lukiko," or levee. All this time I was mounted on the donkey, and we pushed our way onward through the throng of hurrying courtiers, till we approached a second gateway. Through this I caught a glimpse of the scarlet coats of several stately chiefs. But just as we were about to enter, a sliding gate of reeds was rudely drawn across our path, and immediately fastened with the thin leather thong used for the purpose. My companion, Mr. O'Flaherty, however, was quite equal to the occasion, and whipping out his pocket-knife he cut the thong and forced open the door, then seizing the bridle of the donkey in one hand and waving his stick in the other, he led me triumphantly through, the guards fleeing right and left upon our approach. We soon squeezed through another gateway. Here I dismounted, and we now entered the third court, and made straight for one of the largest houses which it contained—the usual straw-built, pole-supported, beehive-shaped hut of the country. Within this, on a mat, was sitting a splendid-looking man with a very handsome face ; all about him were seated chiefs, like himself, blazing in crimson and gold, and so thought I this must be the far-famed Mutesa. He motioned me to be seated near him, and then entered into conversation with my companion. The space behind the chieftain was occupied by a miscellaneous assemblage of peasants, retainers, litigants, slaves, and minstrels. The supposed king was evidently of the Bahuma tribe, or else, like so many of the Baganda, had much Bahuma blood in his veins. When we had sat here for some time, Mr. O'Flaherty got up, saying, "Let us go now and see the 'Katikiro,' 'chief judge.'" On getting outside I asked him who the handsome chief might be. "That," he replied, "is Kyambalango, the 'Kymbugwe' or keeper of the palace."

Passing through yet another gateway we came to the chief judge's court-house or "Kigango." The chief judge or chancellor, like the chief whom we had just left, was seated on a mat and surrounded by a still greater crowd. On our approach he rose and came out to meet us, and received us very graciously; he was dressed in Arab costume, a snowy white gown of fine cotton, over which he wore a long mantle or robe of rich black cloth, heavily embroidered with gold. He was small, very handsome, evidently of Bahuma blood, though darker than the Bahuma usually are. This is the man of whom Stanley has given so admirable a description— suave, polite, shrewd, far-seeing; but also cold, cruel, cunning, false and treacherous. The Bismarck of Buganda and virtual ruler of the kingdom—this was the man of boundless ambition and intolerable pride whose self-will and masterdom would not endure to be thwarted, and woe to any one who crossed his path! This was the man who in stormy passion had flung down his cap in presence of the king, and had refused to relinquish his suit until Mutesa had stripped a powerful rival chief of everything to gratify the spite of his imperious chancellor.

The Katikiro made room for me on his own mat—a high honour which I am afraid at that time I took as a matter of course.

I watched the great man as he listened to the counsel who were arguing the cases on which he was to give judgment, "sala musango," "cut judgment," he all the while playing the game of "Mweso."* He was never-

* The game of "Mweso," or "Bao," is played on a board, in which are cut thirty-two square holes; hard nuts, beans, or bullets are used as counters. It is common all over East Africa. The object of the game is to secure your adversaries' counters. It requires quickness in counting.

theless listening carefully, though you would hardly think so to see his lithe fingers gathering up the counters with which he played and dropping them into their proper holes. He would suddenly stop, arrange some small white sticks in order on the ground to mark the points of his summing up, and then give judgment, though the scale could be made to incline this way or that by a timely bribe. On hearing the verdict, both plaintiff and defendant and their supporters energetically thanked the judge. Kneeling before him and clasping their hands, they moved them up and down, crying out, " Neyanze, Neyanze, Neyanzege," or, speaking in the plural, " Tweyanze, Tweanzege," " We thank you."

Suddenly there pealed out a long rolling tattoo from the deep-toned royal drums, accompanied by a loud blare of trumpets, which had been a present from England to Mutesa. The music was what might be expected from the tuning up of such instruments preliminary to the production of some melody or air; but possibly the musicians may have been playing a composition of Wagner's which my ear was not well enough trained to recognise. At any rate this was my first summons to the great " Lukiko " or " levee " of the king.

Immediately the chief judge arose, and in another minute his Kigango was deserted, as he, accompanied by the other earls, entered the precincts of the great court of the Kabaka. The chief judge, besides being Katikiro of Buganda, held also the Earldom of Kyagwe. We followed in the rear of the earls, jostled with scarlet-coated Buganda nobles and tributary kings.

Among the throng hastening to pay their respects to the majesty of Buganda were representatives of the Bahuma lords or Bakama, as well as chiefs from Busoga. The fair-faced Lubambula of Koki from the west, and the scowling Wakoli, paramount chief of Busoga, who divided with Luba—known as being the captor of Bishop Hannington—authority to the east of Buganda. Here too were obsequious smiling Arabs from Muscat—men who can smile and smile and be villains with it all; pale-faced Englishmen from the cold North; runaway Egyptian soldiers from the Soudan; adventurers from the east coast and Madagascar; mountebanks, minstrels, dancers, dwarfs. This rabble found seats in the best places they could command outside, while we followed the earls through Mutesa's body-guard, which were drawn up in line, forming a passage reaching up to the entrance to the king's palace.

CHAPTER VII.

INTERVIEWS WITH MUTESA.

KING MUTESA's great reception-house was a vast
beehive-like building, supported on lofty wooden posts
which ran in four not very regular rows. I was
disappointed at my first view of the Kabaka's straw-built
palace. Here there was no attempt at ornament of any
kind such as I had seen at Mirambo's Gwikuru, no
Arab wood-carving, and no stone or plaster work. The
workmanship of Buganda was, however, represented in
its highest excellence—fine grass and string and reed
work, exquisite indeed, and perfect of its kind, but
nothing enduring.

I could not help thinking that this hill on which
was built the city of the king, in a few more years
would be as desolate and deserted as Rubaga now was.
The whole nation might pass away without leaving a
trace of its existence, except perhaps in a few metal
ornaments and weapons, which might come to light in
some future age.

But enough of my reveries. We entered the wide
doorway of the house where Mutesa was. The king lay
reclining upon a low couch, beneath a shabby canopy of
dirty bark-cloth. The couch was placed at the right-

hand side of the entrance. The king was clothed from head to foot in a snowy white robe, and lay back holding in his right hand a small round looking-glass, in which he could see reflected the faces of the courtiers who clustered round the doorway without. At the foot of the couch were two handsome boys, their bodies shining with a superabundance of oil. They too were dressed in snowy cotton robes. One was clasping his royal master's feet, and warming them with his hands, while the other held himself in readiness to brush away any miserable fly whose brain was too undeveloped to comprehend the awful majesty of its fellow-mortal, upon whom it sacrilegiously dared to settle. It is the custom that every great chief shall give some of his sons to the king to be his pages or "bagalagala," and it is from these that future lords and nobles are recruited. Little Nyonyi Entono ("the small bird"), not allowed yet to enter the presence of the king, but a sub-page in one of the great houses outside, in no long time will reach man's estate, and find himself standing in the mighty Katikiro's shoes. And little Kagwa, quickly grown to manhood, by the strange turn of fortune's wheel will find himself a mighty earl— Mukwenda, Lord of Singo; but before they reach that uncertain eminence, they will have to suffer much both of torture and of shame.

At the head of the couch, kneeling half outside, and with his head inclined so as to be near the king's ear, was Kolugi, chief storekeeper. He, though not noble, and therefore not allowed inside the presence-chamber, was a man of great influence and power, and was always more or less our staunch friend.

Inside, and sitting on a mat near the king's head, was his favourite chief Kyambalango ("Leopard-clothed") or "Kyimbugwe;" whilst facing Kyambalango, sat the imperious chancellor. On the left of the doorway, on entering, were seated also on the ground two or three rows of the great lords, while in the space between the chiefs and the king camp-stools were placed for Mr. O'Flaherty and myself.

Further away, in the interior of the house, and facing the entrance, were seated a bevy of black beauties— the ladies or Bakyala of the king's household.

Strange to say, that while Europeans and Arabs immediately single out the light copper-coloured, beautiful hazel-eyed Bahuma women as bearing the palm of beauty, Mutesa and his chiefs admired rather the stouter-built women of a more decidedly pronounced negro type.

When we came into the royal presence, I was duly introduced to the king. I took off my hat, and made him a bow, which he acknowledged Arab fashion with an inclination of his head and by placing his hand upon his heart. He then motioned me to be seated on the camp-stool, a high honour rarely conferred even upon native chiefs, but generally granted to European visitors, though the Arabs were always made to sit on the floor.

I was the bearer of a handsome present of some fine scarlet cloth, which the Church Missionary Society had sent to the king. This Mr. O'Flaherty presented, at the same time dilating upon my virtues, dignity and importance; though I of course was quite ignorant of what was passing.

After a little, a skilled male dancer appeared, and went through the surprising evolutions and contortions of the strange body dance, which I had seen the women of Unyamwesi performing. However, whether it was watching the mazy motion of the dance, or whether it was my own weariness coupled with the heat of the reception-hall, I became intolerably drowsy, and was only awakened to the realities of my position by being addressed directly by the sovereign. I felt like a person at church suddenly conscious of having been caught napping, and tried to look as if I were quite wide awake. I did not of course know what Mutesa said, but my companion explained that he was commanding me to turn round that he might get a better view of me. This I did. "Now to the other side." I did so. And then his majesty pronounced the pleasing verdict that I was "Mulungi," a word which means good or beautiful, to which all the chiefs assented cordially, as they would have done had the monarch been pleased to say the reverse.

I have no doubt that important business of the kingdom was transacted at this Lukiko, but the language was utterly unintelligible to me, so that I was not sorry

when we were all suddenly dismissed by a quick motion
of the king's hand.   Out we streamed as we had come
in ; and thus came to an end the great duty of the day,
and every one was now free to follow his own devices
until the next "baraza," levee, of the Kabaka was
announced.

A few days after this, I went again with Mr.
O'Flaherty to see the king, and on this occasion we
had a private interview.   A great number of the king's
wives and other members of his harem were present.
His Majesty was most affable and agreeable, and again
repeated his verdict of the former occasion, that I was
" Mulungi," and even said that I was worthy of one of
his own daughters.   He had thoughtfully, a day or two
before, sent down to offer me a wife.   I was ill at the
time, and so Mackay kindly or unkindly, according to
the view taken, refused her for me.

When Mutesa remarked that I ought to have a
Mumbeja or princess, there was a shrill chorus from
the ladies of " Wewawo,"—" Yes, indeed."

Mr. O'Flaherty remarked, in making polite excuses
for me, that white people like to marry white people, as
black people like to marry those of the same colour as
themselves.   Again the shrill chorus of female voices—
" Oh no, but we like white men very much."   After a
little more badinage the interview was concluded.
Mutesa never in the presence of any women indulged
his perverted taste for vile conversation, which at any
rate was one of many indications that there existed in

Buganda a respect for women, and also showed that the king felt and knew that such conversation was really shameful and wrong.

I used generally to visit Mutesa once a month, and to his amusement, one day, I read him a fable which I had been told by one of the people, and which I had printed in a small press which we had. I used also to take up a translation of a few verses of the Bible, and he always most courteously allowed me to read it to him. The Arabs used to bring the Koran, and intone passages which neither they nor the king understood; still Mutesa's verdict was that the Arabs' rendering of the Koran was vastly superior to my poor translations into his own language. I have no doubt that if I had intoned the Litany in English for his edification, I should have run the Arabs very close in the competition.

I remember being present once at the king's levee when news arrived of a severe defeat which the Baganda had suffered on one of their raids, at the hands of a people called Bakede, to the north-east of Buganda. The news was received by the king and his nobles with the utmost composure. Mutesa could lose an army with as much outward equanimity, at any rate, as a chess-player would lose a pawn.

On this occasion the Baganda had raided the naked Bakede, they had taken them at a disadvantage, and had collected vast numbers of cattle and little children. The Bakede women would not accompany the successful warriors, and preferred death, be it said to their honour, to the shame that awaited them—a fate which was speedily meted out to them.

The first party got safely across the frontier; but the Bakede meanwhile had gathered in force, and intercepted the second division; and the Baganda, in spite of their guns, were utterly annihilated by the spears of their warlike assailants.

I may here give an account of my last interview with Mutesa. We had heard that there was to be a grand "Kiwendo," or human sacrifice, at the next feast of the Lubare, or Demiurge of Buganda, who, unlike the sublime "Katonda" ("Creator"), interests himself in the affairs of men, and to whom sacrifices and offerings are constantly made. We thought it our duty to remonstrate with the king, and to attempt to dissuade him from so great a crime. We accordingly wrote him a letter, which I was deputed to deliver. As a rule Mutesa liked receiving letters, though this time he utterly refused it. We had sent a letter to him on a former occasion to ask him not to take revenge on the Bakede for having annihilated his army; no revenge expedition as a matter of fact was sent, but whether from fear of God or fear of the Bakede I should not like to hazard an opinion.

As I made my way to the king's enclosure, a little incident occurred which aptly illustrates one of the customs of the country. When I turned into the main road leading to Nabulagala, I overtook a large party of women, the harem of some great chief, preceded by a small boy. In Buganda, small boys are the custodians of the women. The Arabs had tried to prevail upon Mutesa to copy their own customs with reference to the custody of his harem; and though the king followed their evil counsel in the case of a few of his pages, the general custom still was that young boys should hold the office of the keeping of the women.

The little boy in question carried a large thick stick, not altogether for ornament, and marched at the head of his convoy. A poor peasant was coming in the opposite direction, carrying some sweet potatoes on his head, doubtless his day's food. At a signal from the Kadu Lubare (head wife), the youngster in charge swaggered up to him and ordered him to stand and deliver. The man, not liking to lose his dinner, demurred, whereupon the urchin began to lay his heavy stick across the back of this insolent slave who dared to refuse his potatoes to his superiors. I had stopped my donkey, and was watching the scene with much interest and amusement, but when the peasant began to receive a cudgelling, I thought it past a joke, so I slipped down and came up suddenly behind the young brave and put my arms round him. He at once became powerless, and the owner of the potatoes made off as quickly as he could. The ladies and their young squire began to abuse me roundly for having so rudely interfered. I replied by grabbing the boy's fine stick, and then remounted the donkey and went on. He came and begged hard for it: "Munange sebo mpa

F

mugo gwange" ("My friend, sir, give me my stick"). But I said, "No, I was good before I saw you, but you have taught me to steal, and I like your stick." He had to content himself with my reply, and I left him to digest this practical sermon on the eighth commandment. I had seen a similar party a few days previously meet a little girl, and quietly strip her of her clothing, and leave her to go her way without a single rag. It is the custom that the great and powerful have *carte blanche* to seize people on the road, and take whatever they are carrying. Sometimes women, hoeing near the road-side, will capture a passer-by, and, on pain of a severe castigation or of robbing him, will make him take a turn at the spade while they have a smoke.

This custom leads to endless litigation, for if B.'s wives rob A.'s slaves, and A. happens to be a bigger man than B., there is material for a very pretty quarrel and lawsuit.

Soon after arriving at the great enclosure, the king's baraza was announced, and the crowd of chiefs, courtiers, peasants, foreigners, dancers, musicians, and others surged through the doors into the royal court of reception. On this occasion the Kabaka was keeping great state, and was sitting, dressed in native costume, upon a rude chair, over which a leopard skin had been thrown. A costly dark-red scented lubugu, or bark-cloth robe, was knotted over his right shoulder; he wore a collar or thick necklet of finest bead-work round his neck, and he sat with a long scimitar between his knees. Possibly he was sitting up, to make people believe that he was recovering from his illness, and to give Kabarega the idea that he was strong and able. Kabarega is the present King of Bunyoro (described by Sir Samuel Baker), with whom the Baganda wage incessant warfare. Kyambalango, the favourite, sat at the king's feet, while the other great earls sat opposite. We were not in the usual reception-hall, but in a smaller and less roomy building.

When the crush was over, I walked in and made my bow to Mutesa, but was rudely bidden by some of the earls to go and sit outside with the inferior chiefs and with the Arab teacher, or Mwalimu, as he called himself, who had lately arrived, and been very favourably received by the king. Such an indignity had not been offered to any European before, though on another occasion, when Mackay and I attended a grand lukiko, the insolent chancellor had made us sit far behind, and had refused us chairs, saying, " Do not I sit on the ground, and who are you ? " On that occasion, Mackay got up and appealed to the king, and made such an impression that he gave an order, and, amid the acclamations of the servile earls, chairs were brought, and we were allowed to sit quite close to the king himself. The chancellor gave us his hand, and congratulated us with a smiling face, saying, " Muli Baganze lero " (" You are favourites to-day "). Knowing that the kindly Kabaka would probably be inclined to treat me politely, and that this was only an officious order prompted by the jealousy of the chiefs, I simply turned to Mutesa and said, "Sikiriza okutula ebweru" ("I do not agree to sit outside"), and then turned away to walk off in a huff. I was called back immediately, and the king said to me, "Where do you want to sit?" "Here, in your presence," I replied; and the gracious monarch immediately motioned to me to sit down beside Earl Mukwenda.

The proceedings began by a display of native dancing, as already described, accompanied by a Musoga minstrel on the "Nanga," a kind of banjo. When there was a lull in the music, I thought that it would be a good opportunity to present my letter, which I produced, and the king's eye fell upon it. I said, "I have brought a letter;" but the king pretended not to hear, and looked away from me, so that he might not see my outstretched hand.

At this juncture, the king's Koran was brought and handed to the little Arab mwalimu; but before reading he turned the book over, and pointed out something to the king. Mutesa's countenance, usually so benign, suddenly changed to scowling anger, and with flashing eyes he caught the book from the Arab, and shook it in his outstretched hand towards me, saying at the same time, "You have spoilt my book. Do you wish to insult me?" As may be imagined, I was perfectly astonished at this unlooked-for outburst of anger, nor did it dawn upon me at first what connection there could be between the king's Koran and myself. I suddenly remembered, however, that the king had sent the book down to the Mission to be mended, and Mackay had turned the covers the wrong way about to facilitate the operation. The Arab had pointed this out to the king, and sat with a meekly satisfied air, enjoying my discomfiture, although he was a particular friend of mine, and used to visit me constantly.

I took out a new linen pocket-handkerchief, and told Kyambalango that this was for the king. The chief received it, but said that the king was angry, and would not accept my peace-offering. It did not, however, occur to Kyambalango to return it. Pocket-handkerchiefs are quite an institution in Buganda, but it is not etiquette to use one in public. So, unless you wish to be thought an ignorant boor or foreigner, you retire for a minute or two to blow your nose, the handkerchief being a small square of bark-cloth. I have seen a chief make use of the garment of one of his attendants. Colds are very common, and as it is considered impolite to speak of certain ailments, they are euphemistically described as " colds," (" sen-yiga ") in which condition a large majority of the adult population constantly remain.

But to return. The king refused both my letter and my pocket-handkerchief, and I was not sorry to see him raise his hand and wave a signal that the reception had come to an end. Rather sadly I left; and this was the last time I ever saw the king. As I mounted the donkey to return home, the little laddie whose stick I had stolen was waiting to beg for it back again, and I was very happy to return it to him, so we parted mutually satisfied. Mutesa did not live very long after this reception and died in the autumn of 1884.

CHAPTER VIII.

MUTESA'S DEATH.

MUTESA had long been ailing, and seemed to grow daily worse and worse; the Arabs, however, assured him that there were some traders from Zanzibar, now at Unyam-yembe, in the Unyamwezi country, who possessed a marvellous medicine which could cure him. Messengers were accordingly despatched post haste to bring these great doctors with their potent prescriptions, and they arrived in due time, and at once commenced operations. It was given out that the medicine was "dungi enyo" (very good), but that no one would be allowed to see the king whilst the drug was working. Mutesa was ordered a particular diet, and forbidden to eat salt (black people as a rule never eat salt when they are ill, why I do not know). It was reported that Mutesa endured the treatment for some time, but, as the new regimen prevented him from enjoying the society of his wives, he grew tired of his doctors, and refused any longer to follow their advice.

The condition of the king was kept a profound secret, and even when he died the event was not made known till some time after it had taken place. Whether, as was reported, the Arabs' medicine had proved fatal rather than curative, or whether he was smothered by some of his wives, will never be known. The latter alternative is by no means impossible, for, as Emin Pasha shows, the practice is not confined to Buganda.

The possibility that the king's death might prove a very serious matter for us had of course been in our minds, though we did not suspect that the end was so near. From the inquiries which we made of the converts, and from the accounts of previous visitors to Buganda, we were led to expect that there would be a wild scene of anarchy and confusion upon the death of Mutesa, and probably a bloody civil war. However, as the sequel will show, these apprehensions were not fulfilled, and the interregnum passed in comparative calm.

One night, as Mr. O'Flaherty was sitting up late writing home letters, at about half-past twelve, he heard a low voice outside his window, and on going out he found one of the native Christians who had come down with a friend to warn us that the king was dead. I slept in a room up-stairs, and he came up immediately and aroused me. When I opened the door, he seemed much agitated, and said, "Mukassa of the drum has just come down to tell us that the king is dead." He added in a dubious tone that he did not suppose that they would kill us. We could now hear the quick beat of drums, sudden and alarming, and the sound of a great cry swept fitfully and wildly across the intervening valleys, as ever and anon a gust of wind stronger than usual brought it to our ears. We got out all our available guns, fearing that the rabble, now let loose, might make a sudden attack upon the mission; and I loaded my revolver, putting it at my head, and then lay down to restless sleep and troubled dreams.

In the morning, Tom the coffee-maker before mentioned, was early stirring, and when I looked out of my window, he saw me, and put his hand to his mouth, and said in a stage whisper, "Sultani amekufa." (the sultan is dead). Soon afterwards I awakened my little boy Lugalama, who slept upstairs near me, and told him that the king was dead; he said with great consternation, " Munange tunakola tutiya ?" My friend, what shall we do? It was indeed an alarming piece of news for us all. It might mean the total destruction of the mission property, and possibly the loss of our own lives and the slavery or death of our boys.

When the great earls met in council, it was debated whether the strangers should be attacked—namely the Arabs and ourselves. Kyambalango, our supposed friend, and Mukwenda of Singo, were in favour of robbing us; but the clear-headed Katikiro (chief judge) combated their proposal on the ground that it would discourage the visits of strangers and the development of trade.

The Arabs were all expecting an attack, and had spent the night armed to the teeth. They had also armed their slaves and given them gunpowder. The next day, two men arrived from Mackay, who was down at the lake about twelve miles off overhauling the mission

boat.   On the way they had been robbed of their
clothing and had had to run for their lives.   When
Mackay heard the news, he launched the boat at once,
and made her ready for sea, in case the mission should
be destroyed and we should be compelled to seek
refuge on the lake.   The people who brought him news
of the king's death assured him that his place would be
plundered.

At this time every one in the country was standing
on the defensive, awaiting the onset of his neighbours,
so that there really remained nobody to make an
attack.

Meanwhile, we at the mission had gone to see the
chiefs, and to express our condolence upon the death of
Mutesa.   Mr. O'Flaherty went in the morning, and I
in the afternoon, taking a present of fine calico to offer
for the king's obsequies.

As I drew near the court, I heard the sound of bitter
wailing, and on my arrival found myself among a
weeping crowd.

The principal chiefs were collected together in a little
temporary hut, sitting on the floor dressed in dirty bark-
cloths, and shedding tears piteously, while, in the great
house where the dead king lay, his wives were crying
and loudly lamenting him.

I had been told it was the custom to kill the
unsuccessful candidate for the throne, and as I was
personally interested in Mwanga and another lad, sons
of the late emperor, whom I knew, I begged the

chiefs to let that custom be omitted on the present occasion.

Great credit is due to the chancellor for his firmness and for the good order which he kept throughout the country, owing to which very few lives were lost and very little property destroyed.

The next day the chiefs sent for Mackay, with the request that he would make a coffin for Mutesa. He had already won extraordinary fame by the coffin which he had previously made for the late king's mother, Namasole. He has described the circumstance; and what follows is almost entirely in his own words.

The morning after the death of Mutesa's mother, Mackay and Mr. O'Flaherty had gone to pay their respects to the king. They found all the chiefs with their hands clasped above their heads, roaring and shedding tears with all their might. When they entered, the king bade these chiefs be silent, which they were instantaneously. His majesty then asked Mackay how royalty was buried in England. Mackay endeavoured to describe three royal coffins with cloth coverings, and one of them of lead to preserve the remains. At once the king asked him if he would be undertaker and make the coffins; and, thinking that they would be of ordinary dimensions, Mackay agreed to do so, at which Mutesa was much pleased. Mutesa, however, had no lead, but plenty of copper, which Mackay told him would do well enough.

The court was dismissed, and soon after there arrived at the mission a host of fine bronze trays of Egyptian workmanship (probably presents from General Gordon), and copper pots and water jars of Zanzibar (Hindu) make, with copper drums made in Buganda by coast artisans. These were to be manufactured into a coffin.

Next morning, he went off to Rusaka, the residence of the late queen-mother, some five miles distant, to measure the body. Much objection was made by the royal ladies there, at his going in to measure the corpse, but his friend, the chief Kyimbugwe, was the master of the ceremonies, and he explained that Mackay had been commissioned by the king to do so. Mackay was, however, somewhat taken aback, when he was told by some of the other chiefs that he ought not to have measured the corpse, but the dimensions of the grave, and have made the coffins to fit the latter. He told them that there was not copper enough in the land to make a box larger than what was necessary for the body alone, but that, if there were, he would willingly make one as large as a mountain, but that, as it was, he would make the inner coffins to suit the body, and the outer one as large as a house if they liked.

The grave was a huge pit, some twenty feet by fifteen feet at the mouth, and about thirty feet deep. It was dug in the centre of the late Queen's chief house, an enormous hut some hundred and fifty feet in diameter, as usual all roof, with no walls, and a perfect forest of poles inside, the centre ones being large enough for frigate masts. Rusaka stands on a hill of dry sandstone, clay, and gravel. It was well that the stratum was so firm, otherwise serious accidents might have happened if the sides of the grave had fallen in.

Nearly all the excavated gravel had been carried away, while the monster pit was neatly lined all round with bark-cloth. Into this several new bark-cloths were thrown, and carefully spread at the bottom, filling up much of the hole. Then the segments of the huge box, which, with the other coffins, had taken more than a month to make, were lowered in with much trouble, and Mackay descended and nailed the corners together. After this, he was summoned to the ceremony of putting the corpse into the first coffin. Thousands of women were yelling with all their might, a few with tears in their eyes. Only the ladies of the royal family were near the body, which by this time had been reduced to a mummy, by constantly squeezing out the fluids with rags of bark-cloth. It was wrapped in a new "lubugu," bark-cloth, and laid on the ground. The chiefs half filled the nicely padded coffin with "bufta," finest Manchester shirting, then several bunches of petty charms belonging to the Queen were laid in, and the body was placed in the coffin, which was immediately filled up with more calico. Kyimbugwe, Kawuta, and the other chiefs in charge, carried the coffin to the court where the grave-house was, when much more yelling took place. Mackay then screwed the lid down, but such was the attachment of some of the royal ladies to the deceased, that he had to have them peremptorily ordered away, with their crying and tears, and hugging of the coffin, before he could get near to perform his duties as undertaker. Then came the copper coffin, into which the other was lowered by means of a huge sheet, and the lid of which had to be riveted down, a process that was new to the chiefs standing by. " He cuts iron like thread," they said, as the pincers snapped the nails. "Mackay is a proper smith," they all shouted.

With no mechanical contrivances, it was astonishing how they got this copper coffin, with its ponderous contents, lowered into the deep grave, without letting it fall end foremost into the great box below. The task was effected, however, by means of the great multitude of men. Thousands of yards of unbleached calico shirtings were then filled in, round and over the copper coffin, until the big box was half full. The remainder was filled up with bark-cloths, as also the space round the outside of the box. The lid was lowered, and Mackay descended once more to nail it down. Several thousands more of "Embugu," bark-cloths, were then laid on, until within three feet of the surface, when earth was thrown in, to the level of the floor of the house where the grave was.

Mackay and his companion returned at dusk, but the burying was not completed till nearly midnight. Next morning, every man, woman, and child in the land had their heads shaved, and put off their mourning dress of tattered bark-cloth, "luzina," and belt of plantain leaf.

The amount of property in calico and bark-cloth, buried with Namasole, was estimated at fifteen thousand pounds. Mackay ends this most interesting description by saying, "Who would have thought in the civilised world of burying fifteen thousand pounds worth of cloth in the grave of even a queen?"

But to return to the subject of Mutesa's own obsequies. At first the native smiths and carpenters undertook to make the coffins by their own unaided efforts, but the attempt was such a miserable failure that the chiefs had to beg Mackay to show them how the work was to be done. They said that there must be three coffins at least; but Mackay begged them to allow two to suffice. He then made a huge chest, on which he nailed brass and copper trays flattened out, and copper sheathing, together with the zinc lining of old cases which we had received filled with various stores. The copper and zinc represented the metal coffin, and the whole was covered on the outside with the fine white calico which in Buganda is only worn by the upper classes. The effect was considered satisfactory, and so the dead king was placed in this novel coffin, and buried in a grave which was dug in one of his largest houses.

The whole country went into mourning, and every one allowed his hair to grow.* No white or coloured cloths were seen; the men were all clothed in the national costume of bark-cloth, knotted over the right

---

* In mourning, the ancient Egyptians allowed the hair and beard to grow. Herodotus, II. 36.

shoulder, but girded as a sign of mourning, with withered plantain fibre, an emblem of decay and death. The women also wore the bark-cloth wrapped round them, under their arms so as to cover the bosom. A casual observer would not notice the way in which the different sexes wore this costume; hence perhaps arose the scornful saying, among the surrounding nations, that the Baganda were all women, and their inveterate habit of keeping dogs, doubtless gave rise to the still more insulting taunt, that they were the offspring of these domestic pets.

The women in mourning wore girdles of tattered green plantain leaves, perhaps an emblem of the life shattered by death, as the leaf is broken by the storm, though black people are not poetical. The struggle to obtain necessary food leaves little room for romance; and no doubt the genial current of many a noble soul is frozen at its source, which, under happier conditions, might have become a life-giving stream.

Though the king was dead and buried, the scene was not yet wholly ended. His old palace, Nabulagala, now became the " Kasubi," a kind of pale unreal image of the new king's glory and grandeur. Here at Kasubi, were old deposed chiefs, possessing the simulacra of empty titles, but without any position or influence. Their master was now a dead king, before whose tomb they did homage, yet from whom they could expect but little favour. One of the deposed chiefs was now keeper of the grave, another the spirit's " musenero," chief butler. His beer and food were regularly brought. His drum was beaten, and these living ghosts of chiefs came into the presence of the ghost of their deceased monarch, bending low before the spirit, and thus the strange pageant of giving glory to the dead is kept up.

Truly a part of the whole passionate longing of mankind to be immortal, and of that deep craving expressed in so many and such various ways, in all ages and countries, comes out here in the court and homage paid to the dead Kabaka. I ought not to say "dead," for it is not polite in Buganda to speak of the king, or other persons of position, as having died—people must say "agenze," he is gone.

Of Mutesa it is difficult to give an accurate judgment. To say he was great would be hardly true, but to say that he showed some fine qualities, and that he was, in spite of his clogging surroundings, a man who sought after better things, is to give him no more than his due

Some of his acts showed a certain breadth of view His institution of a market, and his endeavour to encourage the missionaries in bridge building, by giving them the right to levy toll on foot passengers who made use of their bridges, were indications that he wished to advance. His generally courteous treatment of all Europeans, and his forbearance, with myself for example, showed a generous spirit. I knew he disliked my intruding religion on him; I did not know the language well enough to put it in a humorous or amusing manner, even if I had possessed the wit to do so; and as Mutesa

G

looked upon religion as an amusement and recreation, my readings about a great White Throne of Judgment, before which even kings were to stand, must have been most distasteful to the easy-going potentate. There was much that was good and loveable in him, but his education had been a training in cruelty, brutality, and lust. Such edicts as that every man was to wear a bead on his wrist, on pain of losing his head; and every woman, a bead on a string round her waist, on pain of being cut in half; such brutalities as shooting his wives, practised in his earlier days, and such vile obscenities as make daylight ashamed, which he caused to be performed in his open court, show that his training in these vices had born a plenteous crop of fearful crimes.

Some of his vilest abominations, I believe, he committed by the advice of the Arabs, but what was frequent and notorious in his unhappy successor, was seldom practised by himself. What a fearful picture was presented in reality in that gay and bright-looking palace of pleasure built upon its sunny hill!

Daily went up the terrible cries of unhappy victims, as they were deliberately hacked to pieces, with strips of reed, sharp enough to be used as knives, condemned very often for nothing, or merely for some breach of court etiquette. Frequently furnaces were smoking, in which the agonised bodies of persons, innocent of any crime, were writhing in slow torture, till death, more merciful than their tormentors, ended their anguish and despair. Sometimes scenes of hideous shame were enacted which make the heart sick to contemplate. But yet, in judging of these things, it is well to remember that there are none to whom the fearfullest crimes are not more than possibilities, for in every human heart are all these things, and out of every human heart they may proceed at any time, as He well knew, who bade His people pray, " Lead us not into temptation."

CHAPTER IX.

THE POLITICAL CONDITION OF BUGANDA.

BEFORE proceeding to describe the new king, it may be interesting to glance at the political condition, as far as I understand it, of the Kingdom of Buganda. First, then, in order and constitutional importance, comes the divine figure of the Kabaka, or Emperor, or Czar, of Buganda. Theoretically, he is, like his Russian counterpart, an autocrat; but, like most autocrats, he is hampered on all sides by restrictions, which, in the nature of things, have arisen to limit his absolute power. He is elected on a principle which, I believe, was law in our own country in former times, namely, that the best man should be chosen, and not necessarily the eldest son of the previous king. Certain Radical politicians might, if they pleased, find in the Buganda constitution a standing protest to the world against the law of primogeniture, for, by its immemorial provision, the king's eldest son can never be king. Still, strange to say, in these revolutionary days the latest news we have from Buganda tells us that the impossible has taken place, and that the king's eldest son has been elected to the throne.

The emperor is elected by an assemblage of the great

earls, Pokino of Budu, Kangao of Bulemezi, Sekebobo of Kyagwe, Mukwenda of Singo, Kyimbugwe, keeper of the palace, Kasuju, keeper of the king's children, and possibly other principal chiefs, such as Mugema, Kibare, and Gabunga, the latter being Lord High Admiral of the king's great war canoes.

It will be simpler, perhaps, if I first try to explain how one candidate for the throne may be more likely to succeed than another. The Baganda are split up into families called Ebyika, or clans. Every Kyika (clan) has, so to speak, its distinguishing crest. There is the kyika of the grasshopper, "Ensenane;" the kyika of the sheep, "Endiga;" the kyika of the crocodile, "Engonya," and so on. It is a curious thing that no person may eat the animal after which his kyika or clan is named. The kyika of the king is the royal tribe of the Bahuma, or Balangira (princes), as they are called in Buganda. Hence we can understand how it is the Bahuma herdsmen, though utterly despised in Buganda, are yet called princes, and have the royal privilege of paring their nails to a point, and of wearing brass and copper rings upon their ankles. Strange to say, there is a rule that a man or woman must not marry in their own kyika, and marriages with cousins are viewed as marriages with sisters, and are strictly forbidden. Now every kyika presents the reigning king with one or more virgins, "Bawala," as concubines or wives, and the child of the wife given by a particular kyika to the king is that kyika's *protégé*, and consequently the candidate whom in an election the chief or chiefs belonging to that kyika are bound to support.

The king is always surrounded by his wives; and, when he is old and feeble, it is often suspected that they give him his *coup de grace*. In fact I think it is not improbable that Mutesa was smothered to death by his wives, so that polygamy, at any rate at the king's court, carries with it certain decided disadvantages.

When once the election to the throne is decided, the unsuccessful candidates are put into durance, and guarded, inside an enormous enclosure, by Kasuju, the chief appointed keeper of the king's children. In former times, it is said, the other brothers, with one or two exceptions, were put to death.

The king has his council, or "Lukiko," answering roughly to our own Privy Council, of the chiefs whom I have just mentioned, with others of less degree. He himself appoints all the chiefs, called " Aba-saza," and all the officers of his court, or " Batongole." Besides these, he appoints the under officers in the households of these chiefs. Thus these vassals, as they hold their appointments at the pleasure of the king, and not of their actual masters, are consequently largely in the power of the king; and this gives him enormous power over them, and, through them, over their masters also.

It is invariably the policy of an able Buganda king to play off one chief against another, and one party of his subjects against an opposing party. Even in dealing with foreigners, the same astute course of action has often been followed with great success. How shrewdly he guesses that it is the devoir of one party to counteract the teaching of heresy by the other, and of the latter party to protest against errors. In similar fashion, the same subtle calculation causes him to foment and foster discord in the surrounding countries. Then, when one party comes craving for an army to help its particular faction, the Kabaka accedes, and sends his horde of savage soldiers, as cowardly as wolves, to combine with the powerful friendly faction which he favours, and the two together can hardly fail to conquer. Then the men, old and young, of the defeated party are butchered in cold blood, and when all resistance has ceased, women and children are dragged away in numbers to a shameful and degrading servitude.

In Buganda, as I have already stated, there are three persons who bear the royal title of Kabaka, namely, the king, the queen-mother, and queen-sister. The king must always have a mother, "Namasole," and sister, "Lubuga." If his actual mother be dead or out of favour, another woman, probably an aunt, is chosen to support the title. The Lubuga is chosen from the " Bambeja," or princesses.

The Bambeja are an important body of women, often very numerous. They are condemned to perpetual virginity. Sometimes, however, a great chief, as a mark of special favour, is presented with one of these princesses for his wife. They live in some style, having

usually large grants of land, and they often own large
numbers of slaves. They are, naturally, among the
highest in the land, but, with the exception of the
Lubuga (the king's sister), have no actual official
position. The fact of their being forbidden to marry
may, by the more charitable, be looked upon as some
palliation for the scandalous lives which most of them
lead. They often use every blandishment, and even
force, to secure some young peasant, the unhappy
object of their affection; but, should he be discovered
with them, he must meet the awful fate of death by
fire, the common capital punishment in Buganda.

Having spoken of the royal personages, the three
" Bakabaka " (sovereigns), the Balangira (princes), and
the Bambeja (princesses), I come now to the next in
order, namely, the Bakungu, or great chiefs. The
whole country is divided into five parts or earldoms—
first, Buganda proper, the district in the neighbourhood
of the king's capital, the Kibuga or Lubire; second,
Kyagwe, to the east; third, Bulemezi, to the north-
west; fourth, Budu, to the west; and fifth, Singo, to the
north. These are governed by chiefs, whose titles are
the following:—Sekibobo, Earl of Kyagwe; Kangao,
Earl of Bulemezi; Pokino, Earl of Budu; and Mukwenda,
Earl of Singo. The other great chiefs are Kymbugwe,
Mugema, and Kasuju, Kitunzi, and the admiral
Gabunga, Mutanda, Kolugi, Mujasi, and Musalo salo,
captains of the guards, and other sub-chiefs too
numerous to name.

In addition to the five earldoms, there are other official positions, appointments to which are made by the king, which confer on their holders the rank of chief—for example, the Musenero (chief butler), and Mufumbiro (chief baker whose name is Kawuta).

The under chief, the second in command in any earldom or barony, is the Mumyuka; and So-and-so is said to serve, as subordinate or Myuka, such-and-such a chief. The other offices held *by the appointment of the king* are the Sabadu, head of the slaves; Sebatimba, head of the upholsterers; Sabakaki, chief of the gate-keepers; Mutuba, chief of the bark-cloth beaters; Musali, the guide on the march; Sabagabo, &c. These are a few of the officers of a chief's household.*

The great earls themselves take honorary offices in the king's household, in this respect following the example of their European counterparts. One will be Sabadu, another Musali, and so on. The great chiefs are obliged to spend a certain number of months out of every year in waiting at the Kibuga or capital, just as the high officers of our own Queen's household. At other times they visit their provinces or chieftainships in the Kyalo, or country place. They are all feudal lords, and possess privileges analogous to those of our old feudal nobility, and are empowered to exact taxes or tribute from their numerous retainers. The

* In the chief's household, women sometimes hold positions of importance. The principal wife is always called the Kadu Lubare.

king has certain royal tax-gatherers, called "Basolozi," who collect brass and copper wire, bark-cloth, and cowrie shells. If, however, the people are slow to respond to the demands of these worthies, the king himself will go on a royal progress, and exact enormous benevolences from the delinquents much after the fashion of our Tudor sovereigns.

Each chief has his own drum, with its own peculiar beat, which all his vassals know. The drum is a very important feature in African political life, and in more than one county the entering on a chieftainship is expressed by the phrase, So-and-so has eaten the drum.

Pages may be found in every chief's establishment, but except in the case of the arrogant chancellor, whose pages are called "Bagala-gala," I imagine that they are merely called Balenzi (boys), and not Bagala-gala, which are an appendage of royalty.

Chieftainships are mostly hereditary, but a few, such as the Katikiro, Mukwenda, Kangao, etc., are held at the king's pleasure. Among the hereditary chieftainships are those held by chiefs of the Bataka, or landed gentry, a class of which I shall speak presently. The chiefs have absolute power of life and death in their own baronies. But any one possessing a slave may kill him for anything or nothing. I recollect Mackay telling me how a chief named Munawa killed one of his slaves for dropping a gourd of plantain cider. When Mackay pointed out to him the evil of it, old Munawa was ashamed and denied having done the deed, and sent for another slave, who he said was the one Mackay accused him of having killed, in order to try and prove that he was innocent of the crime.

The chiefs, when they go to the king's grand levee, array themselves in their best fine cloth gold-embroidered coats and Sunday breeches. The cut of these garments would horrify a London tailor, and a missionary who had served his apprenticeship in Bond Street would no doubt find his vocation in Buganda. When the chief returns from the king's presence to the bosom of his family, he immediately doffs his finery, and betakes himself to his graceful and comfortable " lubugu," barkcloth robe, and finishes the day with the help of his " Kita," an enormous gourd of " Mwenge " (plantain wine), which before nightfall leaves him in rather a sottish condition.

The armies which the king sends out from time to time to ravage the neighbouring countries are commanded by the principal chiefs in rotation. These armies carry fire and sword, blood and iron far and wide. Vast herds of women and cattle are swept in, as well as thousands of children, to be from henceforth chattels—chattels, perhaps, of children, and slaves possibly of slaves. So miserable is their fate, so wretched, so dulling to the senses, so destructive to all feeling, that one can scarcely be surprised that in a few years the unhappy creatures have given way beneath the weight of their misery, and have even actually lost all desire for freedom. After a raid of this kind, the

Arab, ubiquitous, heartless, bloody, finds his opportunity for buying the children and women, and is ready to purchase with his borrowed barter goods the slaves who in other countries he is able to procure more simply with his sword.

If the poor Indians at the coast are ruined by the Germans, and can no longer lend to the Arab traders, as in former times, at least some compensation may be found in the fact that it will probably result in lessening the power of the Arabs for slave-hunting; and I for one, though I sympathise with our Indian fellow-subjects, have seen too much of the bitter suffering of the victims of these Arab traders to make me regret anything which cuts off even one source of supplying them in their inhuman traffic.

The king, during his great " Barazas," will do what is termed " Give out an army " (" Gaba egye "). The chief appointed to the command is called the Mugabe. In returning home after victory, the spoil taken is divided. For the king a large proportion is set aside, and a smaller share for the chiefs and officers. The peasant soldiers often fare very badly, and what between the fearful ravages of smallpox and the frightful coughs and colds which the troops suffer from on the march, it is doubtful whether as many lives are not lost in obtaining the slaves as are gained in the influx of human spoil. Scenes of awful horror are perpetrated on these expeditions, which are unenlightened by a single ray of human kindness. Lust is lord, and wrong is right, while love is lost in the wild struggle for wealth. Illustrations might be multiplied indefinitely, but it is enough to say that it not unfrequently happens, as natives who have taken part in these raids have told me, that when some wearied woman carrying her babe is unable to keep up the rapid pace of the hurrying warriors, the child, too young and useless to be worth its carriage, is flung far into the forest, to perish with hunger or to fall a prey to some prowling hyena; while the agonised mother, when she would at all costs seek her child, is kept back and driven on by the spears of the brutal warriors.

The Bitongole are great offices under the king, and each Kitongole, as it is called, has its proper name. There is the Kilangira, so called after the princes; and the Kitesa, called after the late king. One of the Batongole* is called Namfumbambi, and always wears little bells jingling on his ankles. The origin of this practice is that a favourite of a former king was caught eaves-dropping, and his royal master humorously ordered that from henceforth his Kitongole should be distinguished by the wearing of bells, so that his inquisitive favourite should always give timely notice of his approach by his musical accompaniment.†

* "Batongole" are officers. "Bitongole" are offices.

† This story is given for what it is worth, but the practice may be derived from the Wanyamwezi, among whom the wearing of these small iron bells is very common; but, with this single exception of Namfumbambi, I never saw any one wearing them in Buganda.

A chief is buried in one of his houses, where the grave is dug, and the body is squeezed and kneaded till all the moisture is extracted, and then the mummy is wound up in strips of bark-cloth, and quantities of bark-cloth and cotton cloths are buried with the body, the amount varying according to the wealth and importance of the deceased chief.

The umbilical cord of all persons of high rank is carefully preserved, and pedigrees are kept by these relics of ancestry.

At this point I may redeem the promise I made a little while back, and say something about the Bataka or landed gentry, an important class in the country, most of whom are chiefs (Bakungu), or sub-chiefs. The Bataka, literally people of the soil, are the old landed gentry of Buganda, and are hereditary owners of the land. They are protected from eviction by the king, and may not be arbitrarily put to death by him.[*] Gabunga was one of these Bataka chiefs; and two other Christian sub-chiefs were also Bataka, namely the jolly old giant Kamanya, keeper of Suna's father's grave, and Kinyoro, an early though not altogether satisfactory convert to Christianity.

We now come to the second great class in the country, the Bakopi or peasants. The name Bakopi seems to be derived from a tribe who formerly came from the north

---

[*] The king has authority over Bataka within certain prescribed limits; he may depose one brother from the headship of the clan or chieftainship, and put another brother in his place.

of Bunyoro, Kopi, or Chopi as it is sometimes spelt, and which Emin Pasha identifies with Shifalu. The peasant class in Buganda are, I suppose, named from this probably conquering people, as the slave class, Badu, are called after the country of Budu, or Udu, as people who only know the Swahili language usually pronounce it.

The Bakopi usually attach themselves to some "Mwami," master or chief. They have the right to "senga," serve whom they please; and if they are dissatisfied they have the privilege of "senguka," that is, to leave the service of their master and attach themselves to some one whom they fancy more. It is not always a safe thing to do. One of my friends, a Muhuma herdsman, who kept the Katikiro's cattle, left the chancellor's service to enter that of the king. On some lying pretext he was seized, his ears cut off, and his eyes put out, as a warning that the imperious chancellor would allow none of his servants to prefer any one else to himself, not even the king.

The duty of the Mukopi is first to follow the chief to war, armed with two long spears and the beautiful shield, which the Baganda are so skilful in making. His work at home largely consists in building houses and making the fences which I have already described.

In return for this service, the chief will give him a wife, and sometimes two; but she may be taken away from him and given to his neighbour, for any or no reason.

The Mukopi is free; but often loses his wife and children, and even his own liberty, by getting into debt, when he descends to the miserable class of Badu or slaves.

If not taken out of the country by the Arab traders, the native born slave has certain facilities for redeeming himself, and such redemption is often effected.

The sons of chiefs are in the Bakopi class, and have no recognised position in the country. Those whose mothers are of high rank are presented to the king, and also any boy remarkable for good looks or any other valuable quality.

Most of the peasants own two or three slaves. An ambitious man will quietly accumulate a number, and quarter them on his friends, who give them their scanty pittance of food for the use and show which they can make of them. Then, if their owner is given an office or Kitongole, he collects his slaves, and blossoms out with quite a train of followers behind him.

The effect of thus owning slaves, and being a hanger-on of some feudal lord, is to make these Bakopi cringing, abject, servile, and toadying to those above them, but arrogant, domineering, proud, and overbearing to those whose unhappy fate it is to be their slaves.

Lastly are the slaves, drawn, I suppose, originally from the conquered people of the country of Budu, south-west of Buganda.

How shall I speak of them?—and slavery, what can

be said of it ? The deepest degradation that strength can inflict on weakness, the utmost depth of shame to which an unhappy human soul can be dragged. Who will not sympathise with those savage Bakede to whom I have already referred, whose women's hearts rejected with loathing the life which lay before them, and who chose death cheerfully to being the concubines of those whom they scorned and hated ?

The slaves have no rights. What have they to do with riches and honour, or home or hope ? Their bodies are not their own, and the jewel of chastity, did they ever so much desire it, lies for ever out of their reach.

Shall we say it is well that their feelings should become so blunted that they dumbly acquiesce in their shame ? Dare we say that because they often seem light-hearted they do not therefore feel their own degradation ?

The slaves in Buganda are drawn from the surrounding countries, chiefly Bunyoro and Busoga, a few from Busàgara, Ihangiro, Buzongora, and Buzinja. They fetch from ten thousand to twenty thousand cowrie shells, equivalent to between three and six pounds in English money, according to description. A beautiful Muhuma woman will fetch far more. I recollect one day being offered three slaves in exchange for my Muhuma boy Lugalama. The idea of this exchange was not pleasant to me, and I replied that, if the gentleman threw himself into the bargain,

H

I should not care even then to do business with him.

We had a good number of little boys, some given to us by chiefs, some sold to us. Little Lwanga we bought for a padlock and four yards of calico. Some were redeemed by us. For instance, one of the apprentices whom Mutesa sent to Mackay, to learn how to work in iron, purchased a slave. The position was rather curious, having slaves living at an English mission, so we had no hesitation in redeeming the boy and setting him free. I suppose legally we were not justified in buying a slave even to redeem him, but as the English law gave us no protection, and as we were actually outlaws, we felt quite at liberty to behave as such in particular cases of this kind.

Another little laddie, whom I christened James Greenway, or Jimmy, I redeemed at a great price; I gave for him a gun, a white box, a looking-glass, and a few other things. I used often to tell him that he had cost far more than his market value. When my new purchase came home, he wanted to go back to the chief who had sold him, so I said, "All right, you shall go back in seven days, if you wish it; if not, you can stay here." A day or two afterwards I asked him if he wanted to go, but the good feeding and clothes he got with us and, I hope, kind treatment made him more than willing to stay, and he promptly replied, "Neda Munange," "No, my friend," "njagala kubera wano," "I want to remain here." I had a special interest in him, for I supposed, though mistakenly, that he was the brother of the boy Lugalama who was killed by Mwanga's and the Katikiro's orders. Lugalama had told me that he had a brother in Buganda, a slave somewhere, and I had promised to do all I could to find him and redeem him.

CHAPTER X.

ACCESSION OF MWANGA.

As soon as the breath was out of Mutesa's body, the three young princes who had enjoyed their liberty by favour of the late king were at once seized and made prisoners. Of these, one, Mwanga, was to succeed Mutesa and to be future king of Buganda. Kiwewa, the eldest son, not being eligible by the custom of the country, which I have already explained, was left quietly in his own compound, little thinking that the course of events would in a few short years place him, also, on the throne of Buganda. The Council of the great Earls was summoned immediately, and deliberated under the presidency of the Katikiro, or Lord High Chancellor, while the whole country awaited with breathless expectation the result of their deliberations. After a time the sound of vociferous cheering was heard, and soon some of our friends came rushing in to us with the news: "Mwanga alide Buganda," Mwanga has eaten Buganda.*

* This metaphor of eating a drum or a country was one of the arguments sometimes used by us to demolish the doctrine of transubstantiation. It is astonishing to think that these people, who only a few years before had never heard of any one whiter than a Muhuma herdsman, should be arguing with an Englishman on the

The newly-elected king, Mwanga, at this time was a lad of some eighteen years of age. He had visited us several times, and I had tried to teach him his letters; but, wayward and flighty, he seemed unable to concentrate his attention on the same thing for any length of time. As to his moral character, there were some very evil reports current which shocked even a people so lax in morals as the Baganda.

I recollect, one day when he was paying me a visit, asking him how he would treat us if he became king? He replied, "I shall like you very much, and show you every favour." In appearance he was very like Mutesa, only shorter, and with more of the negro about him; but he lacked the common-sense and experience of his father.

The circumstances in which he was now placed may be some excuse for his subsequent tyranny, and certainly the sudden marvellous change in his condition, from a position hardly better than that of a peasant, to the autocratic authority of an African emperor, could hardly have been without deterioriating effects, and might well have turned the head of a much stronger-minded man.

---

meaning of *hoc est corpus*. As the Roman Catholic priests expressed it, it was their devoir to counteract our heresy, and they did it to such purpose that they got one or two of our converts, one especially who was most clever in argument; and on one occasion answered my objection to the Pope by asking, "How I came to have a bishop?" This was a fine handsome young chief named Bali Kudembe, who was the fourth Christian to fall a victim to the cruelty of the young tyrant who was now ruler of Buganda.

How as a god to his subjects he ruled from his slippery eminence, and how he imbrued his hands in innocent blood, at the cruel suggestion of the murderer Mujasi (whose zeal for Islam at length led to his own miserable end), until he had filled the cup of his crimes to overflowing, and how he was as suddenly hurled from his autocratic power as he had been suddenly raised to it—all this makes up the terrible tragedy, fearful scenes of bloodshed and slaughter, strange vicissitudes of fortune which I have now to unfold.

When we first paid a visit to the new king, we happened to arrive after the chiefs and other courtiers had been admitted; so, finding ourselves shut out, there was nothing for it but to return home. The reason he would not see us was no doubt his desire, by such insolence, to show his sense of his new importance. At this time we were the only white men in the country, for the French priests had left in Mutesa's time and had not yet returned, though they came back some months later when Mwanga sent for them.

Mackay now left the capital and returned to finish his work on the boat which he had been obliged to abandon in order to superintend the burial of Mutesa. It was a time of much rain, so "Bwana Filipo" (as Mr. O'Flaherty was always called) and I did not again venture to pay another visit to the king, as we thought it better to await Mackay's return. Our enemies, meanwhile, were busy maligning us at the court, for it must not be forgotten that ever since our arrival we had met with the bitterest hostility from the Arabs and from those natives influenced by them, who believed the lying slanders which the Arabs never ceased to pour into their ears.

On one occasion, indeed, during the late king's reign when Mackay brought some boxes of provisions in the boat from Musalala, the Arabs told the king that we had just received a great many loads of gunpowder, and so Mutesa sent down some of his officers to have everything examined. There was, of course, not a single ounce of gunpowder to be found; but this circumstance shows how strong even then was the feeling of suspicion against us. For in Africa it is thought a serious breach of good manners to search a stranger's private goods, and Mutesa would never have done so unless he had believed that there was sufficient ground for the gravest suspicion. Of the general causes of suspicion against white men, and against ourselves in particular, I shall speak in more detail later on.

The report which now reached the ears of King Mwanga was that Mackay was going along the coast in the boat, and was making small raids for purposes of stealing goats and plantains. As a matter of fact, the boat was beached at the time, receiving a coat of paint, and Mackay was ill with fever in his tent.

At last Bwana Filipo and I thought that we had better put in an appearance at court and tell the king ourselves how the matter really stood. Therefore, in the beginning of November, in the year

1884, we paid our first visit to the new Kabaka or emperor.

When we arrived at the king's enclosure, we were kept waiting outside for about two hours in a wretched hut where the great earls—men who are virtually kings in their own provinces—had gathered together. One of their number, Pokino, ruler of Budu, was amusing himself and the company with obscene jests. I told him it was a shame for a great man so to lower himself, and he accordingly refrained.

After we had become thoroughly tired of waiting, one of the pages came to fetch us, and we were duly ushered into the presence of our quondam pupil, now our king. It was with something of anxiety that we entered the presence-chamber of the new monarch. He was holding his court in a small house, as his new capital, or "Kibuga," had not yet been built. As we entered, he was sitting on the chair which his father had used the last time I had seen him, and looked very much like the late king. This likeness naturally helped, I believe, to determine his election; many of the chiefs wished to choose a younger boy, but the others asserted that he was not nor could not have been Mutesa's child, while of Mwanga there could be no possible doubt.*

* It sometimes occurred that as a mark of royal favour the king would send some one of his wives to a favourite chief, such as the chancellor; and, besides this, the notorious unfaithfulness of Baganda matrons made the question of paternity a doubtful and difficult one to decide.

Mwanga received us smilingly, and told us we had "kyeju"—an admirable word which perfectly depicts the character of your ordinary negro, and which includes anything between unconscious self-complacency and brazen-faced insolence. Our "kyeju," or insolence, consisted in not having sooner come to see him.

The king was dressed in Arab costume, and had a gilded mirror near him, such as may commonly be found in the front-parlours of small lodging-houses, in which he could admire his gold-embroidered vestments. In the course of conversation he praised the Arabs, our bitter enemies, and said he wished the French priests to return to Buganda, and that we must bring them. He wanted a house built for himself as well as a boat. He then asked me if I knew how to sew; fortunately I did not, or he might have set me to make him a pair of trousers. Then he inquired if I were able to make guns. He knew perfectly well that I was not, but it was his "kyeju" which made him ask these questions. Bwana Filipo and I replied that we were all three only teachers; but that, if he were willing to pay people in Europe to make these things, they would be glad to do so. The king did not like this way of putting it, so he changed the subject by asking me "if I possessed a gun." I not very wisely replied "that he had seen it when visiting us," thus reminding him that he had once been only an ordinary mortal such as ourselves.

After a little more conversation of this kind he

waved his hand, and at this signal of dismissal we left him. The next day Mr. O'Flaherty went to see the king in his new palace, and Mwanga at once began begging, and made Bwana Filipo promise to give him a field-glass which he had seen on one of his visits to the mission.

In all the trouble and confusion of the change of sovereigns the old chancellor had managed to keep his place, and even called Mwanga his "mtoto," child. The consummate art of flattery of which this ambitious man was master was something astonishing. Mwanga was afraid of him, and knew that the velvet paw concealed cruel claws, and that the obsequious lord who was ready to wipe the moisture from his face, or to brush away a fly with a white pocket-handkerchief, or to perform any other menial office, was in reality his master.

Meanwhile Mackay had returned to the mission-house, and he and I went together to pay our respects to the Kabaka. The king had now built another temporary enclosure on the slope of Nabulagala Hill, and quite close to Mutesa's old palace. When we reached the entrance, we found ourselves among a turbid swaying crowd, and our ears were deafened with the din which a motley band of musicians were making. Kettle-drums and hand-drums were rolling, horns braying, flutes screaming, and the "madinda" (a kind of dulcimer played by striking with sticks pieces of wood arranged in a scale) gave out a not unmusical accompaniment, while blind minstrels twanged away on their banjos, the whole making a most discordant harmony. It is the custom to put out the eyes of the court performers, as it is supposed that they will thus become more proficient in their art. There is, however, some accusation preferred against them, possibly true, but if not, no great matter: plenty of false witnesses can soon be found to represent the Crown. I have never heard of any arbitrary act of cruelty being performed in Buganda without some show of justice, even if it were only of the Star Chamber type.

Through all the noise of the other instruments we could hear the booming of the king's great drums. We made our way through an enormous crowd, till we came to the small house where the reception was being held. The king was sitting facing the door, the royal " jembe," or magic horn, a very white tusk of ivory, placed at his feet, and the chiefs in rows at each side, still dressed in mourning, that is, wearing shabby bark-cloths; but as a mark of honour to the new king, over these were thrown rich finely-dressed skins, Mwanga himself wearing a splendid leopard-skin.

Mackay and I pushed our way to the king's presence, and sat down, one on each side before him. On entering we made polite bows, which he duly acknowledged. The uproar was tremendous, and the crowd were kneeling outside in front of the king, with their hands upon the clay ridge which surrounds the house and serves to keep out the rain. Like all Buganda houses, this one was built on the slope of a hill, with the door facing the ascent; so that this clay ridge is a very necessary precaution in case of a flood of water rushing down.   This house had, however, two doors, one in front and the other at the back; ordinary people are only allowed one doorway, so that, when the king's officers come to search for delinquents, they may not escape by the back door.   The crowd of sycophants were screaming for places and promotion; and I suppose here, as sometimes happens in Europe, those who screamed loudest obtained the desired posts.   It was on the same principle, I imagine, that Dr. Lemuel Gulliver, in one of the countries which he visited, was informed that those who could jump the highest were thought most worthy of being ennobled.   As we were jammed up in very uncomfortable positions, half crouching and half kneeling, Mackay tried to make a little more room, and unluckily happened to kneel upon the carpet on which the sacred " horn " of ivory was reposing; immediately three or four fussy chiefs eagerly warned him off.   There was no intentional discourtesy in this action of theirs, for the Baganda are most particular, as indeed are all Africans, to see that their customs are strictly observed, and that the rules of etiquette are respected; so that an unhappy foreigner is almost certain to do something dreadful in their eyes.   A few days before, while sitting in a house with some of the chiefs in which was one of the king's great sacred drums, I chanced to put my sun-helmet upon it; at once there was a cry of horror at the desecration, and the Earl of Bulemezi snatched it off, and handed it back to me with a reprimand. I apologised for the mistake I had unwittingly made, and so the incident terminated. In the same way I may mention that Bwana Filipo, also, while visiting the late king's tomb, chanced to turn his back upon the grave, and so incurred a sharp rebuke from the chief in charge for insulting the deceased Kabaka, whose spirit was there. So much do they hold the idea of reverence to a deceased monarch, that every chief who received any promotion was obliged after saying "neanze, neanze," etc., to the three Kabakas, the king and his mother and sister, to go and "Kweanza" before the tomb of the late king. These instances will serve to show how easily, from ignorance, a stranger may give offence. The people of Buganda, however, had the good sense and delicate feeling to pardon errors that we frequently made which would have met with severe punishment and fines, had their own people committed them. Other tribes will make a breach of custom an excuse for exacting a heavy fine. I recollect when travelling in the Usukuma country, south of the Nyanza, one of our party shaved his head. The people assured us that this was "mwiko," or unlawful, since they had not yet sown their corn; it was most annoying, if slightly amusing. But they made him pay ten cloths, or forty yards of unbleached calico, for the breach of custom.

But to return—the present public "baraza," or reception, did not last long, for Mwanga got up suddenly and, retired; presently he sent a page to call the Katikiro, or chief judge, Mackay, and myself to a private interview. We were conducted through several reed-built courts, until we came to another small house where the king received us. We found him lying on the ground stretched upon some rich carpets obtained from the Arabs. The old king Mutesa used always to allow the Katikiro and other honoured guests to sit inside the house with him; but this young Rehoboam had no such intention, so we were all stationed in the doorway. My stool happened to be nearer him than Mackay's; he bade us change places, and then the conversation began. Mackay was chief speaker. In front of the king was his favourite large mirror, while he held a small one in his hand.

Mwanga was inclined to be self-willed and rude, while Mackay was perfectly polite and firm. "Do you want to go to Musalala (at the south of the Lake) to bring more white men?" said the king. "No," replied Mackay, "but if you wish it I will go." "Very well," rejoined the King, "I will give you a 'mubaka'" (messenger), and he named Kadu Mayanja, a man whom Mackay knew well, a turbulent and murderous character. Mackay said "he did not wish this person to accompany him; would the king appoint some one else?" "Oh, I see," said Mwanga, "you think he is too clever, and that is the reason you do not like him."

Mackay said, " Give me Bijugo," "little bells," this was
the king's confidential page. Bijugo, however, modestly
said that his " magezi," " cleverness," was not equal to
that of Kadu Mayanja, to which the king, and consequently the company, assented. Mackay replied by
saying, " Very well, if Kadu Mayanja is so clever, he
can go by himself with the boat, and I will remain
behind." Mwanga then gave way, and called
Sematimba Michah, one of his Christian pages, who
afterwards became a sub-chief, and appointed him to go
with Mackay. After a good deal more desultory talk,
we were dismissed, having formed not too favourable
an opinion of our new ruler.

CHAPTER XI.

CAUSES OF SUSPICION.

THERE is an old prophecy current in Buganda that the country is to be conquered by a people coming from the East. How strongly this idea seems to have possessed the people may be seen in the jealousy with which they tried to keep strangers from going in that direction. Mutesa said to Mackay when the subject of a direct easterly route was mooted between them: "I know you white men want exceedingly to see what there is beyond Busoga, but I will never permit it." Possibly this astute monarch feared that his ivory preserves would eventually be tapped by the agency of Europeans, and that the Busoga ivory would find an outlet other than through Buganda.

It is therefore not a matter of surprise that the Baganda people and their rulers should look with suspicion upon the advent of foreigners so unlike any people whom they had ever seen before; nor that our teaching and the marvellous influence which that teaching gave us should be viewed with suspicion and dislike by those in power.

Our methods seemed to them as contemptible as dangerous. We were willing to teach "balenzi" and "badu," boys and slaves, and with dismay they saw the very flower of their nation and the young aristocrats who would hereafter be powerful chiefs flocking about us, and hanging upon our words and eagerly reading our books. Sebwato, the Katikiro's most trusted sub-chief, and Mayanja, lately a powerful chief and still keeper of Kamanya's (Mutesa's grandfather) grave, were openly baptized, while in no short time many chiefs, of whom the most powerful was the boy-admiral Gabunga, followed their example.

Had the royal personages and chiefs known what we knew of the tremendous new power which had entered their country, they would have agreed with the adversary quickly while in the way with him; but of this they had yet much to learn. They could see indeed a dim danger ahead looming fearfully in the distance, but they knew not how to meet it. It is merely a truism to say that mankind are universally actuated by self-interest, a fact in human nature which the Divine Teacher recognised, and to which He made His appeal.

But of any interests beyond the present, and of any gain besides that of wealth or comfort or power, the Baganda had no conception, any more than the fanatical Arabs, who never tired of telling them that we were simply agents of the British Government.

Unfortunately the Arabs thoroughly believed this themselves, and therefore they spoke with that sincere conviction which only a belief in their own statements could give; and hence the coming of white men

I

in response to the invitation given by King Mutesa through Stanley in 1875 could only be viewed by that ruler and his counsellors as an advent for some interested purpose, a purpose which to their eyes became more and more evidently that of seizing upon the country. It will be seen that there were many circumstances, slight in themselves and insignificant, which, when taken together and viewed through the medium of native fears, heightened by Arab hostility, combined to give colour to the growing suspicions entertained by the rulers of Buganda.

The arrival of white men was particularly grievous to the Arabs, who looked upon us as possible rivals in trade as well as actual rivals in religion, and who believed that one of our main objects was to thwart their paramount interest, the slave trade.

It was indeed natural that we should be looked upon as direct agents and representatives of our country, since the white men of whom the Baganda had any knowledge were rulers and governors—Baker, Gordon, Emin. Moreover, the gradual encroachment of Egypt from the north with her powerful white pashas was a constant source of alarm to the Baganda people. Buganda was indeed for a while occupied by Egyptian troops, and theEgyptian flag was hoisted by their leader almost under Mutesa's nose. Gordon Pasha removed these troops, and I am under the impression that one of Emin Pasha's visits to Buganda was for this purpose. We were told that when the Egyptian leader came to

visit Mutesa, the king brought some hundreds of his
"bagazi" (gate-keepers) and "bamboa" executioners,
and ordered that a couple of them should stand behind
each Egyptian soldier, and on the least sign of hostility
they should attempt to bind the Egyptian troops.
Great fires were kept burning all night through, and
the whole country was on the alert, awaiting an attack.

When the first missionaries arrived (under the leader-
ship of Shergold Smith—than whom no braver man has
set foot in Africa) in June 1877, they presented to
Mutesa a letter of introduction from the English Foreign
Secretary, and also a letter from the Church Missionary
Society, signed among others by the Archbishop of
Canterbury. Whether the missionaries made clear to
Mutesa who or what the Archbishop was, I very much
doubt. But these letters naturally could only have
given the King of Buganda one impression, namely
that the bearers of them were ambassadors of the
Queen of England. There were in addition always
present hostile Arabs with their explanations of such
credentials.

The next advent of missionaries was by way of the
Nile in 1879, when Mr., now the Rev. Charles Pearson,
the Rev. G. Litchfield, and Mr., now Dr. Felkin, were
enabled to reach their destination by the generous
kindness of General Gordon, who provided them with
an Egyptian escort, and commanded all the "Vakeels,"
or governors of the various stations, to treat them
with every consideration. Mutesa had sent some of

his people north, who naturally concluded that the mission party was a political embassy, and told the king on their return that the "Bangereza" (Englishmen) were bringing him a large present from the Queen. When the party reached Buganda with their baggage, which looked like untold wealth to the ignorant people of Buganda, Mutesa sent down messengers to ask for the gift from his friend Queenie, whose people the new-comers were. Still further to increase the already strong conviction as to the direct relation between the missionaries and the Government, Mr. Pearson's party produced a letter from the Foreign Office, recommending them to the favour of the King of Buganda.

Her Majesty's Consul at that time in Zanzibar apparently considered that, perhaps unconsciously, the missionaries were giving native rulers the impression that they were accredited agents of the British Government, in which it is obvious from what I have already said he was perfectly correct. I do not think the missionaries were necessarily to blame, nor do I think that the Consul in Zanzibar blamed them ; but I think I am correct in saying that he wrote to Mutesa, telling him that he was the only accredited agent of her Majesty in Eastern Equatorial Africa. On receipt of this letter Mutesa at once accused the missionaries of presenting bogus letters, and of being impostors. The missionaries in turn wrote home to complain to the committee of their society that their position was a false and unpleasant one, and pressure was apparently brought to bear upon the Consul at Zanzibar by the Church Missionary Society, so that he wrote to Mutesa the following letter :—

"H.B.M. Agency and Consulate-General,

"Zanzibar, Nov. 24, 1879.

" To King Mutesa of Uganda.

" Sir,—The directors of the Church Missionary Society in England, by whom Messrs. Wilson, Mackay and others now with you were sent, have received reports from these gentlemen to the effect that their lives have been endangered in consequence of letters which, they say, I wrote to you, stating that no Englishman in Uganda came from the Queen, or had letters from the English Government. I am directed if this be correct to write and explain that the letters presented were given to the missionaries by the English Government.

" Your Majesty knows that what has been reported is not correct, and I have the best reason to be satisfied that so far from these gentlemen's lives being in danger, they were, long after my letters reached and up to a recent date, well received and in favour at your court. In proof of which your Majesty had allowed some of your people to accompany one of them to Europe.

" As to a letter addressed to your Majesty by the Marquis of Salisbury, dated May, 1878, I have to inform you that, on receiving a copy thereof, fearing the original might be delayed, I wrote and explained its

contents, in order that you might be encouraged to
extend to the missionaries the protection and assistance
you had already shown to all Europeans.   I have only
now to repeat what I have said, and ask your Majesty
to encourage and protect all travellers, traders, and
missionaries who may visit your dominions, and to allow
one and all of them to travel where they please, and to
leave the country, should they wish to do so, by any
route they may select, either by way of the Nile or
Unyamwezi, or by any new route they may have a
mind to try.   " I have the honour to be,
        " Your Majesty's most obedient humble servant,
                (Here his signature),
            " H.M. Agent and Consul-General."

This letter shows so admirably the state of muddle
which had now been reached, that, at the risk of being
tedious, I have given it in full.   Reference is here made
to the envoys brought to England from Buganda by
Messrs. Felkin and Wilson.   Their idea in persuading
Mutesa to send some of his people to Europe was that
such a visit would do more than anything else to give
the Baganda people a better knowledge of their relation
to the outside world.   Had Messrs. Felkin and Wilson
been able to prevail upon Mutesa to send some of his
chiefs or superior officers, the experiment might have
proved a success ; as it was, Mutesa sent some utterly
insignificant people of the " Bakopi," or peasant class.
Long afterwards, when speaking of this to Mackay,

he said, "You Bazungu, white men, can make many wonderful things, but my 'magezi gezi,' cunning, is much superior to yours. Did I not send some slaves to Bulaya, Europe, and did the Bazungu not believe them to be chiefs?"

The fact that the two missionaries undertook to conduct the King of Buganda's envoys to England, with the letter which Mutesa wrote to Her Majesty, naturally gave them, in Mutesa's view, the appearance of being the accredited agents of the Queen, and although Her Majesty only received the envoys at a private audience, and the Foreign Office refused to receive them officially, it was quite enough for Mutesa to know that his messengers had been received and his presents accepted by the august woman-ruler who held sway in Bulaya.

The further fact that Mutesa's messengers were brought back to Buganda in charge of a missionary, who was the bearer of return presents to the King of Buganda, and of a letter from the then Foreign Secretary, must have removed any little lingering doubt from the mind of the people of Buganda that the white English missionaries were, or could be, anything else but direct agents of the British Government.

It was only natural and right that the British Consul-General at Zanzibar should wish to keep up friendly relations with so important a native ruler as Mutesa, and, to secure this end, he corresponded with the King of Buganda, sending him occasional presents.

When Mutesa died, the Consul wrote to congratulate Mwanga upon his accession. Subsequently I wrote to our Consul to ask him to write and explain to Mwanga what we really were, a request to which he promptly and courteously acceded.

The Consul-General's position in the matter was somewhat difficult, since I asked him to do what he had been apparently blamed by other missionaries for having done some time previously; nevertheless, he wrote distinctly to Mwanga, telling him that we were only teachers of religion and nothing more.

We were the only Englishmen in Buganda at the time, and he requested us to ask Mwanga to forward letters which he sent with our mail to Emin Pasha. We were thus the natural channel of communication between the beleaguered pasha in the north and the east coast, and so the suspicion which had hardly slumbered was again awakened, that we were in league with the dreaded "Batuluki" (Egyptians) from the north.

Rumours of troubles in which Bazungu played a prominent part reached Buganda from all quarters. In the north there was news of fighting in the Soudan in which the English were implicated; news of German annexations in the east; news, uncertain, undefined, of Bazungu advancing from the west, and the advent of English missionaries and German traders in the region south of the Nyanza made the outlook in all directions stormy and uncertain. Mr. Thomson had suddenly appeared in Busoga, and had as suddenly retired. He had sent no present and no message to Mutesa, who died shortly afterwards.

But the news of Thomson's coming, distorted and magnified by the terrors of the narrators, together with the other circumstances already mentioned as operating to make us objects of fear and suspicion was, I think, the immediate cause of the terrible tragedy which I shall relate in the succeeding chapters, and of which two young Christian lads especially dear to me were the first innocent victims.

CHAPTER XII.

LUGALAMA.

WHEN Rumanika, King of Karagwe, died, the succession was disputed between two of his sons. One of these, Entare, "the lion," sent to Mutesa and obtained his help. By means of a Baganda army, supplemented by his own faction, Entare overcame his brother, who took refuge on an island in the lake Mwutanzige (?). The supporters of the conquered brother were handed over to the tender mercies of the Baganda raiders, who swept the country far and wide, and so, by means of the swords of their own tribe, managed to enslave a large number of the lighter-coloured Bahuma. While this raid was proceeding, the news reached the zereba where Lugalama's father and mother lived that a Baganda war-party was close at hand, and they could hear the sound of the hostile drums as the raiders came on to the attack. Immediately there was a hurried flight of women and children. Soon the Baganda came up. The Bahuma men could only fight and die (for there is no quarter given in African warfare), and then there only remained the easy task of hunting out the spoil. Lugalama and his little brother ran and hid themselves in the long canes, and soon, with breathless horror, they heard the yelling of the painted warriors close at hand beating the long grass. Soon the children were spied and dragged out. The thirst of blood is on their cruel captors, and they cry, "Kill the bigger one, kill him!" A spear is raised—but a darker fate awaited him. These raids showed only the brute man with cruelty not yet refined and hardened by the dogmas of a fanatical religion. Lugalama was yet to learn more of the wickedness of the world and to be mocked and taunted and slowly tortured to death on account of a creed of which he could hardly judge. At this time, however, a chief, Sebwato by name, came up and seized him, bidding his would-be murderers begone. He, good man, snatched the little charms, "ensiriba," the child was wearing about his neck and flung them away. He had already thrown away his own, for he had begun to learn at our Mission. He was a superior man and very kind-hearted, and afterwards became one of my warmest friends. For the present he took his little prize and tied his hands, and the march back was begun. The mother was seized by some one else, the other children by others. Thus this peaceful little family was broken up and ruined, and its members separated to go away into slavery and shame, and this child to a cruel, lingering death.

Sebwato gave him some small thing to carry, but it was very burdensome to him, for he could not eat the new kind of food which they gave him. The

Bahuma, like the Masai, live entirely upon milk, and now no milk could be obtained, only scanty supplies of sweet potatoes and plantains. Many of the little children perished on this pitiful march. If they survived, what lay before them ? To be bandied about from owner to owner, at last, most likely, to fall into the hands of the most abject of the sons of men—the mongrel descendants of slave-dealing Arabs, or Arabs themselves almost as low.

And so the caravan of captive women and children went on, leaving the Kagera River behind choked with the corpses of husbands and brothers who had died in their defence, the way marked by the emaciated bodies and whitening bones of helpless children who died on the terrible march. This is Africa left to herself. Livingstone, Stanley, and Cameron have told us what Africa is when left to the Arabs. If such recitals as these have any meaning, it is that the most powerful appeal is made to civilised nations to take the African tribes under their fostering care. It is an appeal to England to do for Africa what she has so triumphantly effected for the peoples of India.

Sebwato, Lugalama's captor, sent him on before with a part of his following, but when the boy reached Buganda he was quickly kidnapped from his new owner; but Mugaju or Lugalama, having appreciated the kindly disposition of Sebwato, managed to escape from his kidnappers and return to his first captor. Now Sebwato had determined to set the child free, and show his appreciation of the teaching he had received at the Mission by sending him to us. He knew that we hated slavery, and thus his sending him to the Mission was practically manumitting him. There were not wanting mischievous boys who told Lugalama (Mugaju, as his new master called him) that the white men were most cruel, and would certainly cut off his ears. This horrible practice is so common in Buganda that the child might well believe it possible. I remember the first day that he came with his master to our house. He was dressed in ragged bark cloth, but not even rags could make him look common. I was at once struck by his face, so different from the other followers of the chief. When he came to live with us he soon showed himself quick at learning. At first he wished to return to his first captor (the story of the cutting off ears was, I think, haunting his mind), but he soon learnt that this was untrue, and lost his fear of the strange-looking Bazungu (Europeans). I remember that some time afterwards Sebwato came and told me that the boy belonged to one of the chief families of Karagwe, and that the King Entare wanted to get him back again. I said I did not think it right to keep him from those who had so strong a claim upon him, if he wished to return to them. Lugalama was listening to this conversation, and when Sebwato had gone he came up to me and said, "Do not agree to what he says, they only want to take me back to sell me to the Arabs." This boy was one of the few Africans I have met with who seemed really to care much for his parents. He told me the story of his capture, and when I asked him about his father he could hardly speak, and his beautiful eyes filled with tears at the thought of his death.

Speaking of the sensibilities of Africans, it may be worth while to relate that when I was last at Usambiro, at the south of the Nyanza, there was a young Muhuma, whom the Katikiro had given to Mackay for doing some work for him. This little fellow's name is Ndongole, or Timoteo. I had given an order to kill a sheep which was ailing, in order to save it from dying a lingering death, when Ndongole, or Kayima, as we always called him, who was standing by, began to whimper and cry. "What on earth is the matter with you?" I asked him; and he said, "I am so sorry for its little lamb, which will be left an orphan." I immediately, though perhaps weakly, reprieved the poor sheep, which, however, died in a day or two, but I could not resist such eloquent pleading.

Mugaju Lugalama soon became a great friend of mine, and was a general favourite. On one occasion, when Mackay and I visited the Katikiro, he came with us, and the Chancellor's eye immediately fell upon the handsome Muhuma boy, and he asked who he was, and how we had got him; and when we said he had been given us by Sebwato the Katikiro seemed displeased and vexed, but let the matter drop. At the time we suspected nothing, but we discovered afterwards that the chief was annoyed that we should receive gifts of boys, as if we were chiefs, forsooth! I mentioned in a former chapter the practice of sending pages to the king and powerful chiefs. About the time of Lugalama's coming to us we were visited by a large number of the king's pages who were learning to read, and among others two who deserve especial mention, Mukassa, who was named Samweli, and Kakumba, named Yusufu. Kakumba always took much interest in our teaching, and was very fond of coming to see us. After a time his master died, and he told us that he wished to come and serve, "senga," us. This we allowed. Now people only go to "senga," *i.e.* serve, a chief or person of authority in the country, and our allowing young men and boys to stay at the Mission gave the chiefs, who were always listening to the slanders of Arab enemies and others, the impression that we wished to gain a position of power and influence in the country by attaching a number of followers to ourselves. Kakumba was a very religious boy, and, though somewhat weak, was a very willing and obedient scholar and servant. Mukassa, whom I first knew as the "guava boy," was a very nice gentlemanly little page. He used always, unlike the usual run of visitors, to bring a little present of guavas, or "mapera"* as the fruit is called in Buganda.

* "Mapera" was the name by which the French priests were always called. When they were first asked their names they replied, "Mon père," and the Baganda immediately made it into the word most like a word with which they were familiar.

Mukassa was a most eager and anxious little learner, and I soon gave him our small first lesson-book, containing the Lord's Prayer, Ten Commandments, and Scripture texts. A day or two afterwards Mr. O'Flaherty met him in great tribulation, and found that poor Mukassa had lost his book, and was in deep grief about it. I comforted him by giving him another copy. He and many more candidates were baptized the following Christmas Day, when we had a great feast; and this was magnified by our enemies into a seditious gathering. I have indicated in previous chapters other occurrences such as this, which, though small in themselves, taken together, helped to strengthen the growing suspicions entertained against us. How these suspicions led to a terrible calamity I shall tell in the next chapter.

Mwanga had not long been on the throne of Buganda before he began to show himself in his true colours He constantly kept sending down to the Mission for things he wanted, and asked Mackay to make him a lightning conductor for the top of the vast straw-built house in which Mutesa was buried. These demands, however, upon our property and our time were but precursors of worse treatment which we were to receive. We were getting on well with teaching and printing, but evil rumours of coming ill were thick in the air. The name of the Mission was Natéte, a pretty English-looking house on the sloping side of a hill, a ravine below, banana groves all about us. A broad road ran past our own garden fence, opposite

this road was an old fellow named Gomera, whose
dependents robbed us on the right hand, while another
set of people robbed us on the left, and at the back an
Arab had a number of slaves who partly lived on what
we cultivated. This Arab, Hamisi by name, was a
friendly old fellow, and had formerly supplied one of
our missionaries with food and cloth when he was in
great extremity. He was but a very lax follower of
Islam, and not a little given to the bottle. Later, he
offered an asylum to some of our terrified little
Mission boys when the murderers were abroad.

Immediately above us lived Bugalla, a great friend
of Sebwato's and consequently of ours. He had a
curious history, which he related to me one day.
When Bugalla was quite a little boy, Mutesa had
determined to become a Mahometan, and so the whole
country was set to work at the Koran; the king's
pages were circumcised by the score, as well as many
others, and Islam looked triumphant; and poor Lubare,
the divine guide of the Baganda, was for a time in
the background. But one of the holy and important
points of Islam is, that every animal that is killed
for food should be turned towards the sacred city
Mecca, and that the slayer must be circumcised.
Now the functionary who killed the king's beef
happened not to have embraced the belief in the
prophet, and consequently did not kill his beasts in the
orthodox way, and hence the Baganda Mahometans
could not now, and (to their credit be it said) *would* not

K

eat the defiled meat of the king; and when the haughty tyrant sent them beef of his own cattle, they more haughtily refused it. Now they knew one whose words were weightier even than the Kabaka's. When Mutesa heard it he was troubled, and all Buganda with him, and soon the awful edict went forth that every follower of Islam was to die. Then there was a sickening scene of ruthless slaughter, and a strict search was made for every one who had the damning evidence of his having accepted the new belief. Bugalla managed to hide, and so to evade the inquisitors. Soon, as was always the case in Buganda, the storm spent itself, but Islam had received a blow from which it has not yet recovered. Bugalla afterwards became a chief, and finally was created Kyimbugwe, keeper of the palace, by Kiwewa, the monarch who succeeded Mwanga. How he afterwards behaved to the missionaries, and how he met his death, must be related in a subsequent chapter.

Another of our neighbours was the boy-chief Gabunga, who was a regular attendant at the Mission and a thorough little gentleman. Though he was one of the biggest chiefs in the country, he was quite simple and unaffected. He, alas, later on met with a tragic fate.

Before new dangers arose, we had just passed through a time of trouble in a terrible visitation of the small-pox. This frightful malady, and the plague, a kind of "black death" called "kaumpuli," from time to time decimate the population of Buganda. Kaumpuli is recognised by the swellings in the armpit and in the groin, and by a terrible rise in the temperature of the patient. The fever runs its course in about twenty-four hours, and usually proves fatal.

Small-pox perhaps kills more people, yet it is not so much feared by the natives as kaumpuli, of which they have the greatest terror, as it is supposed to be frightfully infectious.

Speaking of the kaumpuli, I may refer to an incident recorded in the admirable book containing Emin Pasha's letters. Emin describes a conversation which he held with the Baganda guides who led him to Mutesa's capital. He asked them why Mwambia's land was totally depopulated. They replied that there was in Uganda a powerful magic called "Kampódi"—no doubt this very "kampoli" or "kaumpuli." The letters *r*, *l* and *d* are under certain conditions interchangeable in the Lake languages.

The mistake which follows is, though very natural, a little amusing. Emin, believing the magic spoken of to be simply one of Mutesa's notorious raids, asked the guides if it affected goats and cows or household utensils, "and both gentlemen were silent." If an intelligent Chinee were to ask us if the measles affected our silver spoons we should perhaps hardly be so polite as to keep a reserved silence. Emin draws the conclusion that Mutesa always enveloped his plundering expeditions in a veil of mystery.

To return to this epidemic of small-pox, "kawali,"

Mr. O'Flaherty's attendant, a young married Christian, was the first to fall sick, and he had the disease in the most virulent confluent form. When I visited him I saw that he had all that he wanted, but asked if he needed anything more. He beckoned me to come near, and then said, "I want you to pray with me." This man was never forsaken by his faithful wife, who tended him all through his loathsome disease until his death, though he had been often unfaithful to her.

Soon another boy was attacked, then a woman, then Lugalama showed unmistakable symptoms of the dread disease. We removed the patients, five in all, to a good-sized house which had been formerly occupied by one of the missionaries. An old woman, together with the wife of one of our converts, and a little Munyoro girl, who was a source of constant trouble on account of her bad behaviour, and the two boys, made up the complement of the sick. During this critical time Mackay was away, and I had to become sick-nurse. Poor little Lugalama became quite light-headed and delirious, which my companion assured me was a certain sign that he would die. The poor boy was filled with the idea that one of the women patients was going to bewitch him and so cause his death. However, she did not succeed in doing so, and they all made a good recovery.

After this somewhat lengthy digression I return to the rumours of coming ill which were now gaining strength. The king at this time expressed a wish for a box, so I took him a long white tin box, which I first neatly lined with white paper. My friend Kakumba went with me to the royal enclosure to carry it. I was admitted into Mwanga's presence, and I heard the king give a quiet order to the executioners. Then he looked at the box. He was polite enough, but said he wanted a different kind, so I said we would look for another of the sort he preferred. I then took my leave. On coming to the door I found poor Kakumba in a state of great terror, saying, "My friend, they are going to seize me." I tried to reassure him, and passed out, while he almost clung to me. When I got home I found that orders had actually been given to seize all followers of ourselves and the Arabs. Immediately there was a stampede, and Kakumba and other Baganda left us. I did not credit the rumour myself, and thought it only an idle scare; however, Lugalama came to me, and, taking my hand, said, "My friend, you do not understand Luganda;* Mwanga did give orders to seize Kakumba."

In the beginning of 1885, Mackay had arranged that he would go down with the boat to Musalala, at the south end of the Nyanza, and take our letters; but first he had to go up to Mwanga to obtain per-permission. When he was admitted he asked the king to give him the required leave; but Mwanga told him he must bring back a white man, which Mackay re-fused to do. The king then asked him if he wanted

* Luganda is the language of Buganda.

a messenger, to which Mackay replied that he did not.
We wanted to be able to come and go when we
pleased, and to 'send the boat when we wished, without Mwanga's messengers being on board. Mackay
did not of course say this, but remarked that Baganda
could not comfortably eat the food that was supplied to
the boat's crew, who were Zanzibaris. The king then
said he might go; but this trifle light as air con-
firmed his suspicions already aroused by busy slander,
and a page was at once despatched to the Katikiro
privately, telling of Mackay's refusal to take a messenger. Our position was now most difficult, as we
were working quite in the dark, and dealing with
people who could not be straightforward, and who
never believed what we said.

The king then bade Mackay to go to the Katikiro,
the haughty chancellor, to obtain his permission as
well. To him accordingly Mackay applied, and this
arch-hypocrite and murderer, this crafty, clever, subtle,
smiling master of dissimulation received him blandly
and politely. He gave him the required leave, and
actually sent a slave to bring a couple of goats as food
for the voyage which he had already made up his mind
that Mackay should not take. Mackay returned to us
in the evening and packed up the things that he required
for the journey. I intended to accompany him to the
lake to see him off, and to spend the next day with him
on the Nyanza. Kakumba and Lugalama, my two
faithful young followers, were to come with me.

While writing letters late at night we heard the beating of war drums and wondered what it could mean, since we had heard of no contemplated raid, yet it sounded as if an army were being collected. As I went to bed I passed the ante-room where Lugalama, and Benjy and Lwanga, two other little freed slaves, slept. I shall never forget how I stopped to look at Lugalama's peaceful sleeping face. Though one can hardly believe in presentiments, I somehow felt the shadow of an overhanging calamity from which I could not free myself. I held the candle above him. How still he is—how quietly he sleeps—how like sleep is to death! He moans uneasily, dreaming perhaps of his murdered father, or his mother worse than dead. And so good-night, young Lugalama—for the last time good-night.

CHAPT

DEATH O

THE next morning was t
Soon everything was reac
for the lake. Our caravan consisted of the one
boat, and three or four boys besides Lugalama and
Kakumba, while Mackay and I brought up the rear.
One of our friends called Paulo and one or two other of
the native Christians accompanied us on the way. A
rumour reached us that the Mahometan chief Mujasi
(the miserable Sawaddu who proved such a coward and
miscreant in his dealings with H. M. Stanley, and who
is mentioned in that traveller's account of his visit
to Uganda) was out with a large armed following.
Paulo and his companions, fearing some danger, bade
us a hasty farewell and departed, but we kept on our
journey. As we walked along we saw every now and
then men armed with shields and spears hurrying past
us as if hastening to some rendezvous. We called one
of the warriors and asked him where these soldiers
were going. He looked a little confused, but replied
that some of the king's women had run away, and that
they were going in pursuit of them. Mackay lingered
a little in order to get some bearings with his compass,

we were left pretty far behind the rest of our
As we neared the lake and were about to enter
ngled forest, which lay between us and the Nyanza,
armed throng suddenly confronted us, headed by
Mujasi himself, wearing a dirty old pair of European
trousers and a shabby coat. I did not know that this
miserable-looking object was a Muganda chief, although
he carried a long sword. The armed men pressed upon
us and blocked the way, crying out, "Go back! go
back!" ("Mudeyo! mudeyo!"). We replied, "We
are the king's friends, we have received the king's leave.
How do you dare to insult the king's guests?" and we
attempted to proceed. On this we were rudely hustled,
and the sticks which we were carrying were in eager
terror snatched from our hands. Mackay and I offered
no resistance, but went and sat quietly down at the side
of the path. Our enemies grew bolder; soon they seized
us and pulled us to our feet. Mackay simply allowed
them to carry him for a little distance, while I walked
slowly on. Then Mackay regained his feet, and we
were dragged and pushed along for some distance, a
guard of five or six men placing themselves between
the two terrible-looking Bazungu. After a while, when
they saw we offered no resistance, they allowed us to
walk quietly together, and we heard them commend
our prudence in going so peaceably. We now asked
the men to let us see the leader, and when he came
we offered him a present to let us go quietly on our
way. When we had proceeded some eight miles on

our return to the capital (Mengo), we came to a
point where two roads met, one leading straight to
Mengo, and the other more to the left to Natéte, our
Mission headquarters. Here we were halted, and soon
our porters and boys, who were behind, came up. The
boat's crew were free, though their guns had been
taken from them, but our Mission boys all had their
hands tied. When I saw my little Muhuma friend
with his hands bound, without thinking, I went straight
to him and began to undo the cord. It was, I am
afraid, a most foolish proceeding on my part, in the face
of the armed and angry soldiers. Their leader seized
his sword and seemed beside himself with fury. He
had lost all self-control, and danced and brandished
his weapon in my face, crying out, "You're drunk!
You're drunk!" "I am not drunk," I replied. In
my excuse it must be remembered that I did not know
that this wretched-looking creature was in reality a
powerful chief, and so, standing perfectly still, I scornfully added, "Come with your sword, you slave." This
was too much for Mujasi's dependents, and they began
to push me violently, though no blow was struck.
Mackay tried to come to me, but the loaded guns of the
soldiers were thrust before him, so he called out,
"Come away." I turned and went towards him, and
saw the sorrowful face of poor little Lugalama for the
last time on earth. The word was given, and still
guarded, we resumed our march. After a while,
when we had come to another road that led to Natéte,

we were bidden to go back to our own house, and the Mujasi and his triumphant guards marched on to Mengo, the king's enclosure. Mackay and I sat down to consider our position. It was about three o'clock in the afternoon, and we had been hustled and marched under guard for the last two hours and a half, besides the two or three hours' walk towards the Nyanza before our arrest, and we were very weary and despondent. The Rubicon had at length been passed by Mwanga's insolent soldiers, and the terror with which we, as Bazungu (white men), had hitherto been regarded, seemed to have disappeared. Now, the Baganda could see that we were merely helpless mortals, and that it would be an easy matter to make an end of us. Truly this was a serious crisis for us, but it consoled us to think that we had not suffered this insulting treatment by the order either of the king or the Katikiro, though we found out later our delusion on this point. We decided to lose no time, but to lay the whole matter at once before the Katikiro. When we reached his enclosure we were bidden to wait. A few Arabs were sitting in one of the houses, and we joined them. They were of course discussing what was now the most absorbing topic, for the news had spread rapidly through the country that the Bazungu had been entrapped by Mujasi. No one dared to announce our presence to the Katikiro, as Mujasi was having a private interview with him, reporting his success in the late encounter. After waiting some time, we got up and

went to the doorway, and Mackay called out loudly,
'Katikiro, my friend, I am your friend. We are the
white men." After calling once or twice we were
admitted and invited inside the house, and Mackay
stated our case and asked why we had been so badly
treated. To our surprise the judge rather defended
Mujasi, and wanted to know the meaning of Mackay's
having threatened him with his gun. As Mackay
had had no gun, and as the stick he was carrying had
been immediately wrested from him, he simply replied
that it was false. The judge then asked what we
meant by taking Baganda out of the country. Again
Mackay explained that Kakumba, the only Muganda
in the party, was carrying my mat, and that he was
not going in the boat. The subject was then dropped,
and another case came on for hearing. When this was
disposed of, Mackay returned to our affair, and told the
chancellor that it was a bad thing to treat guests as
we had been treated. The judge listened, but said
little. However, as Mackay proceeded, the chancellor's lips were tightly compressed, and suddenly
with flashing eyes he turned to Mujasi and said, "Take
the Bazungu (Europeans) and send them away, and let
them return no more." This was a terrible blow, and
we sought now in vain to deprecate the great man's
wrath. His anger grew, or he made it appear to grow,
more fiery, and calling Mujasi forward, he said with
suppressed passion, "See, Mujasi, dress yourself to-
morrow, and seize Mackay and Filipo, and this one,"

pointing to me, "and bind them and send them and all their things out of my country, and return them to Bulaya (Europe)." Immediately Mujasi arose, and his men with him, and seizing long reeds, they went through evolutions as if attacking an imaginary foe with spears, while they shouted, "Neanze, neanze ge." Mackay and I were utterly taken aback and astounded at this decision, and we begged the chancellor to hear us and tried to take his hand to plead once more. But he waved us scornfully aside, and, with a cry of triumph from Mujasi's soldiers, we were hustled and dragged from the great man's presence, a dangerous and angry mob momentarily growing thicker about us. Soon they were actually quarrelling for our clothes. "Mine shall be his coat," shrieked one; "Mine his trousers;" "No, mine!" and there was a scuffle to get nearer the clothing they coveted. However, the chancellor did not wish matters to go quite so far, and sent his head executioners to warn off the vulture soldiers. The order was instantly obeyed, and dazed and amazed we found ourselves alone. It was now near sunset and we made our way back to Natéte in a very unhappy frame of mind. When we reached our house, the three of us held a council as to what we should do. Should we try and make for the Nyanza, and get on board our boat? Should we quietly wait the coming of Mujasi to carry out our sentence in the morning? We knew well that he would use his power with the utmost rigour, and our final decision was to send up a a large amount of cloth and try to propitiate the authorities. So we made up six loads, which we sent to the king, and six more to the Katikiro, and in great suspense we awaited the result. Soon our messengers came back bringing the cloth. Is our gift then refused? No, it is only that it is late, and the king will receive it to-morrow. The Katikiro graciously accepts his bales, and sends back to say we are his brothers. When Mackay and I reached our quarters, the first thing we did was to warn all our adherents and all who were staying at the Mission to take flight. But, one young fellow, named Seruwanga, would not go. Like Lot, he lingered. I went out and asked him what madness it was that possessed him and made him loiter when there was such danger. His kindly reply was, "I'm going, my friend." A little later I again went out, and there he was; I became angry, and bade him leave at once, and he left, but alas, too late, and that evening he was seized. Mukasa Samweli, of whom I have spoken, hearing of our trouble, came down late at night under cover of darkness to show his friendship. Edward, another Mukasa, one of the first who accepted Christianity, also came to offer his sympathy. He was now keeper of Mutesa's mosque, a house which was built for the worship of Allah, and to the honour of his prophet, but which was always used as a Christian school. Afterwards Edward was made a powerful chief, but he met with a violent end, the fate of many of the actors in the scenes which I am relating. The next day, Mr. O'Flaherty went up to see the king and Katikiro, but met only with disappointment and failure. Mujasi came down with him, and the insolent chancellor had the effrontery to appoint Mr. O'Flaherty to search our house for Christians, the Katikiro supplying him with his own myrmidons to aid in the quest.

When no one was found, Mujasi returned, and soon afterwards Sambo, Mackay's boy, was set free, but Lugalama, Balibanange, and Bikutula, the others who had been seized the previous day, were still in custody. That afternoon Sambo came and told us terrible tidings, that he had heard Mujasi was going to burn the boys to death. This sad news grieved me to the very soul, and I went out and sought some place to be alone. After a while a sub-chief appeared with Bikutula. I gave him a reward, and promised that if they brought Lugalama back we would pay the price of five slaves and redeem the others as well. Later, they brought Balibanange. There remained only Kakumba and Lugulama and Seruwanga, but these were doomed; their only crime was that they had been living with us. Lugalama was really condemned because his master had given him to us and not to the king or Katikiro.

When the messenger saw how eager I was to redeem Lugalama he suggested that, if I gave him a larger present, the child's safety would be ensured; so I gave him some of the fine gold thread of great value, used for embroidery, and promised him more when he came with Lugalama; and, though he must have known all the time that the lads were dead, he accepted the bribe, and appeared to undertake our errand. I made no attempt to go to the authorities myself, as I knew that my doing so would only irritate them and make the murders more certain than ever, while in my heart I could hardly believe that they would actually take place. Lugalama and Kakumba, when first arrested, were taken into a house, and Kakumba was beaten in accordance with a common Buganda custom in the treatment of prisoners. They had compassion on Lugalama and gave him some food. Next day they were taken to the king's enclosure and their sentence was pronounced, Mujasi being the chief accuser. Sebwato, Lugalama's former master, tried to save him but in vain.

And so the three boys, Seruwanga, Kakumba, and Lugalama, were led away to death, a mocking crowd following them. "Oh, you know Isa Masiya (Jesus Christ)," said Mujasi. "You know how to read." "You believe you will rise from the dead? Well, I shall burn you and see if it be so." These were some of the mocking taunts which they endured, and loud was the laughter which greeted such sallies. But the young Christians, as some reported, answered boldly and faithfully. Seruwanga was a daring fellow, and I can well believe that when Mujasi mocked he would sing, "Killa Siku tuusifu" ("Daily, daily sing the praises "), as all were reported to have done. Kakumba too had come to us when all others were afraid, and perhaps his voice joined in the song. But what could have been in poor little Lugalama's heart but the haunting, over-mastering horror of death—and such a death! What a *via dolorosa* was that which these doomed captives were now to tread! But there were none who dared to beat upon their breasts and show the sorrow that they felt, though there were many sympathising friends who followed, many compassionate hearts that God had touched with a pity which perhaps before they had never known. One of these was Kidza, Mujasi's "musali" or guide, and it was from him, gentle, loving, and brave, one of God's noblest martyrs, that I heard this story.

He told me how the mob, carrying gourds of banana-cider, wound on their way till they reached the borders of a dismal swamp called Mayanja, a place I had often visited with Lugalama. Here they halted. Part of the crowd bring firewood, others make a kind of rough framework, under which the fuel is heaped. Then the prisoners are seized, and a scene of sickening cruelty is enacted. Some lay hold of Seruwanga, others of Kakumba, and others of Lugalama, brandishing their long curved knives. Seruwanga has committed his cause to Him who judgeth righteously, and the cruel knife cannot wring from him a cry; bleeding he is cast into the fire. Kakumba appealed to Mujasi. Mujasi believes in Allah the All-Merciful—he pleaded a

L

relationship with him; but, alas! there is as much mercy in the knife in the executioner's hand as in Mujasi's heart, and he too undergoes the short agony and the flame.

And now the saddest scene of all. Mujasi bids them treat Lugalama as they treated the others. Surely even these men, hardened by frequent executions, have never had to do a deed like this. They come nearer and he cries out, " Oh, do not cut off my arms; I will not struggle—I will not fight! Only throw me into the fire!" Surely this was the saddest prayer ever prayed on this sad earth—" Only throw me into the fire!" How like young Arthur pleading for his eyes!

> " Alas! what need you be so boisterous rough?
> I will not struggle—I will stand stone-still,
>
> .   .   .   .   .
>
> And I will sit as quiet as a lamb.
> I will not stir, nor wince, nor speak a word."

The butchers do their work and mar what was so wonderfully made, and the poor bleeding boy is placed on the framework that the slow fire may finish what the cruel knife has begun. A wail of anguish goes up, becoming fainter and fainter—a last sob, and then silence.

Musali stood sadly watching the sorrowful scene, wondering perhaps whether his turn may be next, when Mujasi, drunken with blood, came to him. " Ah, you are here! I will burn you too and your household. I know you are a follower of Isa (Jesus)." " Yes, I am," said Musali, "and I am not ashamed of it!" Never a truer word was said, and never a braver man spoke. Mujasi then left him.

What shall I say of that day of waiting, hoping, praying, fearing—praying not vainly, though at the very time the awful deed was being perpetrated?

> "O mother! praying God will save
>   Thy sailor. While thy head is bowed
>   His heavy-shotted hammock-shroud
> Drops in its vast and wandering grave."

Such prayers are not vain as they may seem, but the answer to them is yet to come.   That was a day when the wrongs of Africa came home to me and burnt themselves deep into my very soul—that day when Lugalama fell asleep, January 31st, 1885.

He Fell Asleep.

He fell asleep.   No troubled dreams oppress him,
  He moaneth not; lying in Jesus' breast,
No terrors of the darkness now possess him;
  He lieth in the light at perfect rest.

Sometimes he lay so still that I would listen
  With a strange awe, and half suppose him dead;
And at the thought my eyes with tears would glisten
  As I stood o'er this loved child's little bed.

O God of Love! Thy Love no shadow knoweth,
  No evil cloud of darkness o'er it lowers,
No bitter blast of coldness o'er it bloweth—
  Forgive the sin of love so weak as ours.

And yet our love, tho' by corruption clouded,
  Is still a spark of flame that fell from Thee,
Which yet shall shine, no more by shadows shrouded,
  In Thy great light, O God, eternally.

CHAPTER XIV.

INTERVIEWS WITH MWANGA.

THE Arabs sent down a message of sympathy with us in our trouble, and Hamisi and Ali bin Sultan came themselves to see us the following day. Ali bin Sultan afterwards showed us the bitterest hostility, but at this time the Arabs all visited us, and, whatever their real feeling may have been, nothing could have been kinder than the way in which they acted towards us.

A few days later Mwanga sent for Mackay, and when Mackay spoke of the murder of the boys, declared that he knew nothing about it, and said that the chief judge and Mujasi were only peasants, while he himself alone was king. This denial on his part was untrue, for the outrage was committed, if not at his instance, at any rate with his connivance. During these dark days the many faithful friends whom we reckoned among the native Christians still continued their visits. Among these were Samweli, most faithful of all, Sebwato, Gabunga the young admiral, and several others. They came usually at night, for our house was guarded all day; but in less than a fortnight this terrible storm had blown over. The Katikiro sent down to remove the guards who were watching our house, and permission was given to all who wished to bring us food for sale and to come for medicine. This was practically granting us permission to teach.

In spite of these favourable signs it was quite clear to us that our position was very precarious and uncertain, and so we determined to try and get as much printing done as possible. Mackay, with great foresight, had, on first coming to Africa, brought out a printing press with him. During the eight years which had elapsed it had passed through various adventures, and parts of it had been damaged and destroyed in a fire at the mission. Mackay, however, now made the missing pieces and put the whole together, and we were able to make printing our principal occupation; and it was well that we took this opportunity, for the cruel outrages which I have described in the last chapter, so far from deterring others from coming to us to be taught, bore immediate fruit in largely-increased numbers of learners, and redoubled the interest felt in our work. We printed hundreds of reading-sheets and spelling-sheets, which were eagerly bought, and we began to put into type the Gospel of St. Matthew. From morning till night, eager and intelligent readers surrounded us. Mukasa was a constant visitor. He said to me one day, "Do not call me Mukasa—Mukasa is dead. I am Samweli." This boy went home and taught his mother, who idolised him, and then the two together taught his old grandmother. He also taught his half-brother Engiri (peccary), and Ali Wali, a very nice little boy, who was afterwards accidentally burned to death in one of the fires which are so frequent and so fatal in Buganda. The whole family, in spite of the displeasure and vexation of their relations, decided to throw aside all their ancestral relics and charms, for their new religion did not allow them any longer to consider sacred the animal which represented their kyika or clan, the explanation of which I have already given.

Mwanga's sisters, too, were eager readers; but whether they reformed their evil way of living I much doubt. One of them, named Mwafu, who chose the name of Eve when baptised, was very unassuming and modest—she was duly married with Christian rites; but the queen-sister, though clever and intelligent, scandalised the Church by her lack of chastity, for which she was degraded from her high position by Mwanga's order. Another princess also brought disgrace upon the Church by the same scandalous behaviour. She finally was won over to his faith by her Roman Catholic lover; yet, in spite of her weakness, she proved herself our true friend, and on one occasion, as will be seen hereafter, saved the mission by a timely warning and practical advice which we found of great value.

Mwanga for the present showed us no increased hostility, and bad as he was, we yet felt that his deposition would mean the utter ruin of the mission, a belief which was fully borne out by the events which subsequently took place in Buganda. Rumours that Mwanga's position was uncertain now began to multiply, and reports that his deposition was imminent reached us continually. Earnest and thoughtful men were at this time coming to us in large numbers, and not a few were baptised.

One of the old king's counsellors, Engobya, the father of a large number of most earnest readers, advised that we should be killed, for the chiefs with some show of reason looked with the gravest suspicion upon the new teaching, which they said induced " Kyeju," insolence. And no wonder that the philosophy which opens the eyes to see the substance of things, and which sets up a glass wherein all things are reflected in a strange form, filled them with supreme fears. A teaching which put great for what they believed small, and noble for what they thought mean ; which, lacking the heroic aspects of Islam, could yet make men calmly appeal to a spiritual power and brave without excitement the direst death, was a puzzle to the rulers of the country ; and there need be no surprise that the new superstition appeared to be a height of Kyeju hitherto unattained in Buganda.

The next news which we heard was of the disgrace and banishment of Mukwenda, Earl of Singo, the chief agent in the plot to depose Mwanga ; and the day following some sixteen of the principal chiefs were driven from power. The rebellion was thus nipped in the bud by the sagacity and foresight of the astute chancellor, and his wayward and wilful puppet was still kept on the throne.

The chancellor or Katikiro was all along a believer in the old gods of his country. He had all the subtility of Arabs; he adopted their dress, learned their language, outdid them in the suavity of manner and politeness which characterises them; but in his heart he hated them as he hated us for being foreigners, and for their religion. I remember at one of my last interviews with him, he sent for his Christian books, and read a little. He had learnt his letters at the time when Christian reading was so much the fashion in Mutesa's day, but he and many other chiefs still clung to their old belief in Lubarè.

When the rebellion was crushed the king began to talk of sending some of his pages to England, and apropos of this asked why we never went to see him. A few days afterwards we heard that he had given orders to rob our cattle, which had the desired effect of causing us to decide to attend his " baraza," levee. I had determined never to see his face again if I could help it. So Mackay went up to the enclosure, and had a satisfactory interview with both king and chancellor. Not long after this, Mwanga sent a messenger with compliments and a couple of cows; and the day following he sent another cow— ample compensation no doubt in his blind eyes for the murder of our boys. Mackay again went to see him, and the king said that he would never part with the English, and directed him to write and invite the French priests to return to Buganda. To which of course Mackay agreed. Not long after this, the king again sent a couple of cows, with the request that we should go and see him.

Towards the end of April of 1885, news reached us that Emin Pasha was making his way to the coast with five ranks (regiments) of soldiers. This information came from Sembuzi, who may be remembered as the officer who deserted Stanley. A few days later, we heard that Emin and another European (Capt. Casati) were at Mruli with only thirty men. On the 3rd of May, in the afternoon, a rumour reached us that the Katikiro had given orders that the people who came to us to learn should be seized. But the next day Mackay had a favourable interview with him, and heard that Emin Pasha had been refused leave to pass by Kabarega. The Katikiro promised he would send an armed force to relieve him.

One of the pages came one day in great glee, this was Mwanga (Silas), to tell how a priest of Lubarè (of the old religion) had been beaten by the king's orders. I pointed out to this young enthusiast that persecution was wrong, and that what happened to the followers of Lubarè to-day might happen to the followers of Isa (Jesus) to-morrow.

About the middle of May, Mackay went to Musalala in the boat. While he was away, Mwanga sent for me. One of his favourite pages came out to meet me when I arrived at the king's enclosure to ask if I could mend a clock. I sent back to say I was a teacher and not a clock-maker. Mwanga desired to ignore this, being misled by the representations of those who were hostile to our creed, but it was a point we always wished to maintain. The king held that the privilege of living in Buganda at the court of so great a monarch as himself was quite reason enough for our remaining in the country without teaching our religion; our contention was that we only consented to stay in order to teach.

Had I known, however, that the clock only wanted winding up, I should gladly have done that for him. Kato, the page who took my message, "re-delivered" me in a very polite manner. He was one of the Frenchman's pupils, and a great friend of mine, as was also Nyonyi Entono. These lads frequently sent presents of goats as a token of their kindly feeling. The king simply said "Very well." I waited all day for an audience, which was not vouchsafed. This was the first time for six months that I had been up to the king.

About this time, June of 1885, there was another rumour abroad that the Christians were to be seized; and on Sunday the large numbers who attended church quietly dispersed. The Arabs' slaves and our Mahometan coast men (servants) had a fight the same afternoon, and the Arabs went up to the king to lodge a complaint against us. The king sent down to say we were to come and plead the case against the Arabs. We sent back to say that our servants and the Arabs were all Wangwana, coast people, and that we had no quarrel with the Arabs—let them settle it between themselves. So our men went and pleaded, and gained the case. That day Mackay arrived from Musalala in the boat, bringing the news of Gordon's death and the fall of Khartoum. The fight between our servants and the Arabs' slaves of a few days ago now broke out again, and many heads were broken on each side, and the captain of our boat badly speared.

On this occasion Mackay went and complained to the authorities, and judgment was again given against the Arabs. The chief ground of the quarrel probably was that our Zanzibar men were in the pay of Christians; though the immediate cause was some dispute at the market which was held just above our house, on an open space, where you could buy beef and vegetables, cloth or slaves—anything, in fact, from a Muhuma girl to a bundle of faggots.

Mackay took up a present to Mwanga as was customary on the arrival of the boat. He suggested to me that I should go and see the king. I told him how much I loathed the thought of looking upon this miserable murderer; to which he replied that it was no pleasure to him, but that he looked upon it as a needful duty. To this there was no replying, so I armed myself with a musical album—a present from some Liverpool sailor-boys—which Mwanga had seen and consequently coveted, and which I had refused to give him. Having gulped down my feelings, I went one morning; and though I was not admitted to the royal presence, my gift was accepted. I waited patiently the whole day, and the conditions for waiting were not unpleasant. The place we used as a waiting-room was the royal store-house;

and the king's store-keepers were nearly all Christians, and were most polite and kind. Little pages, Kibebefu, Mwanga, Kago, and others, were lying about on the floor of the house learning their A B C. During these times of waiting I made the acquaintance of Kiwewa, eldest son of Mutesa and elder brother of Mwanga, who has been made king in the recent changes. I met also Mwanga's two younger brothers, who were at large, one of whom, Kayondo, was also afterwards chosen to be king, though he does not appear to have actually reigned. That day Mwanga did not grant me an audience, and the three following days I went up to the enclosure, but did not see the king. I met, however, Alexandro, one of our converts, who held the chieftainship of Namfumbambi, of which I have spoken elsewhere. He told me that he had been accused of being a Christian, and that he had been beaten by the Katikiro's orders and driven out of his chieftainship.

Alexandro was soon given another office. He was of noble blood, and was never long without some post in the king's service. He, like the majority of those of whom I speak, was in another year to meet with a bloody death for his faith.

Another Christian chief, Mulya gonja ("eater of the sweet plaintain"), was at this time lording it over all the chiefs in the country, having been appointed to "kuba" the "kibuga" (set up the king's enclosure). He had the right to command the services of all the king's vassals in the making of the royal enclosure; and to seize and imprison delinquents. He was of a very proud and overbearing nature, and rigorously put in force his authority. We feared much for him, as he was naturally most unpopular. He was the Edward who visited us in our first great trouble, and was one of Mackay's earliest pupils, and among the first five baptized in Buganda. He was afterwards killed by another chief, for which Mwanga caused his slayer to be hewn in pieces.

The fourth time I visited Mwanga my perseverance was rewarded by an audience. After keeping me waiting the whole day, he sent for me. There were only a few boys with the king, and an elderly woman, probably some lady of distinction. Nyonyi Entono, and Kagwa, now young men, were sitting in the door-way. When I entered the house, Mwanga bade me be seated. I had brought him a hat with which he was much pleased. After some talk about the hat, he said, "Has Mackay gone to the Nyanza?" I replied that he had. Then he said, "Can you swim?" I replied, "Yes, a little." He then asked about Gordoom (General Gordon) and Abdul Emin (Emin Pasha). He also asked about Baker, whose name he knew, as there were some wonderful stories afloat in Buganda as to Baker's prowess. He then asked about Bishop Hannington, and Godoli, the missionary Gordon and Wise, and the trader Stokes, and also about the French priests. This conversation was interspersed at intervals with the two first questions, "Has Mackay gone to the

Nyanza?" and, "Can you swim?" He then asked me if I could dive. To which I replied that I could a little. He kept remarking to his boys in a sort of aside, "He is an Englishman," and, "Mackay is an Englishman," "Makai ali Mungereza." He said that I was "Mulungi," to which all agreed. So I said to him, "You are king, and we must all bow to what you say, so you should always say what is good and right." He agreed to this; then he said, "Is the bishop an Englishman?" I said, "Yes; but that we teachers did not reckon our, selves of any country, but only people of 'Katonda,' God." He then asked about the death of Gordoom (General Gordon) and about the Mahdi. Then he said, "If I go and fight with Nakaranga, will you come with me?" I told him I thought it wrong to go on an expedition to fight; if the enemy came here, it would be a different matter. "If the Madhi comes here," I said "and you fight him, I will help you." But I said, "I thought the Madhi would eat us all up, that he had many guns and cannons." He then remarked my beard and my hair, and asked me if I could do a high jump. I told him that I was getting too old to jump, at which he laughed, and said, "Why, you're only a youth! I am also a youth," he added. But I said, as I had said to Roma, "Have I not a beard, has a youth a beard?" He pointed to a few hairs on his own chin, and said, "Have not I a beard, and yet I am a youth?" "You," I said, "are a man." He then asked where the Frenchmen were. To which I replied, that they

were on the Nyanza. Then he finished off by
again asking if I could swim; a point as to which he
seemed very curious. He wanted to know whether I
could make cloth. At this time Mackay was making
a loom, and a most marvellous spinning-jenny which
worked admirably. He was attempting to make
cloth out of plantain-fibre; but before he had time to
give the machinery a fair trial, the storm of persecution
and trouble broke upon us, and prevented its being
continuously worked. After this long conversation,
the king sent for a fat goat, which he presented to me.
And I took my leave.

Mackay had been down to the lake and got the boat
ready to receive the king, who had expressed a wish to
go on board. However, the priests of Lubare would
not allow the king to go on the lake, as they said that
Mukasa, the Neptune of the Nyanza, had not yet been
propitiated. Soon after this the French priests arrived,
Pères Lourdel and Jeraud, together with a lay brother.
We were always on very good terms with them, and
I think by that time we all recognised that there was
room for both parties, and that they had learnt the
lesson that however much they objected to our doctrine,
public denunciation of it was of no earthly use. Their
former attacks had been made with an honest purpose,
of frustrating what they held to be a dangerous and
deluding heresy. But now there was nothing of the
kind, and all our dealings with them were of the
pleasantest description. I was at the king's enclosure

when the priests arrived; they were called in by themselves and were well received, and Mwanga promised to build them a house.

After they had gone I was summoned, and after some not very interesting conversation, the king reverted to the topic of swimming, "Can you swim?" "Yes, a little." He sent for a fat goat and gave it to me. Then he said, "Will you swim for me?" Swimming, by the way, is a very rare accomplishment in Buganda. Then he added, "Will you swim in my pond?" I said, "I should be most happy." "When will you?" said the king. "Whenever you wish," I answered. "Will you come now?" he eagerly asked. "Is it not too late," I replied. "You will not come now?" in a disappointed tone. "Yes, now if you like." So up got the king, stepped from his throne and took my hand and led me out, followed by a crowd of pages. and we made our way to the pond. It was rather muddy, but I took off my clothes and gave them to a bystanding boy to hold, and then I plunged in and swam about to the king's great satisfaction and delight. The king took my habiliments and critically examined them. He pronounced them to be "biyambalo birungi," beautiful garments, a praise I was not so much pleased to hear, as the tailor who made them might have been, for I feared the next thing would be a polite request for them. The king, however, was in high good humour and did not beg for anything. He praised my patience for waiting so long to see him ; and as I was going away I was warmly congratulated for having swum and for having shown the king that my saying I could swim was not a lie, which I suppose he suspected.

In July of this year the Christians met and balloted for certain elders or church council. We felt this to be a very necessary step, for in case of our being sent away, we wished them to have some organisation of their own. These elders were authorised to conduct service, and to preach in the absence of the missionaries. Shortly before this, my servant Tom had taken his departure. He had been engaged for two years, but waited with me several months over his time. I had a little boy named Benjy, a Musoga, who used to sweep my room. I had got so into the habit of leaving everything with Tom and my Muhuma boy, Lugalama, that I allowed Benjy, a lad of about twelve or thirteen, to have the run of the place. He began a course of systematic robbery on a large scale, and I discovered him at last, owing to the fact of his stealing a needle. When I once suspected that he was a thief, I began to look at my things, and found he had rifled every place where he could lay his hands. He had been induced by some men who lived near to rob me. I gave him a thorough good thrashing, and chained him up for nearly a month. After that I trusted no more small boys for a time. Towards the end of August of the year 1885, Mackay was busy superintending the making of a rope for

M

the king's flag-staff. A Madagascar man, named Toli, who was the King's " fundi," or carpenter, was to put up the mast. He utterly failed, since he cut the good rope which Mackay had made and then tried to join it. The rope gave way, and the whole thing came crashing down and killed one or two men.

Mackay had warned them that it would not do; but they turned a deaf ear to him. The king was disappointed and vexed, and, we heard, abused us roundly. After failing in rearing his mast, he suddenly gave out that he was going to "Kutabala," literally raid; but when carried out in his own country it was more of a royal progress. He gave orders that Mackay and Père Lourdel were to accompany him, the others were to stay at home and keep the house. The chief Kibare was the "Musigere" (*locum tenens*, or regent in the absence of the king).

Mwanga, having already begun to kill people, appeared as if he could not stop. There seems to be a frightful fascination in this passion for blood, which fortunately is as uncommon as it is unspeakably horrible. Accounts now came in of repeated butchery committed by the orders of the rapidly deteriorating tyrant. And rumours of discontent with the king were rife—one chief reason being " teyazala abaana" (" he had no children ").

At the beginning of September our letters arrived, but the news which they brought and what came of it I must relate in the next chapter.

CHAPTER XV.

NEWS OF HANNINGTON.

THE letters which we received brought us definite news of the German occupation of Usagára, and the startling intelligence that Hannington, now Bishop of East Equatorial Africa, intended to make his way to Buganda, following Thomson's route through the Masai country.

It was clear that the Bishop could not have received our letters warning him that he should exercise caution, and telling him about the late outrage, one of the reasons of which the Katikiro had said was that we were hiding white men at Buvuma to the east. However, there was one reassuring point in the Bishop's letter; he announced his intention of proceeding to Kavirondo, south of the jealously guarded territory of Busoga, and ordered that the mission boat should meet him there in October. A Mahometan Belooch had obtained a passage in our boat, and knew all the coast news, so that Mackay and I thought it would be better to tell Mwanga about the German occupation, and the Bishop's coming to Kavirondo, before the Belooch had time to do so. The Bishop had been assured that the Germans would thwart our missions in every way, and had therefore determined

M 2

to find another road to the lake rather than pass through territory occupied by Germany.

It is, however, only just to the Germans, who occupied the East African stations, to say that they have always treated English missionaries with respect and courtesy and have even gone out of their way to show us kindness.

On the 25th of September, 1885, Mackay and I took Mwanga a present, and were granted an audience. We told him our two important items of news—of the German occupation and the Bishop's coming, which made him and his counsellors appear somewhat perturbed. The king asked if other white men would come with the Bishop. We thought that probably two or three might be coming, so we could only reply that we did not know ; but that he was an important person and not likely to travel alone.

"Will the Askofu (Bishop) come to Busoga ? " asked Mwauga. We thought we were fortunate in being able to reply at once in the negative, and to assure the king that he would only come to Kavirondo, pretty far to the south. It will be seen, however, that the Bishop's change of plan made our statements appear like deliberate lying. We then told Mwanga that Ismail the Belooch had news, and the king sent for him.

October, 1885.—The next day, Saturday, the king summoned a great council of chiefs to discuss the whole matter of the coming of the Bishop, and Sematimba, the king's messenger, was called and instructed to go and meet the Bishop, and report upon him, but not to bring him.

I think, since the subject is one of deep interest, that it will be well to subjoin Mackay's very graphic account of the whole affair, which he sent home to the Church Missionary Society. After giving a description of Mwanga's character, and telling something of the work, he goes on :—

"Only a week ago I returned from a tour with the king and army through the west of his dominions. We were away twenty-six days in all. Père Lourdel also accompanied the expedition. We went by water from Busabala (Stanley's Usavara) to Ntebe, thence through Busi and Bunjako to the mouth of the Katonga. From there we struck north to Kyango and Nkanaga. At that place we halted some twelve days, a great review of the troops of Singo and Bulemezi being held. After that we returned N.E. and E. back to the capital. The route by water was the more pleasant, but that by land, though wearisome, the more interesting, as I was enabled to see the country as I had never seen it before. There was much of interest to record, and if I can find time to make a sketch and write out my notes of the tour, I shall do so for the sake of your geographical friends.

" On the road the king gave me several goats, and after returning he presented us with five head of cattle. There was no pillaging or robbery on the way. Much else, however, took place; more than enough to make one think with horror of what another such journey might be productive of.

" While we were still at Nkanaga, our mail arrived

here by the *Eleanor*. The brethren forwarded the letters
to me overland. I read with alarm of the German
doings at the coast, as we had telegrams to 17th June
mentioning that the German fleet had been ordered to
Zanzibar, while Lourdel had information that a force of
700 men was to occupy Usagára. Stokes had sent on
(giving him a free passage) a Belooch trader in the boat.
I meant to tell the king and Katikiro at once the news,
before the Belooch would have the opportunity, as were
he to tell his story first we would be suspected of being
implicated in the German designs, seeing we kept the
matter secret. I was, however, anxious to find out first
how much the Belooch really knew. I pumped some
of our men who had seen him, and from them I found
that the Germans had demanded from Seyed Burgash
the port of Bagamoyo, meaning to purchase it, but that
the Sultan had refused : hence they meant to fight him.
Further, that the Arabs of Unyanyembe were ordered
to return to the coast. Lourdel and I talked over the
matter and agreed to defer making the matter public
until our return to the capital. The matter was besides
much complicated by the letters from Bishop Hannington informing us of his intention to cross the Masai
country and strike the Lake at Kwa Sundu near Busoga.

· " It is only natural that these natives be very jealous
for their land. In Buganda they look on the Lake as a
natural barrier, preventing invasion from the south.
When the Egyptians were north at Mruli, Mutesa was
ever trembling. From the west they fear nothing.

The Congo State may some day alarm them not a little. But the sore point is Busoga. From there they know the solid ground stretches off east all the way to the coast, and an army coming in that direction would find an open road. Mutesa used to twit me by saying: 'You white men would like much, would you not, to see the country behind Busoga? That I would never allow.'

"I could see well how much our deep troubles this last spring owed their origin to the rumour of Thomson's visit to Busoga, although he was home again before they hardly knew here. What would it be now when the report came out that a great man was coming with a large party that very way to Buganda, while, at the same time, the white men were making war on Seyed Burgash? The case looked serious. For it must be remembered that Baganda have no acquaintance with the geography of Europe, and look on all pale faces as of one race. All are called Bazungu. The Arabs have ever averred that we are only the pioneers of annexation—spies in fact. When Lieutenant Smith came here, Hamadi bin Ibrahim advised Mutesa to kill him and Wilson, as, he said, 'wherever these English put their foot, the land becomes theirs in time.' From that day onwards Mutesa was ever suspicious, yet prudent. When the Arabs continually reiterated their warnings as to our ultimately eating the country, Mutesa replied, 'Let the Bazungu alone. If they mean to eat the country, surely they will not begin at the interior.

When I see them begin to eat the coast, then I shall
believe your words to be true.'

"Now, the beginning has been made at the coast—
Bismarck *versus* Burgash. Who will win? And then,
too, the English are coming to the jealously guarded
land of Busoga, at the other side of Buvuma. One
white man is supposed to be a host in himself.

"On Friday (25th inst.) Ashe and myself went to
court to congratulate the king on his safe return, taking
with us a box of sundry small articles as a present, it
being our custom to give both him and the Katikiro
something every time the boat brings us goods. His
majesty expressed himself well pleased with the gift.
We then told him that we wished his permission to let
the boat go to Kavirondo to fetch his guest whom we
had been expecting for some time. He was our Bishop,
a chief of the Church, and our superior. We mentioned
that his reason for coming that way was to avoid the
Germans (Badutchi), who had some misunderstanding
with Seyed Burgash. We did all we could to remove
from the king's mind suspicion as to our having any
connection with the Germans. We were cross-questioned as to the German's quarrel with the Sultan, and
as to what they wanted there at all. Our information
being very meagre, it was difficult for us to say much
definitely, only we told simply what we heard, viz. that
they had acquired a piece of territory, with the consent
of the native chiefs, inland from Bagamoyo, that they
had no designs against Burgash or his territory, but

that the Sultan was provoking them by planting his flag in hosts of places where he had never done so before ; and then they wished to purchase a port which Burgash refused to sell. 'Will Burgash fight ?' asked the king. Answer : 'You are a king, and can best decide such a matter.' King : 'I believe he will come to terms with them without fighting.' Answer : 'We think you have judged rightly.' Kibare was present. He was regent at the capital in the king's recent absence. Kibare suggested that Burgash would fight. King : 'What are these Baduchi ? Are they Bazungu ?' Answer : 'Yes, they are Bazungu ; a very powerful nation. They fought the French not long ago, and beat them, even capturing their king.' 'Which is the stronger, the English or the Germans ?' 'The Germans are the stronger, especially by land. The English could not beat them if they went to war.' 'Ah,' said Kibare, 'if the English could not beat them, Burgash need not try.' King : 'Is the Bishop an Englishman ?' 'Yes.' 'Is he bringing much bintu (goods) ?' 'He will not come empty-handed, but he is a chief not of this world's goods, but of religion ; he is a great teacher.' 'Do you want to go to fetch him ?' 'I do not want to go myself, but we should like the boat to go to Musalala, where Mr. Stokes will join her and go to Kavirondo to try and find the Bishop.' 'Where is the Bishop just now ?' 'He is probably at Chagga.' 'Is he coming through Busoga ?' 'No, he means to reach the Lake somewhere in Kavirondo, leaving Busoga far to the north, and Ukerewe to the south.' 'Is he coming alone?' 'Not likely; he is a great man, and does not travel alone; he will have one assistant (chaplain?) with him, and perhaps another.' 'Is Stokes coming with him?' 'Perhaps; I don't know.' I then asked if he would kindly send a "mubaka" (messenger) with the boat, and to this he consented. He gave us a cow on leaving.

"Next morning the king had a council of his chiefs. Present—Kibare, Kangao, Mukwenda, Pokino, Mugema, Nsege, Ngobya, Kyimbugwe, and Kolugi—all important personages. The Katikiro was absent. Mwanga made a speech to them on his relations with white men from the beginning. When he came to the throne he wanted Bazungu, and had sent Sematimba with me to Musalala to bring three Englishmen. They refused to come. He therefore sent for the Frenchmen at Ukumbi. They came at once. He then narrated every word of our conversation with him yesterday, adding, what I have omitted to mention above, that we had asked him to build a house for the Bishop, as we were short of accommodation. The chiefs then expressed their opinions on the situation. All seemed to be of one mind, that white men were all one, and that we and the Bishop were only the fore-runners of war. We were only waiting for our head-men to come, when we would commence to eat the country. Kangao would go and fight the Bishop. Ngobya said that when you see running water you may expect more to follow; the only way was to stop it at the source. We were drawing these white men here : hence he counselled that we should be killed so as to stop the evil. It had been said that if white men were killed the country would be ruined. No such result had followed the murder of two white men in Ukerewe ; Lukonge was still there. Mugema remarked that our house had been a year and a half in building ; who would undertake a like work again ? The general opinion was that the Bishop was not to be allowed to come, especially as he was coming by a *back door* through the Masai and Busoga. [N.B. —The Baganda call the Masai ' Basaba,' and know of their presence to the north-east of Busoga. They do not know that the tribe extends also southward, as far as the Wahumba.]

"The king suggested that Sematimba be sent in the boat, to inquire and spy how many men the Bishop had with him, and what goods, and return in the first instance to report. Kolugi's advice was that the whole party proceed first to Musalala, instead of establishing themselves over there, behind Buvuma ; and that the king might send there for them, if he liked. Kangao remarked that seven ships of Bazungu had been lost off the coast of Buvuma, as the Lubarè (Lake spirit) would not allow them to come here.

"Kolugi's advice was adopted, and Sematimba received instructions accordingly not to bring the Bishop's party direct here, but to convey them to Musalala, and return here to report.

"Next day was Sunday, and we had our hands full with classes and services all day. On Monday we meant to go again to court and see the Katikiro, if possible, as well as the king, and explain again our absolute non-connection with the Germans, while we meant to assent to the proposal that the party go to Musalala first. Mr. O'Flaherty thought that it was necessary for him to go to meet the Bishop, and try, if possible, to bring him direct to Buganda. He accordingly went to court, and saw the Katikiro in his own place. That official expressed his alarm at the news he had heard, and closely cross-questioned O'Flaherty on what he knew. The king was afterwards seen, and after O'Flaherty's explaining by the aid of a map that the Bishop's route does not lie near Busoga, he obtained permission to go himself in the boat and bring the party straight on here, the king alleging that he wished to have many Bazungu, English, French, Germans, and all, at his court. The Arabs were present, and reported on the doings of the Belgians at Unyanyembe and Karema, and also in Manyuema (now in Congo State).

"Sematimba was not there, however; but he came to me afterwards, saying that he was perplexed, as the king had given him positive instructions to convey the Bishop and party to Musalala, while he had not been sent for to get other instructions to bring them direct to Buganda. He could not, therefore, go until he had seen the king again. I advised him to do so. He waited at court all day yesterday, but did not see his majesty. Meantime Mr. O'Flaherty has changed his mind, and thinks he will not go.

" *Wednesday, 30th.*—Mr. O'Flaherty waited all day at court, but did not see the king. In the evening we together agreed that I should try to see the king next morning and endeavour to get the messenger definitely appointed.

" *Thursday, October 1st.*—Took with me a large school-map of Europe; found a grand "burzah"; king on throne; Katikiro and all great chiefs present; body-guard drawn up, and lords of the cord predominating. Evidently important business on hand. I felt very thankful to have this opportunity of seeing king and chiefs together. It was indeed providential.

" After salaams, unrolled map of Europe; said that I had brought it to show that Bulaya (as they call Europe) was not one country, but contained many kingdoms, each having a different race, language, and king; just as in Africa there were Baganda, Banyamwezi, Bakedi, Bagogo. We were English, and were in no way responsible for the doings of the Germans. We had not brought them to Zanzibar, nor had we anything whatever to do with them. We were accused of wishing to ' eat ' the country, but in all these years we had eaten nothing. We were only friends and subjects of the king, and had no sinister motives.

. " On this from all sides rose the cry, ' Who told you that we said you meant to take our country ? ' ' Everybody says so : besides, I can understand that you have reason for alarm.'

"The king, Katikiro, and Pokino (formerly Kyambalango) then spent some time in animated conversation, but in whispers. After which the Katikiro begged to assure me most positively that they had no suspicion of us, and that I had been misinformed (diplomatic truth!).

"I continued, that 'I had now been in the country more years than any other European; that my first request on arrival was for permission to bring Mr. Pearson and party. They had come and seen the king and had given presents to him and the Katikiro, and all had left without doing any harm. I had asked in like manner for canoes to be sent for Mr. Stokes, and Mr. O'Flaherty, and Mr. Ashe, one after the other; and these had all shown themselves to be men of peace. Now I asked the king to send for our Bishop, who was an Englishman like ourselves; let him send a messenger in our boat and bring him. He was the king's guest.' The king at once replied, 'I have given you Sematimba, he will go.' On Sematimba being called forward, I asked again : 'This messenger will go in the boat and bring the Askofu (Bishop) and his brethren direct to this ?' Mugema said, 'No ;' and others echoed, 'No.' Kolugi was sitting behind the Katikiro. He rose and came forward, and, kneeling in front of the throne, said, 'Sematimba will go to Musalala, where he will find Stokes, and go with him to find the Askofu, and take the latter back to Musalala, where he (Bishop) must wait until the king sends for him.'

"The Katikiro also added that Sematimba was to remain with the Bishop at Musalala, and send on here his assistant, Ensubuga, in the boat to report concerning the new party and their goods. All assented to this finding, which, by the way it was brought forward, was evidently a previous resolution. The king also assented, and so did I. I then explained that Mr. O'Flaherty did not now mean to go, but that if the king wished one of us to go in the boat, I was prepared to do so. To this Mwanga replied, "I wish you to stay where you are." Orders were given for a cargo of plantains to be supplied, and Sematimba left. The court soon after rose."

With reference to the route which Hannington now followed, the Rev. E. C. Dawson, in his admirable biography of the Bishop, is at some pains to defend the choice of this Masai road. Of his eloquence there can be no doubt; but in spite of his enthusiastic manner of writing, he can hardly carry his more cautious readers with him. Hannington, while he acted on the advice and with the countenance of Sir John Kirk and General Matthews, chose this road notwithstanding the adverse opinion of the only traveller who had preceded him—Mr. Joseph Thomson.

Mr. Dawson, too, is surely mistaken in the opinion which he expresses of the ordinary caravan route between Zanzibar and Unyanyembe. Only one missionary, as far as I am aware, has died from the effects of the journey on this route, and his death was due, I have been told, to the same cause which so nearly proved fatal to Bishop Hannington himself, want of proper necessaries.

Physical suffering, and fatigue, and fever are, I suppose, the natural accompaniment of travelling in a new country; but Thomson seems to have suffered more from these than the average traveller on the other route. I do not wish to minimise the difficulties of the road which I myself have travelled four times; but it is my deliberate opinion that for the present it is the more feasible and less dangerous route of the two under discussion, and I think as regards the healthiness there is not much to choose between them.

Hannington, as one of his reasons, mentions that Stokes' caravan had been attacked in Ugogo by robbers. But this was the Bishop's mistake. Robbers, properly speaking, only attack in the forests. In an inhabited district an attack of this kind could never be made, unless with the direct orders of the chief. It was a mistake which the Bishop made in Busoga, and was one of the causes which led to his death.

The occasion he refers to when mentioning the attack upon Stokes was when Stokes had given orders to his caravan to proceed before the "hongo" question had been finally settled.

In the account given of this in a missionary paper

Stokes' men are said to have fired in the air. Most of them did so ; but the writer did not know that it was for the same reason that so many warriors fire into the air, namely that they were too frightened and too nervous and too unskilful to fire anywhere else. Two of their bullets, however, going through the air, struck two Wagogo men by chance and killed them.

To return now to Buganda. The boat was sent off to look for the Bishop, and we settled down again to work. Readers flocked about us, and there were weekly meetings of the Native Church Council, at which various questions were discussed and decided.

And so a month passed away.

As a rule a journal is not interesting, but I think that in this particular instance what I wrote when in the middle of the trouble which was now to fall upon us will perhaps make the situation more clear, so I extract the following from my diary :—

1885. *Oct. 25th, Sunday.*—In the morning, Entanda (Gideoni), one of the court lads, brought the news of the arrival at Luba of two white men, who he says are Englishmen, one an elderly man, and the other a youth, and that they have twenty Wangwana (porters) with them. Later on, Sekajija Marko, a little page, came with the further news that the Englishmen were prisoners, and in the stocks. We were very much concerned, and Mackay and I, when we heard of our countrymen, strongly suspected that it must be Bishop Hannington and his chaplain. Still it might be some

N

other traveller, and we knew that the German explorer, Dr. Fischer, was leading an expedition to the Victoria Lake. It might be he. We called our Native Church Council together, and decided at once to dismiss the congregation, which had by this time assembled for service, and that Mackay and I should go up to the king's enclosure, and endeavour to see Mwanga.

Presently in came Yusufu Nasala, and told us that the king has decided to kill the prisoners, adding that one of them has lost a thumb. Immediately I heard that I said "It is the bishop." For this mark of identification could hardly be mistaken, as a gunpowder accident had deprived Hannington of his thumb in his early days. Mackay and I lost no time in making our way to the king's enclosure. As we entered the Wankaki (great gate) little Sekajija and another page who called himself Noah came up and whispered as we passed, "Bagenze kubatta" (They have gone to kill them). We entered and waited long in Kolugi's store. Kolugi is a person of considerable importance, and can muster some one or two thousand warriors. The king refused us an audience, and bade us tell Kolugi what we wanted. Both Kolugi and Pokino, who were present at the council which Mwanga held to decide upon murdering Bishop Hannington, at first professed entire ignorance of the whole affair. We said, "This is a matter which all Buganda knows; why are you deceiving us?" We carefully detailed to Kolugi the news which we had heard, and besought him to carry our words to the king, and to ask him to grant us an interview. He went to the king, and presently returned, saying, "The Kabaka commands you to go to the chief judge. Our last pleading before the chancellor had been so unsatisfactory, that we refused, saying that we were the king's guests alone, and we added, "The Englishman in Busoga is our brother, and the king knows that we told him the Askofu (Bishop) was coming to see him. For what reason has he now sent to have him killed?"

"The king knows nothing of these words," answered Kolugi. "Why do you persist in deceiving us?" we said; "you are our friend? We have heard the names of the messengers despatched by the King—Wakoli * the gate-keeper and Musoke, the page; the former to kill the Askofu, and the latter to count his "bintu" (things)—and we know that they have already gone."

Kolugi again went and stood before the king, and after some time, came out bringing Mwanga's reply. "The king commands you to come to-morrow, and he will give you his messenger to go and save them." "To-morrow," we replied, "will be too late. Oh, let him send now."

Kolugi offered to return once more; but Mwanga had gone out of his inclosure by the back way, which led to his pond, and did not return till nightfall, when we had to go, since the great gates were closed. As

* Same name as one of the paramount chiefs of Busoga, from whom he must be distinguished. The other chief of Busoga, Luba, it was who captured Bishop Hannington.

our last earthly resource we offered Kolugi a large bribe if he would send post haste and delay the messengers. This he promised to do; but we had little confidence either in his willingness or ability to do so. While waiting, Samweli slipped a letter into my hand which he had written. He was one of the assistant store-keepers, and had heard the chiefs when they told us of the ignorance of the king and themselves of our bishop's danger. The letter ran thus:—

"Munange sebo (My friend, sir)—Believe not their words—they have deceived you; most certainly the messengers have gone to kill them."

"SAMWELI."

"In the courtyard of the storehouses there were sitting some miserable captives taken from Busoga in a late raid. I noticed them carefully to see whether they got any food. It was a fasting day for us, so that a fellow feeling made us sympathise with them; but the livelong day passed by and not a morsel did they get. Some of them were women with young children in their arms. I asked one of the guards if those prisoners would get any food, and the reply was that they would receive some on the morrow."

The above was written at about 4 A.M. on Monday, Oct. 26th, 1885. My diary of that miserable day ends thus:—"Their death—if it be God's will—and ours, which will also probably follow: O God, may it be a step towards better things for this unhappy land! O God, look upon it——"

CHAPTER XVI.

DEATH OF HANNINGTON.

MEANWHILE, Hannington, knowing nothing of the state of things in Buganda, or of the suspicion caused by Thompson's coming, had made his way to Kavirondo, where the mission boat in charge of Mr. Stokes, of previous mention, had proceeded to look for him. Though Hannington himself soon left Kavirondo with fifty men, there still remained the bulk of his porters under the native pastor Jones; but, strange to say, Mr. Stokes heard no news of this caravan, and so he returned to Musalala.

As will be seen, the bishop's change of plan was most unfortunate, though under the circumstances it could hardly have been avoided.

Hannington, after leaving Kavirondo, journeyed north until he reached Busoga; and at Luba's, where he was stopped, he saw his first view of the Victoria Nile.

I give here his own account of his capture, and it will be seen how he mistook Luba's warriors, who were acting under the chief's orders, for robbers.

Strange to say, a few months later the journal came into our hands. Kulugi, the keeper of the king's stores, who had the custody of the things stolen from the bishop was, as I have said, to a certain extent our friend, and we had sent him a present of a small tusk of ivory, after which Mackay visited him and managed to obtain from him the bishop's writing-case, which contained the diary which he had been writing, it would seem, up to the hour of his death.

It was hardly a matter of wonder that my tears should fall as I read the familiar handwriting of the friend who had been a companion in months of weary travel and whom I had learned to know so well and to respect so much.

If you can respect and love a man after living with him in Africa it means that in no small degree he has the highest qualities.   This may seem a strange remark to make; but Africa proves a man, and he who issues unscathed from that furnace is pure gold indeed.

This is the journal of his few last days :—*

"*Oct.* 21*st, Wednesday.*—About half an hour only brought us to Luba's.   The first demand was in a most insolent tone for ten guns and three barrels of powder; this, of course, I refused.   They then demanded that I should stay three days; this I refused, and when the same demands were made, I jumped up and said, I go back the way I came.'   Meantime the war drums beat.   More than a thousand soldiers were

---

* I follow here mostly the editing of Rev. E. C. Dawson, the bishop's biographer, though my copy of the diary and his do not always agree.

assembled. My men implored me not to move, but laughing at them I pushed them and the loads through the crowd and turned back. Then came an imploring message that I would stay but for a short time. I refused to hear till several messages had arrived; then, thinking things were turning my way, I consented; said I would give a small present and pass. My present was returned, and a demand made that I would stay one day; to this I consented, because I fancy this man can send me on in canoes direct to Mwanga's capital, and save a week's march. Presently seven guns were stolen from us; at this I pretended to rejoice exceedingly, since I should demand restoration not from these men, but from Mwanga. A soldier was placed to guard me in my tent, and follow me if I moved an inch. I climbed a neighbouring hill, and, to my joy, saw a splendid view of the Nile, only about *half an hour's distance*, country being beautiful; deep creeks of the lake visible to the south. I presently asked leave to go to the Nile. This was denied me. I afterwards asked my head man Brahim to come with me to the point close at hand whence I had seen the Nile, as our men had begun to doubt its existence; several * followed up, and one, pretending to show me another view, led me further away, when suddenly about twenty ruffians set upon us. They violently threw me to the ground, and proceeded to strip me of all valuables. Thinking they were robbers, I shouted

* "Several" here refers to Luba's people.

for help, when they forced me up and hurried me away, as I thought, to throw me down a precipice close at hand. I shouted again, in spite of one threatening to kill me with a club. Twice I nearly broke away from them, and then grew faint with struggling, and was dragged by the legs over the ground. I said, 'Lord, I put myself in Thy hands; I look to Thee alone.' Then another struggle and I got to my feet, and was thus dashed along. More than once I was violently brought into contact with banana trees, some trying in their haste to force me one way, others the other, and the exertion and struggling strained me in the most agonising manner. In spite of all, and feeling I was being dragged away to be murdered at a distance, I sang 'Safe in the arms of Jesus,' * and then laughed at the very agony of my situation—my clothes torn to pieces so that I was exposed; wet through with being dragged along the ground; strained in every limb, and for a whole hour expecting instant death; hurried along, dragged, pushed, at about five miles an hour, until we came to a hut into the court of which I was forced. Now, I thought, I am to be murdered. As they released one hand, I drew my finger across my throat, and understood them to say decidedly, 'No.' We then made out that I had been seized by order of the Sultan. Then arose a new agony. Were all my men murdered? Another two or three hours' awful suspense, during which time I was kept bound and shivering with cold, when, to my joy,

* My copy has the addition, "And, my God, I am Thine."

Pinto (the Goanese cook) and a boy were brought with my bed and bedding, and I learnt that the Sultan had seized me and simultaneously my men and loads, and meant to keep me prisoner until he had received word from Mwanga, which means, I fear, a week or more, nor can I tell the exact truth of what they say. I am in God's hands.

"*Oct. 22nd, Thursday.*—I found myself, perhaps about ten o'clock last night, on my bed in a fair-sized hut, but with no ventilation—a fire on the hearth, no chimney for smoke; about twenty men all around me, and rats and vermin *ad lib.*; fearfully shaken, strained in every limb; great pain, and consumed with thirst. I got little sleep that night. Pinto may cook my food, and I have been allowed to have my Bible and writing things also. I hear the men are in close confinement, but safe, and the loads, except a few small things, intact. Up to one o'clock I have received no news whatever, and I fear at least a week in this black hole, in which I can barely see to write. Floor covered with rotting banana peel and leaves and lice; men relieving nature at night on the floor; a smoking fire, at which my guards cook and drink pombe; in a feverish district; fearfully shaken, scarce power to hold up a small Bible. Shall I live through it? My God, I am Thine.* Towards evening I was allowed to sit outside for a little time, and enjoyed the fresh air; but it made matters worse

---

* My copy here reads, "1 P.M., good broth, but no appetite to eat it. However, if it was not here, I should no doubt feel starving."

when I went inside my prison again, and as I fell exhausted on my bed I burst into tears; health seems to be quite giving way with the shock. I fear I am in a very caged-lion frame of mind, and yet so strained and shattered that it is with the utmost difficulty I can stand; yet I ought to be praising His Holy Name, and I do.

"Not allowed a knife to eat my food with. The savages who guard me keep up an unceasing strain of raillery, or at least I fancy they do, about the Mzungu.

"*Oct. 23rd, Friday.*—I woke full of pain and weak, so that with the utmost difficulty I crawled outside and sat in a chair, and yet they guard every move as if I was a giant. My nerves, too, have received such a shock, that, hearing some loud yells and war cries outside the prison fence, I expected to be murdered, and simply turned over and said, 'Let the Lord do as He sees fit; I shall not make the slightest resistance.' Seeing how bad I am, they have sent my tent for me to use in the daytime.* Going outside, I fell to the ground exhausted and was helped back in a gone condition to my bed. I don't see how I can stand all this, and yet I don't want to give in, but it almost seems as if Uganda itself was going to be forbidden ground to me.† The Lord only knows.

"*Afternoon.*—To my surprise my guards came kneel-

---

* My copy reads, "I implore to sleep here, but fear not. I said, 'Take away my boots, and how can I flee?'"

† In my copy, "Though I am far in the dominion, I have yet only looked upon the country itself."

ing down—so different from their usual treatment—and asked me to come out. I came out, and there was the chief and about a hundred of his wives come to feast their eyes on me in cruel curiosity.* I felt inclined to spring at his throat, but sat still and presently read to myself Matthew v. 44, 45, and felt refreshed. I asked how many more days he meant to keep me in prison. He said four more at least.† He agreed, upon my earnest request, to allow me to sleep in my own tent with two armed soldiers at each door. The object of his visit was to ask that I would say no bad things of him to Mwanga. What can I say good? I made no answer to the twice-repeated request. He then said if I would write a short letter and promise to say nothing bad he would send it at once. I immediately wrote a hasty scrawl (I scarce know what), but said I was a prisoner and asked Mackay to come. God grant it may reach; ‡ but I already feel better than I have done since my capture, though still very shattered.

"*Oct. 24th, Saturday.*—Thank God for a pleasant night in my own tent, in spite of a tremendous storm, and rain flowing in on the floor in streams. Personally I quite forgive this old man and his agents for my rough treatment, though even to-day I can only move with

---

* My copy has "cruel adversity," which makes sense.

† Here Mr. Dawson and I differ a good deal. May I venture to say that I cannot look on Mr. Dawson's changes as improvements. Hannington's own words, though often rugged, are always living pictures.

‡ This letter never came into our hands.

the greatest discomfort, and ache as though I had rheumatic fever. I have, however, to consider the question in another light: if the matter is passed over unnoticed, it appears to me the safety of all white travellers in these districts will be endangered, so I shall leave the brethren, who know the country and are most affected, to act as they think best. The day passed very quietly. I amused myself with Bible and diary.

"*Oct. 25th, Sunday* (fourth day of imprisonment).— Still a great deal of pain in my limbs. The fatigue of dressing quite knocks me over. My guards, though at times they stick to me like leeches, and, with two rifles in hand, remain at night in my tent, are gradually getting very careless. I have already seen opportunities of escape had I wanted so to do, and I doubt not that in a few days' time, especially if I could get a little extra pombe brought to them, I could walk away quite easily, but I have no such intention. I should be more inclined to stop should they say 'Go,' to be a thorn in the old gentleman's side, and, I fear, from that feeling of contrariness which is rather inborn. I send him affectionate greetings and reports on my health by his messengers twice a day. What I fear most now is the close confinement and utter want of exercise.

" When I was almost beginning to think of my time in prison as getting short, the chief has sent men to redouble the fence around me. What does it mean? I have shown no desire or intention of escaping. Has a messenger arrived from Mwanga? There is just time for him to have sent word to tell them to hold me fast. The look of this has cast me down again.

"One of my guards, if I understand him rightly, is making me offers of escape. He has something very secret to communicate, and will not even take my boy into confidence. I do not, however, want to escape under the present circumstances; but at the same time I take great amusement in watching and passing by various little opportunities. My guards and I are great friends, almost affectionate, and one speaks of me as 'My White man.' Three detachments of the chief's wives—they say he has one thousand nearly—have been to-day to see me. They are very quiet and well-behaved, but greatly amused at the prisoner. Mackay's name seems quite a household word. I constantly hear it.* My men are kept in close confinement, except two who come daily backwards and forwards to bring my food. This they take in turns, and implore, so I hear, for the job.

"*Oct. 26th, Monday* (fifth day in prison).—Limbs and bruises and stiffness better, but I am heavy and sleepy. Was not inclined to get up as usual, and, if I mistake not, signs of fever creep over me. Mackay should get my letter to-day, and sufficient time has passed for the chief to receive an answer to his first message sent before I was seized, the nature of which I know not, probably: 'White man is stopping here. Shall I send him on? Waiting your majesty's pleasure.'

"If they do not guess who it is they will very likely,

* In my copy, "But of the others I scarce ever hear a word."

African fashion, talk about it two or three days first of all, and then send a message back leisurely with Mwanga's permission for me to advance.

"About thirty-three more of the chief's wives came and disported themselves with gazing at the prisoner. I was very poorly and utterly disinclined to pay any attention to them, and said in English, 'Oh, ladies, if you only knew how ill I feel, you would go.' When my food arrived in the middle of the day I was unable to eat—the first time, I think, since leaving the coast I have refused a meal. To-day I am very broken-down both in health and spirits, and some of the murmuring feelings, which I thought had gone, have regained hold upon me. Another party of wives coming, I retired into the hut and declined to see them. A third party came later on, and being a little better, I came out and lay upon my bed. It is not pleasant to be examined as a caged lion in the Zoo, and yet that is exactly my state at the present time. My tent is jammed in between the hut and high fence of the Boma, so scarce a breath of air reaches me. Then, at night, though the tent is a vast improvement on the hut, yet two soldiers, reeking with pombe and other smells, sleep beside me, and the other part of my guard, not far short of twenty, laugh and drink and shout far into the night, and begin again before daylight in the morning, waking up from time to time to shout out to my sentries to know if all is well. I fear all this is telling on my health tremendously.

"*Oct. 27th, Tuesday* (sixth day as prisoner).—All I can hear in the way of news is that the chief has sent men to fight those parts we passed through. I begin to doubt if he has sent to Mwanga at all, but thinks I am in league with the fighting party, and is keeping me hostage. I begin the day better in health, though I had a most disturbed night. I am very low in spirits; it looks so, so dark, and have been told that the first messengers would return at the latest to-day. Last night the chief's messenger said perhaps they might be here as soon as Thursday, but seemed to doubt it. I don't know what to think, and would say from the heart, "Let the Lord do what seemeth Him good." If kept here another week I shall feel sure no messengers have been sent, and if possible shall endeavour to flee, in spite of all the property I must leave behind and the danger of the undertaking.

"Only a few ladies came to see the wild beast to-day. I felt so low and wretched that I retired within my den, whither they, some of them, followed me; but as it was too dark to see me, and I refused to speak, they soon left.

"The only news of to-day is that two white men, one tall and the other short, have arrived in Akola, and the Sultan has detained them. It is only a report that has followed me. I am the tall man, and Pinto, my Goa cook, the short one; he is almost always taken for a white man, and dresses as such. I fear, however, with these fearfully suspicious people, that it may affect me seriously. I am very low, and cry to God for release.

" *Oct.* 28*th*, *Wednesday* (seventh day's prison).—A terrible night; first with noisy drunken guard, and secondly with vermin, which have found out my tent and swarm. I don't think I got one sound hour's sleep, and woke with fever fast developing. Oh, Lord, do have mercy upon me, and release me. I am quite broken-down and brought low. Comforted by reading Psalm xxvii.

" In an hour or two fever developed very rapidly. My tent was so stifling that I was obliged to go inside the filthy hut, and soon was delirious.

" Evening; fever passed away. News comes that Mwanga has sent three soldiers, but what news they bring they will not yet let me know.

" Much comforted by Psalm xxviii.

" *Oct.* 29*th*, *Thursday* (eighth day's prison).—I can hear no news, but was held up by Psalm xxx., which came with great power. A hyena howled near me last night, smelling a sick man, but I hope it is not to have me yet."

His last night of weariness and pain had passed away, and little promise there seemed of morning joy, when suddenly Mwanga's messengers appeared, and coming in, they told him that the king of Buganda had sent for him. The previous night he had heard much beating of drums, as we had heard on the night preceding the day of Lugalama's death.

The messengers bade him come forth from his prison. He is pale and worn with fever; but very quiet now, very patient, but withal very noble; never so noble as now, never so ready to die as to-day. Quite broken-down and brought low, never had he reached so great a height. One of the messengers snatches up his Bible, another his portfolio, and another his sketch-book; and they lead him out, telling him he is soon to join his men.

There are, however, no signs of his men, and the way, is long; another *Via dolorosa* is being passed. He is very weary, but he must not rest. There accompany him great numbers of Basoga warriors armed; these had been summoned by the war drums of the preceding night.

After two hours' walking the party reach an open space without the banana groves, where at last Hannington sees his men, not, as he expected, with their loads, nor carrying their guns and full of spirits at the thought of once more being on the road, but all bound, some with the "kaligo," heavy-forked branch, round their necks, stripped of their clothing, and many with their hands tied behind their backs. They now see their master led into the open where they are. He seems wonderfully calm, and turns as if to sit down—this is not allowed. A gun is fired, doubtless by Wakoli, and Hannington's guards begin to strip him of his clothing. He is quite passive in their hands. He has commended

o

his soul to Him who sits above kings. But the report* of his last words has come to us: " Tell the king," he said, " that I die for Buganda. I have bought this road with my life."

They had now forced him to his knees—fitting posture in which to die; so kneeling

> " And looking upward, full of grace,
>   He prayed, and from a happy place
>   God's glory smote him on the face."

Then the spears are plunged into that heart which had overflowed with such fervent love for his murderers and their race.

Such was the terrible scene which the bishop's followers had to witness, and we can partly enter into the feelings of sickening horror with which they saw the grim death inflicted on another which was immediately to be their own.

One of these men was destined to pass through this awful drama, and return to tell the thrilling tale. The warriors with a wild cry now sprang upon the defenceless porters, and soon the frightful butchery was accomplished; and then, as if half fearing what they had done, the army of the Basoga and Baganda murderers hurried away, leaving the dead lying where they had fallen. Night drew her curtain over the scene, and

---

* This was told us by friends who had many opportunities of seeing those who were actually present. Still, they are only given as a *report at second hand.*

when the moon came out she shone peacefully upon the seeming sleepers ; alas,

"The many men so beautiful,
And they all dead did lie,"

and the long hours passed slowly away. Just before dawn one of the sleepers moves ; seems to awake, sits up, looks wildly round ; sinks back, remembers now what it is, and these all about him are his dead companions. He has a ghastly wound, his bowels are protruding through the gash ; again he painfully raises himself, puts back his bowels, drags himself to where he sees a banana leaf lying, puts it over the wound ; and then, not staying to mark the faces of the dead, with the dim instinct of preserving his life, he crawls away. He cannot get far, he comes to a hut. He is recognised ; but the simple folk who live there have no sympathy with such deeds of blood as have been enacted near them, and so they give this unhappy fellow-creature food and shelter ; and, so a stranger in a strange land, he meets with loving-kindness and hospitality until he is able to reach the Mission station at the south of the lake.

CHAPTER XVII.

BAGANDA CONVERTS. .

To return now to what was passing in Buganda. During these days we lived in constant expectation of being put to death. Reports of earnest conferences on the subject held by the king and chiefs daily reached us. We allowed all our boys to leave us and find refuge where they could. Hamisi, the Arab, our old neighbour, took care of one or two. Mahomet Biri the Tripoli Turk, the bearer of the first relief to Emin Pasha, took charge of some others; so that in this time of great trouble we received kindly sympathy and help from people of Islam.

After our first futile attempt to see Mwanga, the next morning Mackay and I went up again to his enclosure, taking with us the following letter written in the Luganda language :—

[*Translation of Letter.*]

"Natete, Oct. 26, 1885.

"MWANGA, KABAKA WA BUGANDA.
(MWANGA, KING OF UGANDA.)

"SEBO (SIR),

"We, the Englishmen, your guests, pray you to inform us concerning our brother, the bishop, who, we hear is at Luba's. We hear, moreover, that he is in danger. Therefore, sir, we pray you to send a messenger to extricate him, and to protect him efficiently."

This letter we signed, and it was duly delivered to the king. He sent out to say that he would send for the Baflansa (Frenchmen) to read it to him. We knew that this was another put off; he would not see us, how could he indeed. So sadly we came away. In the afternoon Père Lourdel came down and told us that he had seen the king, who commanded Mackay to come and write a letter to the bishop, telling him not to come by the Basoga road. Mackay had at this time a very bad attack of fever; but he immediataly wrote the letter, and I made all haste to take it up to the king's enclosure. Soon after I had arrived there, in walked Mackay. In spite of fever he had hurried after me on the donkey.

The king was only playing with us. We waited till nightfall and then returned, our darkest fears strengthened by what we were told, that the king had ordered the messengers not to return until they had killed the white men.

I quote from my journal, Monday, Oct. 26th, 1885: "The king said, 'What can these (Mackay and I) do if I kill their brethren?' What, indeed, O righteous God; but tell it unto Thee."

At one of his barazas Mwanga accused us of calling our place a royal enclosure. This may have arisen

from Mr. O'Flaherty saying one day in the merest jest
to Ndaula, the young king of Koki who used to visit
us, "Have you come to Kika"—a word used only of
coming to see the king.   Rumours again became rife of
Mwanga's intention to murder all the Christian readers.
On the 5th of November, Père Lourdel, who had done
all he could to save the bishop, sent us a letter
confirming the sorrowful tidings of the death of
Hannington and all his porters, and telling us that we
were to be put to death also.   That night one of
Mutesa's daughters, the "Mumbeja" (princess) Nalamansi, sent down to warn us to make friends with the
king at once, and to send a large present.   Mackay and
I did so, sending a quantity of valuable things to the
king and the chief judge and Kyimbugwe.   The king
accepted his, and the chief judge sent down to say that
we might now sleep in peace as he would protect us;
but Kyimbugwe sent to say we must send him some
more as our gift was not sufficient.   So we sent him
a few more things.

The king, however, sent down a message to command
Mackay to come up at once to the Kibuga (palace).
We felt great uncertainty of what was in store for us,
and quite expected that orders would be given to put
us in the stocks.

When we arrived we found Père Lourdel was also
waiting, and the three of us were admitted into the
king's presence.   To our no small surprise, he ordered
chairs to be brought for us, and we sat down.

There were present Kulugi and Kauta (chief cook), who was a young Mahometan and a faithful servant of Mwanga; he was afterwards burned to death, endeavouring to save his master's valuables in the great fire which destroyed Mwanga's enclosure. Kyimbugwe, now Pokino, Earl of Budu, was also present, a few pages were there as well—some of them our eager little scholars; and it was pleasant to know that though they dared not give us a smile of recognition, they were quite true to us.

The king began by saying to Mackay, "What is the meaning of the present you sent me?"

Mackay: "For friendship."

King: "What is your judgment?"

Reply: "It is not for judgment, it is for friendship."

King: "Have I only 'eaten Buganda' to-day, why give it me now, and not long ago?"

To this Mackay replied that he had finished repairing the king's gun. This was a little diversion, and the gun was brought for the king to look at—yes, it was very good—another gun which we had sent, and which had belonged to Mackay was brought. The king said, "Have you another gun?"

"No," replied Mackay, "I do not require a gun." Then Mwanga looked at it: "But how can I take your only gun? besides, see it is out of order—well, put it right, and send it to-morrow." But the king was eager to return to the matter of the present.

King: "Well now, the present, what is it for?"

I said, "We thought you were angry with us, because when we came to see you, you refused to see us."

Old Pokino now joined in, "Yes, and they sent me a present, and the Katikiro also, because they think we can influence the king. They think we want to kill them, and they wish to redeem their lives. What danger are they in? Do we kill guests? do we kill Baziba, or Basoga, or Arabs?

It was contemptible of this old fellow so to turn against us, for he always professed himself our warm friend. I turned to him and said, " Why, then, did you send back to say our present was not large enough, and tell us to send you more?" Pokino was nonplussed for a moment, and the others smiled a little at this. However they all began to rail against us. At last Mackay said, "Have we done wrong to give the king a present?" This was a telling question, which nonplussed them again. Then I said, " You all know why we sent it. We want to hear about our brother." General chorus: " Who told you about your brother?" " Answer: "Does not all Buganda know it?" Chorus: "Oh, does all Buganda go to your place?" Then the king addressed Kolugi and said, " Question them exceedingly;" so we were pitilessly plied with questions. Some of our informants were sitting by us, Père Lourdel being the chief, also some of the little pages who used to keep us supplied with information. We put off our cross-examiners as well as we could; finally we said, "We have not come here to 'ropa' (inform on) people." Whereupon they waxed angry, and the king called us hypocrites, and added that we were "bagwagwa,"* the most insulting term in the language. Manoga, the king's tailor, now came back to the question of who had told us about the Bishop. The king said, "They refuse to tell; because they think I shall kill the person." Then he tried a wheedling tone. "Tell me," he said, "and you will be 'baganze enyo' (great favourites)." Our continued silence made them very wroth, and then came angry words about killing. "What if I kill you?" said the king. "What could Queeni (the Queen) do? Was she able to touch Lukonge or Mirambo when they killed white men? What could she do, or all Bulaya (Europe) together? How would they come—would they fly?" Père Lourdel now kindly attempted to create a diversion in our favour. He said, "If you killed these white men, then I should not care to stay in your country." "If I killed them," insolently replied the king, "should I spare you? Are you not a white man like them?" The Père reflected on this in silence during the remainder of the interview.

Mwanga then said he would not have the east road used. Was he not the king? Who was Queeni?

We replied, "We are not messengers of Queeni, but messengers of God." Then Kauta began to mock, and they complained that we made the people our children, which led to some coarse humour from Mwanga, the first and last time I ever heard him say anything of

* Lowest of the low.

the sort. By this time we were thoroughly worried and harassed.* The king now addressed us directly, and appointed us "babaka" (king's messengers) to guard our own place, and to see that no people came near us—to see us or to sell us anything—and he added, " If you do not guard your place properly I will seize you and put you in the stocks." "Yes," added Kolugi, "and kill you."

Pokino now returned to his point, and said we lived in constant fear of our lives, and that we could neither eat nor sleep. "Well, look at us," I said, "and say if we appear like people who live as you say, and who fear to be killed." They then turned on me. "What brought you to Buganda, and who asked you to come? Mackay we want, but what can you do?" I said, "I thought you desired teachers, and Mutesa sent his canoes for me." They then took up the question of our teaching, and wanted to know why we did not teach the king and the chiefs. "Why," they scornfully asked, "did you not teach Kataluba (one of Wilson and Felkin's envoys) when he went to Europe? And why do you not teach your own Wagwana (servants)?"

More than two hours of this ceaseless attack had passed, and we were quite tired out, while no conclusion had been arrived at.

Suddenly Mwanga called an attendant, and said, "Take these white men and give them two cows to quiet their

---

* Mr. O'Flaherty had been treated in the same way by the Katikiro; and sent with Mujasi to search our house, see p. 143.

minds;" and then he dismissed the court. And so we went home with our cows, devoutly thankful to God for having brought us through such an unpleasant ordeal.

During this time of deep trouble, when people dare only come to us by stealth or at night, the young Admiral Gabunga sent a message to say that he wished to be baptised, and a day or two afterwards a letter came from Duta—one of the native church council—to say that Gabunga and some of his people had come down to Walukaga's enclosure, and that some other members of the church council were assembled there, and wished the young chief to be baptised. This boy had always stuck to us, and used to come in state with all his retinue, and dressed in his scarlet coat on Sundays, and he never was ashamed of the fact of his being a reader. We decided to comply with his desire, and I then went to Walukaga's and performed the rite, being the only available clergyman. Mr. O'Flaherty, the only other ordained missionary, all this time had been far from well, and the worry and anxiety of this terrible time had brought on severe fever, from which he never really recovered. Mwanga allowed him to leave at the end of the year, and on his way home in the following July, 1886, he died in the Red Sea. *Requiescat in pacem.*

Walukaga was a most remarkable man. He was the king's head blacksmith, and one of the most intelligent Africans I have ever known. Mackay, when making Namasole's coffin, became acquainted with him and liked him, and a friendship sprang up between them. Walukaga afterwards visited Mackay, and listened most attentively to what he told him. It was the revealing of a new and wonderful idea to him, and the opening up of a hope transcending far anything of which he had ever before dreamed. And he cried out, "How is it when we were making Namasole's coffin you told me none of these good things?"

If the teaching of that blacksmith alone had been all that Mackay had accomplished (which it was not), yet even in that case who would dare to say his years of self-sacrificing toil and frequent fevers and unceasing worries had been endured in vain!

Walukaga was a splendid Christian according to my ideas. Yet, according to some English Christians, Christ's teaching was too high for him and such as he.

Some days later Duta again wrote conveying a serious piece of news. His letter ran as follows :—

"We have heard that yesterday the king was in a bad way. Bwana Mapera (Lourdel) gave him medicine for his eyes, and told him not to rub them with oil. Well, at night the king did rub them with oil, and called the Katikiro and all the chiefs, and said to them 'The white men have given me poison, I am in an evil plight.' And all the people wept much, and they said the white men want to kill the king, and now he is ill. But this news is very bad, etc., etc." The same day news reached us that Balikudembe—a young chief who learned to read at our mission, but who joined the French priest's pupils afterwards—had been seized, and that he was under sentence of death by fire.

"That afternoon a whole troop of pages came down from Mwanga bringing 8000 cowrie shells, as part payment for some things which he had bought from us. One of the boys, Tito, drew me aside and told me that Balikudembe was dead. This young hero had dared to tell the tyrant that he did unwisely to kill the white men. Mwanga forthwith sent for the chancellor. "See!" he said, "this fellow wants to insult me," and then the cruel death-sentence was passed. The chief executioner was a friend of Balikudembe's, and mercifully killed him with a sword before committing his body to the flames.

Soon after this, moved by some restless impulse, I went to visit the spot where Lugalama died. It was late, about 1 A.M., as I made my way to the dismal swamp, the scene of that sorrowful tragedy. Once before I had visited the place with a faithful friend, Musali. He and I knelt there and I bade him pray, for I could find no words. He did pray—prayed for the murderer, and prayed for his fellow-countrymen. He himself was soon to die for his faith, true Christian indeed, although of the race for whom Islam is good enough!

This night, however, I went alone. There was a brilliant moon, casting inky shadows and revealing the weird shapes of the plantain trees with their silvery leaves. I could hear the ceaseless sound of innumerable crickets, yet except for this there was an awful silence and stillness. The way led past four cross roads over the brow of a hill, and down to the valley where the swamp called Mayanja lay, and to which I was going. At the cross roads was a sacred building, which I entered and knelt down. Then I came out and went on. That sorrowful procession which had passed this very road only a year before seemed to be with me now, and I the saddest of them all. The path dipped down to the edge of the swamp. I descended the hill and entered the chill and murky atmosphere of the morass and came to the very place. It had evidently been lately used. There was the framework of rough branches charred and blackened, and some of them fallen. The frame-work on which the mutilated bodies of some other unhappy victims had been fixed quivering over the slow flame.

As I stood there my stick struck something hard, and I stooped down and picked up the object which lay at my feet—a human skull. I stood there gazing at it, and again the awful question of the meaning of the mystery of life and death came upon me. I put the skull gently down again, and turned away and made my way homewards, relieved, I think, by this pilgrimage.

On the 3rd of December, 1886, I took to the king a letter from Egypt for Emin Pasha. Sir John Kirk had asked us to endeavour to prevail upon Mwanga to

forward letters to Emin. The king received the letter, and a little later sent it on.

The new year saw things brighter. Mr. O'Flaherty had been allowed to leave in peace, and Mwanga continued to be civil. He sent a present to Mackay one day of 10,000 cowries, telling him he was a muganze (favourite).

Very soon afterwards he gave Mackay another 8000 cowries, and sent a polite demand for my trousers. He had fallen in love with them, when I swam for him. I complied with his request and sent him a pair.

At the beginning of the year Mwanga had sent out an enormous raiding expedition against Bunyoro, of which Kangao, ruler of Bulemezi, was in command. On the 5th of February a letter reached us from the Russian traveller, Dr. Junker, from the north. He was in ignorance of events at Khartoum, but was desirous of coming to Uganda en route for the coast. Mackay immediately went and told Mwanga of the traveller's position, taking a present to the king. Mackay explained who Junker was; but the king said that when he heard that a white man was with Kabarega he had immediately sent to attack him. However, he ordered Mackay to return next day, who promised both the king and Katikiro a present of some cartridges, which seemed to put them into high good humour. On the following day an important council of chiefs was held, and they decided, at Mackay's request, to send to Kangao the general of the Uganda armies to order him to protect Junker.

On the 19th of February Mahomet Biri returned from Bunyoro, whither he had been, and brought Emin's and Junker's mail, which they wished us to forward. Junker wrote to us, telling of his desire to come our way ; he also wrote to the king in Arabic.

The next day Mackay went up with the letters which had arrived from the north, and gave the Katikiro the letter which Emin had written to him. Mackay also spoke to Mwanga of Emin ; but the king seemed much more interested in the coat which Mackay was wearing, and which he coveted, than in the matters of Emin Pasha. It seemed to please Mwanga to treat any other ruler with as much contempt as possible.

A few days later an occurrence took place which we feared might lead to a general massacre of Christians.

In the evening while we were at prayers we suddenly saw a strange glow in the sky, and unable to restrain their curiosity the boys ran out to see what it was, and they came back saying, " Kibuga Kiyide," the palace is in flames. Suddenly there was a loud report —" Mizinga," cannon, they exclaim—then another, and another—" Baruana," they are fighting, was now the cry. There was great excitement ; the reports, however, were dull, and more like the blowing up of gunpowder, which it turned out to be, than the report of small cannon. With characteristic caution the Kabaka kept his stores of gunpowder in a straw-built house in which a fire was continually burning. After a while a lad belonging to the chancellor came down and told us that the whole kibuga (enclosure) was destroyed. A little later Entanda Gideon appeared, he had lately distinguished himself by dropping two of Mwanga's best guns into the Nyanza, where they were lost. Mwanga, to his great credit be it said, did not punish him in any way; but Gideon's story now was, that he and Samweli and the other assistant store-keepers had gone behind the house, according to their nightly custom, to have prayers, leaving the store-house unoccupied, except by a wee Mukedi boy named "Bina." The fire was burning brightly, presently during prayers an enterprising spark floated up and caught on a cobweb in the roof, a straw was ignited from this and burst into a tiny flame. In another minute the straw roof was ablaze. Back rushed the boys and made frantic efforts to extinguish the fire, but the fire was master; wildly they seized the different things of which they were the custodians and rushed out with them. But the great straw-built dome was a sheet of living flame, and the high wind soon carried masses of blazing grass to the next house, where a still larger quantity of gunpowder was stored, it too soon was a sheet of flame, and as the small barrels of powder exploded, burning brands were blown in all directions, and soon the whole of the vast royal enclosure was roaring to destruction. Far off it was a splendid sight: it must have been truly magnificent close at hand.

P

The young Mahometan head cook, Kauta, distinguished himself by his reckless daring in endeavouring to save his master's property, in doing which he sustained fatal injuries; as also another chief called Mulamba—the little child Bina was also burned to death. The splendid donkey which Mwanga had taken from us some weeks before perished in the flames.

Mwanga, when he saw the fire, jumped to the conclusion that it was caused by rebels, and that what, I suppose he daily expected, had happened, namely that the whole country was in rebellion, and that the rebels had fired his capital. Seizing a naked sword he rushed from his flaming palace, followed by some dozen of his boys, these he bade strip off their white garments that they might not be discernible, and then fled away into the darkness. Père Lourdel, the French priest, having seen the fire, at once made his way up to the court [he was allowed by Mwanga to use his private road], and suddenly came upon the flying monarch. He stopped him and tried to reassure him. At this juncture some of the chiefs came up and conducted Mwanga to the Katikiro's enclosure.

The chancellor's store-house was soon struck by lightning. Kiwanuka, the God of Thunder, could not allow the divine Kabaka to be driven out of his houses by fire without sending a thunderbolt into the Katikiro's enclosure—at any rate, both times that the king's enclosure was burnt the Katikiro's place was on fire immediately afterwards.

The king then said that he would go to the Nyanza, where the chief Edward (Mulyagonja) had built him another straw palace. This the chancellor opposed on the ground that Kabarega would hear of it, and say that Mwanga had fled from fear of him. Kabarega, we were told, *planted* a man and a baboon— *i.e.* buried them alive in the road by which the enemy would reach him, as a sacrifice or spell to bewitch the Baganda armies. I am sure Kabarega must have prided himself on the success of his charm, for in the fighting which ensued the Muganda Generalissimo Kangao was killed, as well as many of the Baganda people. The Banyoro getting far the best of the battle.

At the end of February, 1886, a report reached us that Mwanga had ordered Bilali, the overseer of the markets, to seize people who came to us to learn. Nothing, however, came of it.

Mwanga was gradually becoming disagreeable again. He had said after the fire that the white men had bewitched him, and would be the death of him some day. He also said that he knew he should be the last black king of Buganda. About this time he gave his head hangman, Mukajangwa, orders to kill Mackay if he brought the boat to a certain place where Mwanga had himself ordered him to bring it. The king bade this executioner take men and cut off Mackay's head and bring his hat to the enclosure. Mackay heard of it, and did not go to the forbidden spot; and the chancellor,

p 2

hearing of the order, sent down to Mackay to warn him not to go. But things of this sort were only the precursors of a coming storm.

About this time we sent off Emin's letters by one of Gabunga's people who was going south in canoes, while Mackay was visiting the king at Munyonyo, quite near the lake. At this place we had a small grass house near the royal enclosure, and we took it in turns to attend the king's baraza. Mackay had several interviews with him, in one of which Mwanga remarked that if the "Balozi" (Consul at Zanzibar) were to write seventy letters for him, he should not allow him to leave the country.

This point of being allowed to come and go at will was one which we were always trying in a quiet way to gain.

A few days later I went down and had one of my last interviews with Mwanga.

After dismissing the general baraza (levée), he called Kulugi and me back again. I had brought some of our little reading books, which I showed him. He asked if the printing was done with iron. I said that it was, and he remarked that nearly all the wonderful things of the Bazungu (Europeans) were made with iron. I asked him when he was going to read, and told him that our Queen, though so great and mighty, was a humble Christian. This set him off about the Prince of Wales. He tried to say his name. I said it slowly, and he repeated it after me. Again return-

ing to the subject of religion, I asked him what a
man really had if he had no life from God after death.
He replied by asking me if I had any scarlet shoes such
as are worn by Turks; and then if I knew anything
about the white man (Junker) who wished to come to
Buganda. I said I did not. He asked if he were an
Englishman. I said, "No, a Murusi—Russian." After
this conversation, I went to see the chancellor. He
hated me, but was generally freezingly polite—never
more. I believe Mackay was the only European that
he could endure.

Next day, Kagwa (Apolo), one of our converts, now a
trusted servant of the king, sent a little boy named
Lulè down to me with a paper. It had belonged to
Bishop Hannington—a blank letter of orders—"We,
James, by Divine permission Bishop of the Church of
England in Eastern Equatorial Africa," &c. Lulè said
he must take it back, as it might be missed.

About the middle of April, Mackay again visited
Mwanga. He had not done so for many weeks after
the king's order to have him killed. When Mackay
went in, Mwanga began begging for cartridges. Mackay
reproached the king for treating him as an enemy,
saying, " The more we give you, the more you hate us."
"What proof do you offer of that ? " said the king.
"What order did you give to Mukajangwa ? " asked
Mackay. "Who told you about that ? " said the king.
" Is it not true ? " answered Mackay.

Lukoto, an inferior Judge, happened to be there;

and the king said : " Kale tuwoze musango "—" Let us
plead our case."

Kulugi, who was present, then began to state the case
for the king ; and when he was silent, Mackay stated
his side. When he had finished, Kulugi said : " Gutu-
sinze "—" The judgment goes against us," or " over-
comes us."

Mackay then left Munyonyo, and came back to
Natete, the mission station ; and the next Sunday,
Easter-day, there was a report that the Christians
were to be seized, and so they were afraid to assemble
in any numbers. Twenty, however, came to the communion in the morning ; and in the afternoon ten more
came for the same purpose ; and in the evening, fifteen
more faithful people came to the Lord's Supper, made
more solemn than ever by the fact of the rumour of the
morning. There were some there who partook of it
for the last time before dying for the faith, of which
it is a symbol.

CHAPTER XVIII.

BAGANDA CONVERTS AND MARTYRS.

THIS month we obtained a new acquisition in Mwana awulira, a young slave whom we redeemed. Bikweyamba, a scion of the royal family of Bunyoro and a Muganda chief, had lately been seized and put in the stocks on the charge of not bringing in sufficient tribute to the king. He was a friend of mine, and sent his sister, Narwaga, a Mumbeja, or princess, to beg for cloth to pay his guards in order to mitigate his confinement. He was heavily loaded with the " kaligo " (slave fork), and had his feet and hands in the stocks, " emvuba." By paying a certain amount he could release a hand, and by paying still more a foot until he was entirely free. Now to raise money he had been selling his slaves to the Arabs. I told Narwaga that if her brother wanted cloth he had better send one of his slaves to us and we would take him in pawn, and if he liked his slave back he might return the cloth and get him out. I had already given some cloth, but did not wish to be troubled by his asking every day for more. I knew very well that he would never send for his boy again, for the price I was giving was several yards more than he was worth.

A day or two later Narwaga said to the slave boy, "Come and let us visit the white men." She did not say I have sold you for thirty-six yards of cloth. So he got up and followed her. He was a Muhangiro, or Mujangiro, from the south-west of the Nyanza, I suppose about 14 years old, slightly lame, having six toes on one foot. Let him tell his own story :—*

"When I got to the Bazungu's house I saw some strange things. Two outlandishly dressed white men, who kept their fire on a large board which they ate off. They had large black clubby sort of feet; their toes, unlike ordinary people's, were all together in one. I was utterly bewildered by the way which these people ate their food. I could see long things protruding from their hands; could they be nails or some strange growth peculiar to Bazungu? They gave me plenty of food, and then a lot of people followed one of the Bazungu and we climbed up into the roof, or rather into another house, on the top of the one in which they ate their food, and then they began to sing; I never heard singing like that before, and I did not like it much. Then they stopped and every one knelt down, and I did too, and the Bazungu began to say words, praying to some one, some great chief, but I could see no one but ourselves. My mistress then told me I was to stay there. I did not mind much, for there were other boys, and I soon got used to the

* I give the boy's own words.

new life." The fire which Mwana awulira saw on the board was our lamp on the table.

. Mackay on one occasion while on the lake had a ship's lamp with a globe—it was nice and bright. A native of Sesse, seeing the lamp on the ground, and wishing to light his fire, brought a bunch of dried grass and thrust it to the glass which he did not see, and waited a second, then tried again, and found it a complete failure; he said, in a tone of great disgust, " Eh, omuliro gwa muzungu guganye." " Eugh ! the fire of the white man refuses," and went elsewhere to seek a more accommodating flame.

╎ Our new boy's former master had given him the name Mudu awulira, the obedient slave. I called him Mwana awulira, the obedient child. He eventually came with me to Zanzibar.

I make an extract here from my diary of May 1st, 1866 :—

Evil tidings reached us to-day; the faithful Musali or Kidza came and told us that Mwanga had been storming about the number of readers who were learning, so we warned our friends not to come about us. We have heard several times lately rumours of evil, and the storm which had been so long brewing broke at last in awful fury upon the Christian readers of both denominations, Protestant and Roman Catholic. On the 22nd of May Semfuma Tomasi came and told us two items of news: First, that Nalamansi, the Christian Mumbeja, had given great offence by flinging away all her sacred charms, " mayembe," and by burn-ing her ancestral relics. And the other, that a nice quiet lad named Matia, who had lately been baptised, had dared, though indirectly, to disobey the commands of the king. This boy was the son of the chief Mugula, and himself held the office of Sabagabo in the Kitongole of the " bagalagala," or pages.

A Mahometan reader, Kawuta, head cook and a con-siderable chief, made the request at Mwanga's baraza that the page Sabagabo should be handed over to him for an evil purpose, to which the king acceded. Saba-gabo, however, bravely stood out against the shameful treatment to which the chief wished to subject him. And it was this splendid act of disobedience which, when reported to Mwanga, served to set the spark to the train which had already been laid.

The next day, Alexandro Namfumbambi, now Mutebe —his new chieftanship—came and told us that Sabagabo had been badly beaten, and was lying in the stocks. And then we heard the terrible news that the Christian readers had been seized and many of them put to death. Nyonyi Entono, my friend (a Roman Catholic reader), who now held a most important office, " Musalo-salo," was cruelly and shamefully mutilated by the orders of the king. He recovered, and afterwards actually became katikiro, or chief judge, in place of the haughty chan-cellor. That functionary killed two of his pages who had been seen reading. The same day Kagwa (Apolo) was called into the king's presence with another youth; a stormy scene ensued. The king, acting on an impulse of uncontrollable fury, attacked the other lad with a spear, gashing him frightfully, and he was hurried away and murdered by the executioners. Then the king turned to Apolo : "Are you a reader ? " he cried, trembling with passion. "Nsoma, Mukamawange," "I read, my Lord," was the brave reply. "Then I'll teach you to read ! " shouted the angry king, and gashed him too with the spear, and then took the wooden handle and broke it over his back. At last, breathless with the exertion, his anger having apparently spent itself, he told him to begone. And Kagwa's life was saved, and no more was done to him. He afterwards rose to be Mukwenda in the latest revolution.

The noble blacksmith, Walukaga, was seized, and the faithful Musali. Alexandro Namfumbambi, who often gave us trouble by his inconsistencies, on hearing of the seizure of his fellow-Christians, went boldly up to the court, and when the executioners asked if any readers were concealed in his enclosure, replied, "I myself am a Christian ; " and was at once apprehended and made prisoner.

On the morning of this dismal day, I was sitting in a kind of verandah at the back of the mission house, and a number of people were seated round learning their letters. We had just been singing a hymn—

"Bona bona bakusinza   =   "All the people bow
                                                    before Thee,
     Gwe Kakaba wo mugulu"   Thou the Ruler of
                                                    the heavens"—

when Mackay suddenly appeared. He came up to where I was sitting, and said in English: "I have just heard that the king has gone mad and given orders to seize all the Christians." The readers saw our troubled looks, and we turned and told them what it was. I said to them, "Escape quickly lest they search our place;" and they hurried off and made their way out through a hole in our back fence. They had hardly gone when Bilali, a coastman in the king's service, came with an armed following to search for Christians. He conducted his search in a very gentlemanly way saying he was sorry to have to trouble us. He found no one, since they had all effected their escape.

The next news which we heard was that Monseigneur Lavinhac, the French Vicar Apostolique, had just arrived from the south of the Nyanza with another priest. He had taught Mwanga at a former time, and we hoped that his influence might prove of some avail in saving the lives of the poor people now in prison.

But so far from this being the case, Mwanga signalised the coming of the French bishop by killing several of the Frenchmen's most prominent pupils. He caused to be mutilated also one of our converts, a young sub-chief named Musamula, who soon died from the effects of his cruelty. This young man had been a follower of Mwanga when the king was still a "mulangira" (prince). One day his master ordered him to go and "nyagga" (steal) some goats; he refused, since he was learning to be a Christian, so was instantly dismissed from

Mwanga's service. I advised him to return and make it up, which he did, and was received back. When Mwanga became king, he gave Embwa (the dog), for that was his name, the small chieftainship of Kisamula, when he assumed the name of Musamula.

The king gave orders that three of Namesole's (queen mother) pages should be put to death, which was carried out. Daily we heard of the murder of some one of our converts; but strange to say, Sabagabo, the boy whose bravery had immediately led to this terrible outbreak, was liberated. The very last time I was at Mengo, Mwanga's capital, I saw him. He dared not say much to me, as there were generally spies about who would quickly report any one seen speaking to the dreaded Bazungu. Latterly we hardly dared to notice our friends lest we should mark them, and thus lead to their being persecuted.

The 27th of May a very likely and alarming report reached us that the mission was to be sacked. Our boys were in great consternation. "*Sauve qui peut*" was all that we could say to them, and Mackay and I were left alone. Our coast servants had never been touched, and so they did not leave us. But they did not live in our enclosure or compound, so that we two were practically alone. It was a dark day. Mackay wrote to the French bishop, suggesting that all the Europeans should adopt some concerted plan of action; but he replied that he did not think it advisable, and possibly he was right. The chiefs were in an angry and irritated frame of mind; yet we could not bear the thought of passively sitting down without making some effort to save those Christians who were still alive, though under sentence of death.

The Katikiro sent three times to demand that Mugoa, a young chief who had lately been advanced by the king, should be killed. Twice the king refused, but the imperious chancellor seemed to be again in the ascendant, and would take no denial. He would not eat until the murdered chief's hand was brought to him, to show that his orders had been carried out.

The king, in order to revenge himself on the chancellor for murdering Mugoa, sent to demand the life of Sebwato, a prominent Christian, whom I have mentioned as the captor and master and liberator of Lugalama. The Katikiro sent back to say that he would see that Sebwato was dealt with. He was most useful to the chancellor, and was a faithful and discreet servant, who managed his master's business transactions with the Arabs of Karagwe. Sebwato was commanded to appear before the chief judge, and questioned as to his connection with the foreign superstition. He said little, but he was notoriously a Christian, and so the Katikiro commanded him to be beaten publicly, which order was carried out. Sebwato took his castigation patiently. He was a tender-hearted man, and I recollect when they killed Lugalama he was moved to tears, when he came to see me some time afterwards. He subsequently gained great glory in battle. One of the charges brought against Christians was, that they would not fight for their king, nor put bullets in their guns. However, in one of the battles which the Baganda fought, Sebwato greatly distinguished himself by his valour, and then the Baganda said there were none so brave as the Christians.

Père Lourdel had seen the Katikiro, and begged of him, if there was anything wrong in our teaching, to drive us away; "but do not kill your own children," he urged. "No," replied the chancellor; "you are guests, and we will not drive you away; but as many as you teach we shall kill." I had said to the chancellor, after the murder of the bishop: "If you do not wish us to be here, let us go." To me he made no reply. It was this determination on the part of the chiefs which led Mackay and me to decide to ask for permission to leave the country. We felt that if they once saw that we were not staying on against their will, which they often implied, they would be more likely to urge us to remain.

The next convert of whom I shall speak, though not a martyr, deserves mention; I refer to the old sub-chief Isaya, of Kasengeje, a place bright in the Christian annals of Buganda as being the home of quite a community of "Bamasiya" Christians. The head of this community, Isaya, had been deposed from his chieftainship of Munakulya, and succeeded in it by Masudi, a renegade one-eyed Arab.*

I shall never forget old Isaya visiting Mackay at dead of night. It was after the wholesale murder of many of the Christians, and some of his lads, retainers and slaves, were under sentence of death. He came and told Mackay about it; and when he reached this point—that his people were to be seized—he said: "They are going to kill my children! my children!" and burst into uncontrollable tears. Mackay did all he could to soothe and comfort him. As a matter of fact, however, his people were not molested.

On the 29th of May Mackay visited the king, who was still at Munyonyo, and begged for the lives of the Christians who were under sentence in prison. The king promised to spare them, but did not keep his word.

The next day I went to Munyonyo. On the side of the road as I passed there was a human head, which looked as if it had been carefully placed there after being severed from the trunk. It had a sort of fascination for me. I tried to discern the features, but it was the face of no one whom I knew. A little further, on the other side of the road, were the limbs hacked in

---

* Masudi was present at Bishop Hannington's capture. He was one of that insolent drunken set through whom Hannington passed with a high hand. Such mean-looking wretches as he and Mujasi, unless one knew them to be powerful chiefs, could be mistaken for nothing but the lowest of the low.

pieces at the joints. I went on, sick at heart. I arrived too late, and was not admitted to the king's baraza. While sitting outside in the storehouse, I was told of the death of Mukasa, a bright brave boy, who on one occasion had administered a thorough thrashing to a companion who was leading some of the younger pages astray. His Christian name was Musa; he was one of the first killed. He was murdered at the door of Walukaga's smithy. I heard, too, the story of Walukaga's capture. When they came to seize him, his wife Hannah, a most intelligent woman and clever reader, escaped with the rest of the household; but he stood firm, and was taken. He waited for a definite reason, and it was this: The Christians were suspected of disloyalty and sedition. Now the most prominent of them would not run away nor go into hiding, lest they should give colour to this suspicion. They appealed to the laws of their country, and were prepared "Kuwoza Musango," to plead for judgment, before the proper tribunal. It was this spirit and this confidence in the righteousness of their cause which so puzzled the rulers, and which made the Christians such a power in the country.

Then followed the crowning act in the cruel tragedy, when Walukaga and some thirty others met their heroic deaths. A mighty pyre was heaped about the Christian captives. Each was firmly bound, a burning brand was brought, and soon the consuming fire enfolded this company of saints, of whom the world was not worthy;

Q

and so calling, if report speaks truly, on their persecutors to believe in Christ, they were caught away in their chariot of flame.

A little later and we heard of the death of Musali Kidza, who had been warned by his master the Mujasi to make his escape; but, like Walukaga, he refused to do so. He was accordingly taken; the unrighteous sentence was pronounced, and they dashed his brains out with a club, and this was the manner of his martyrdom.

At the time of this horrible butchery the mission premises were utterly deserted. However, Namutwe, the old chief from whom I had bought little Jimmy, sent down a number of children to be vaccinated. They came in charge of a small boy, Kiwobe (death-wail), who had learned to read fluently under the instruction of one of the members of the Native Church Council named Munyaga bye nju. While Mackay was vaccinating the children, Kiwobe came to me and said, "Munange njagala kubatizibwa"—"My friend, I wish to be baptised." This was a most extraordinary request at such a time. His teacher, Munyaga, had just been murdered in the most shockingly frightful manner. I cannot forbear to tell the story :—

When Munyaga was captured he was in his house actually teaching at the time. The little party of readers saw the "Bamboa," executioners, coming up the slope of the hill on which stood the house, where they were. Immediately there was a stampede, and the lads and others escaped. But Munyaga, like Walukaga, would not fly, but sat where he was and waited. The executioners came cautiously up. They saw a gun leaning against the reed lintel of the door and stopped, hesitating, believing it was the possession of a loaded gun that gave Munyaga such confidence. He, seeing their evident fear, told them they need not be afraid of the gun, for he did not mean to use it. So they came up to apprehend him. He begged to be allowed to put on his "kansu" (white robe), which they agreed to, and then they led him away. His trial was a cruel mockery, and he was ordered to be hacked in pieces and burned. His torturers cut off one of his arms and flung it into the fire before him, then they cut off a leg, and that, too, was flung into the flame, and lastly, the poor mutilated body was laid on the framework to be consumed. Ashes to ashes, dust to dust, in sure and certain hope of the resurrection of the dead.

Now to return to young Kiwobe's request for baptism: "Do you know what you are asking?" I said to him. "Mmanyi munange"—"I know, my friend," he replied. "But," I said, "you know if you say you are a Christian they would kill you." Again he said the same words, "I know, my friend." "But," I said, "suppose people asked you if you were a reader, would you tell a lie and deny it and say no?" He replied, "Ndiyatula munange"—"I shall confess, my friend." Mackay and I both thought he was worthy of the rite, for he had a good knowledge of reading and seemed to have been well taught, so he was baptised there and then.   He chose the name of Samweli.

The first Samuel baptised was the " Mapera boy." His native name was Mukasa, but Mutesa called him Muganze Awongererwa.   It is a common thing in Buganda to " wongera abaana "—ask, or perform religious rites, to obtain children.   I therefore understood the name to mean the favourite who was asked of the gods, so I thought " Samuel," or " Samweli," would be an appropriate Christian name.

When Samuel grew to be about eighteen, and the election of the Native Church Council took place, though he was the youngest candidate, he was elected with only one dissentient vote.   Walukaga, I think, was the only member unanimously chosen.

Samweli, Kagwa (Apolo), and Waswa, another Christian, were keepers of the king's stores, under Kolugi, and Samweli had been appointed just before this time to go into Busongora to collect the king's tribute of cowrie shells.   While he was away this frightful persecution had broken out, and his was one of the principal names in the fatal proscription.   The king was only waiting for his return to have him killed.   On his way back he learned the terrible news of the cruel murder of his fellow-Christians, and of the fell intention regarding himself.

I was awakened at about 3 A.M. one morning by a low knocking at the door—it is pitch dark in Buganda at that hour—and on getting up and striking a light,

I found Samweli and Semfuma of Kasengeje, together with Samweli's little step-brother, Ali Wali, and one or two others. I admitted them and lighted the lamp, and then they told me what they had come for. Samweli was naturally in great trouble, and asked what he should do. His companions had urged him to fly for his life; but he was on the king's service, and he could not feel it right to leave his trust, and so he came to consult me.

My decision was soon given. "The king has not the heart of a man, but of a wild beast," I said; "and you are not bound to submit yourself to one who is so vile a murderer. You are perfectly justified in forsaking the trust." Semfuma went over to Mackay's house and roused him up, and his verdict was the same as mine. Semfuma was an "elder" also, and he had urged Samweli to fly.

Samweli sat on the ground looking troubled and dissatisfied, and then asked for a pencil and paper, and bent over his paper and wrote. I am sorry now that I did not keep that bit of paper. However, I said, "You need not write; but tell me what you think." Then he looked up and said, "Munange Siyinza okuleka ebintu ebya kabaka," "My friend, I cannot leave the things of the kabaka." The others began to urge on him the folly of his intention, but I said, "No, he is right; he has spoken well; he must take the tribute." Then we prayed together, and we arranged that Samweli should try and get his men to start early, that he might deposit the loads of cowries at the enclosure of the chief appointed to receive them. This was in order that he might be released of his trust before the executioners were abroad in their search. He said sadly that he was afraid the "Baziba" carriers would not bestir themselves till long after daylight, and then he said good-bye. I wondered if I should ever see this young hero again.

A few days later, to my great delight, he appeared at nightfall, and told us how he had gone boldly to the enclosure of the chief and had deposited the loads, and had then walked out. I said, "You ran when you got outside." He said, "No; for I should have been noticed at once; I walked quite slowly till I got out of sight, and then I ran as quickly as I could, and so I escaped."

The Hon. Roden Noel has kindly allowed me to reproduce here a little poem which he has written on the above incident. It is called "Weak Things of the World," and is taken from his book entitled 'A Modern Faust.'

> "A Christian convert, a boy African,
> Knowing the bloody lord of his great clan
> Sought him to visit with a lingering death,
> Because he had embraced Christ, humbly saith
> To a revered white teacher urging flight,
> He may not bend his soul to feel it right;
> For, since he hath been commissioned by the king
> Ingathered tribute from the tribes to bring
> Home to the sovereign—coin of cowrie shells—
> Whatever cruel personal peril dwells
> Among those evil courts, how dare he thrust
> From him the fatal honour of his trust:

And so he braves the tyrant. Ah, young black,
Spurned as inferior, thou hast e'en put back
Poor human nature on the pedestal
Whence pale dishonour dragged it to base fall.
The lowest whom men trample as the clod
Is of the royal family of God;
The weakest woman sits enthroned above
The proud and wise by dignity of love;
Who liveth well alone hath found the key
To every dim, mind-baffling mystery."

CHAPTER XIX.

FAREWELL TO BUGANDA.

ON the 2nd of June, 1886, Dr. Junker arrived at the mission house. Mwanga had given him leave to take up his abode with his fellow-Bazungu (Europeans), and we were able to let him occupy the upstairs rooms of the larger mission house. He brought us interesting news of Emin Pasha, and discussed the best means of sending him temporary relief. Emin had written saying he thought of sending his people in "little flocks" *via* Uganda to the coast. Mackay, who is a good German scholar, wrote a letter in German to Emin, warning him of Mwanga's treachery, and strongly advising him to stay where he was. Dr. Junker told us of the ghastly sights he had witnessed on reaching Buganda. He had seen many mutilated corpses lying by the wayside, for there had been a kind of inquisition held, and the various chiefs were obliged to give up a certain number of people to be killed for being "readers." It did not matter much whether they actually were readers, so long as the tale of murdered persons was complete. The young Christian Admiral did what he thought rather a clever thing; he gave up an innocent young goat-herd to be killed as a Christian, though the poor child had never heard of such a thing as Christianity. The little chief was very penitent when I told him how wrong this was; and had he known that he was acting improperly, would, I feel sure, not have done so. He himself always confessed and admitted that he was a Christian, but he was not powerful enough to screen his dependents who were fellow-Christians without sacrificing one of them. The young admiral afterwards lost his own life in the same cause. This incident shows how very small is the value the Baganda people and Africans generally set upon human life. It is very pathetic the thought of that poor little, unknown, uncared-for goat-herd dying unwept, a slave in a strange land. Yet how strange that, whoever he is, he has been counted worthy to die in Christ's cause.

When Dr. Junker was with us, the French Bishop Lavinhac and Père Lourdel came and paid us a visit. Dr. Junker very unselfishly offered to go with us and protest in the name of humanity against the massacres, and to demand instant leave for the eight Europeans —five Frenchmen, Dr. Junker, Mackay, and myself— to leave the country. The Frenchmen did not think this advisable, and after all it was none of Dr. Junker's business, and Mackay and I did not feel it right to involve him in our troubles. Still, the intrepid traveller was willing to cast in his lot with us; but the Frenchmen settled the difficulty by declining to act with us in the matter, and as I said, referring to the former occasion, possibly wisely.

Dr. Junker in a few days got together a present for Mwanga of various articles, and he and Mackay went over to Munyonyo, where the king still was holding his court. The capital at Mengo, which had been burnt, was being rebuilt, and was now rapidly approaching completion. Before Dr. Junker and Mackay had reached the enclosure at Munyonyo, Mwanga sent Kibare, a great chief, to tell them to return; for the king was soon going back to Mengo, where he would receive his new guests with proper honours. After some days the king returned, and Dr. Junker went up with Mackay to pay his respects. The king received him in full baraza (levée), and at Mackay's request consented to allow Dr. Junker to leave the country in the *Eleanor* (or *Mirembe*), our mission boat.

Then came on the matter of Emin Pasha and his letters: the first asking for permission to come through Buganda with all his people; the second only asking that a small party might have leave to pass. There was a great deal of whispering among the king and chiefs, and the renegade Arab, Masudi, mentioned previously, had a good deal to say, and insolently remarked that all Bazungu (white men) were liars. Soon after, a powerful Mahometan chief, Ntanda by name, came to demand from Junker Turkish slippers for the king—the red slippers which Mwanga had on a former occasion asked me about. Dr. Junker had only some of Khartoum manufacture, which he produced, but which the chief kicked contemptuously away. Junker then retired to his quarters, leaving the insolent messenger sitting in the verandah outside.

Not long after Junker had left the country, the French Bishop Lavinhac and Père Jeraud, a very quiet, amiable man, who had not been very long in Buganda, also obtained permission to leave. They paid us a farewell visit. Père Jeraud came to a tragic end. He was a very clever mechanic, and when at the south of the Nyanza, built a boat. While in her one day with some of his lads, he saw a hippopotamus, and having a gun with him, he determined to try a shot. A coastman, Mungwana, who accompanied him, advised him not, since the gun which he had was useless against such an enormous antagonist; but he fired at the unwieldy brute, his shot took effect, and the great creature came at the boat open-mouthed and capsized her, and all who were on board were precipitated into the water. The survivors stated that the French père refused to make for the shore, crying out that his favourite pupil was lost, and that he would perish with him. Whether this is true, or whether the survivors thought that they were a little lax in their efforts to save the Muzungu, and so invented the story to account for his being drowned, I do not know. At any rate, the gentle père found his grave in the mighty lake.

At the beginning of July negotiations were going on between Junker and the Arabs, through Mackay, for the purchase of cloth to send to Emin. Several loads were satisfactorily purchased, and Mwanga promised permission for them to be sent. During this time many baptisms took place at night. Samweli came also several times from his hiding-place, and as an example of the intelligent way in which the Baganda people read the Bible, he asked about the many bodies of the saints which were said to have arisen in connection with the crucifixion. Also he wanted to know what I made of our Saviour's saying of S. John—"If I will that he tarry till I come," &c.

We now set to work packing some things for Emin Pasha and Captain Casati. It was a great pleasure to Mackay and me to be able to send them a few European articles, along with the cloth which Junker had purchased. The Tripoli Turk, Mahomet Biri, undertook the charge of the caravan, which a few weeks later left Buganda, and successfully accomplished the journey. This was the first effort made to relieve Emin Pasha. Mackay a second time sent him a small caravan. For this and his other services the Khedive of Egypt conferred upon him an Order of the Medij. For an account of the third and greatest effort to relieve Emin, by the important expedition which has been led by Stanley to Wadelai, we must await the return of the illustrious explorer himself, who will no doubt have a thrilling tale of adventure and discovery to unfold of this perhaps the most interesting undertaking of modern travel.

Dr. Junker left us on the 14th of July, 1886, taking with him four of our boys whom we were sending for safety to the mission station at the south of the lake. When Dr. Junker was well on his way, Mackay and I determined to ask for leave to take our departure ; and after one or two efforts we were at length admitted to the king's presence. I now come to my last interview with Mwanga. As I said before, Mackay and I had come to the resolution of asking definitely for permission to leave the country, in order that the chiefs might see that we were speaking the truth when we said that if the rulers wished us to go we were prepared to do so. They had now shown us unmistakably their feeling towards us by the murder of the people whom we taught, and so we determined on this important step.

On the 3rd of August we went to Mengo, and found the king in full "baraza," with all the great earls of the kingdom about him. The king knew what we had come for, and there was an air of general restraint pervading the assembly. Some preliminary business of the kingdom was transacted, and then, at a pause in the proceedings, Mackay went forward, and kneeling at the edge of the king's carpet, and in front of the king—we always sat or knelt, according to native custom, not stood when addressing the king—Mackay began to speak. He asked for canoes that he and I might leave the country. "Why do you want to leave?" asked Mwanga. "We have had nothing but trouble since we have been here," answered Mackay, and, going on, he waxed warmer, saying, "Our place is guarded, our friends interfered with;" and finally remarked, "Though

I am willing to help you, I am not your slave."
Mackay had always tried to do anything he could in a
friendly way for the king. The last thing which he had
made was a splendid rope out of native fibre. But, so
far from showing gratitude, latterly the king had become
more and more insolent in his demands.

When Mackay said, "I am not your slave," the king
became sarcastic, and the chief judge asked who
guarded our place.

Then the king broke in, "Oh, yes, you have to chop
my firewood, have you not? You have to cook for me.
You are my slave. What is it you wish?"

Mackay replied, "We desire nothing but canoes
that we may go." He then returned to his seat.
The king flatly refused, and then I got up and
knelt down at one side of the king's carpet and
addressed him. Immediately there was an exclama-
tion from the chiefs, "Go in front of the king and
'woza,' plead." I replied, "What is the offence? I
will not plead;" and I, too, returned to my seat.
Then the ordinary business proceeded; but the king
was preoccupied and distrait, and could not hide his
annoyance. Both Mackay and I were surprised at the
change which seemed to have come over the chiefs.
On leaving the presence of the king they showed the
greatest civility to us. One of them carried our camp
stools for us, and the haughty chancellor asked
Mackay to dinner. I went home with Kulugi, and
he was very civil, and said we ought not to mind what

the king said. And when Mackay came back from his
dining out he told me how he had met some of the
great earls and how they apologised for Mwanga's
petulance. Though we had been refused permission
to leave the country, we began to pack up, starting
with the books. We told every one who came near us
that we were going.

A few days later the Arab Said bin Saif's dhow
arrived from Magu, bringing letters, one from the
Consul-General at Zanzibar to Mwanga, and another
from Seyd Burgash, the Sultan of Zanzibar, no doubt
written at the instance of our Consul, who was most
desirous of helping us; but there was no fulcrum on
which to work his lever. British prestige was at a
discount, for the Baganda imagined that Englishmen
might be killed with impunity in Africa. As an
abstract principle, I much question if it is to the
advantage of any great nation to allow its subjects to
be killed without making any inquiry about their
death, even if they be only missionaries. It will be
seen that the Government of our country had encouraged missionary enterprise in Africa, and in the
eyes of the natives, at any rate, had identified itself
with the missionaries by giving them letters of introduction to African chiefs. I know I shall find few
supporters among those interested in missions when I
say that I think it is a mistake, from a political point
of view, for any government to allow its subjects to
penetrate into the interior unless it is prepared to

afford them protection. In case it is not, then, for the sake of its own prestige, it ought to forbid their going.

Under the circumstances no consular letters could be of much value or help to us. We ourselves were far more of a power to be reckoned with than a far-off British Consul, who was writing almost in the dark, since we had much influence with the rising generation, and our following comprised many chiefs, and Christianity was growing every day in power and importance. The rulers found it like a fire; beaten down in one quarter, it sprang up in another with even greater violence.

Mackay and Lourdel read the letters to the king in Kiswahili; and an Arab trader, Said bin Jimè, read the Arabic copy.

The king and chiefs tried to assume an air of indifference, but were evidently listening with interest to the contents of the missive—I need not speak of the letter, for it simply contained polite nothings.

Mackay and I felt that, if we could not both of us get permission to go away, it was necessary that one of us should endeavour to return to England to lay the whole state of the mission before the Committee of the Church Missionary Society at home, and to evoke the sympathy of Christians in England for their suffering and persecuted co-religionists in Africa. It was obviously only right that Mackay should have a change to Europe after his long years in Africa, and so we agreed that he should ask for permission to leave, and tell the king that I would remain.

Mackay started in the morning, taking a present, and had an interview with Mwanga, and told him that he intended to go. "I will never consent to that," said Mwanga, and promised him large gifts of "ensimbè," cowrie shells, and also promised him four milch cows, if he would remain. Afterwards he called him privately, and, when none of the great lords were present, said, twice over, "You shall remain with me, and teach people religion."

When Mackay saw that Mwanga would not consent to his going, he said, "Will you let Bwana Ashe go?" and, after some parley, the king finally consented to this.

Then came a time of sorrowful farewells. Our house was crowded every evening by faithful friends who came to bid me good-bye. But the saddest leave-taking of all was with Mackay, in whose company I had passed through so many trials and troubles, and who had always proved himself my true, sympathetic, and steadfast friend.

The mission boat had not yet returned from her voyage to the south of the Lake, whither she had gone with Dr. Junker and his party, and so I was obliged to take a passage in the dhow which had come to Buganda a week or two before with the letters, and which was now returning to the further end of the lake. I had a fellow-passenger in an Arab trader

R

whose soubriquet was Khambi Embaya (the bad camp).

He and I parted company a few days later, when I had the good fortune to encounter the little *Eleanor* on her way back to Buganda with letters. I forwarded Mackay's mail by land, and got my party on board the *Eleanor*, and made a quick and prosperous voyage to our port near Musalala.

Khambi Embaya, like so many of my companions, met with a violent death. While I travelled south through Unyamwezi territory, he took the Usukuma road, and he and all his people were killed by the Wasukuma natives a month or two later. The quarrel arose, I believe, because the Arab's slaves wished to draw water for themselves before the natives had watered their own cattle. Angry words arose, blows were struck, the natives collected in force, and in vain the Arab endeavoured to restrain his followers. In the end he and his whole party were annihilated. Some say the quarrel arose because the Arab's people had thrown the corpse of a dead porter into the well which the Wasukuma were using. However it happened, the fact remains that poor Khambi Embaya was killed. It is a sorrowful reflection that the fine qualities which many of these Arabs possess should be prostituted to the shameful and degraded purpose to which they are misapplied in slave-dealing.

My little party consisted of the Wangwana (coast-men), one of whom had a wife whom he had married in Buganda. This woman was a native Muganda, and it seems that she ought not legally to have been removed from the country. At any rate, her friends pursued me for days in order to try and recover her. I knew nothing of this at the time, but supposed that Juma—for that was her husband's name—had acquired her lawfully. Mackay wrote to me afterwards, and told me of the pursuit. The rest of my party was made up of four boys, whom I was taking with the intention of leaving with Gordon at the south of the Nyanza.

And so, as I reclined on the little after-deck of the *Eleanor*, and as the boat glided swiftly onwards, I saw perhaps for the last time the deep rich colouring of the gorgeous panorama which lay stretched before me, while the coast line of Buganda slowly became more dim and undefined in the distance. How peaceful and yet how glorious that living picture appeared in the gold and purple of the setting sun; but how could there have failed to be a sense of utter sadness in my heart, as I thought of the scenes which had been enacted in that unhappy land of misery and mystery? How could I fail to call up the familiar faces of the dead—kindly dark faces of faithful friends; and above all the never-to-be-forgotten, sorrowful, appealing eyes of little Joseph Lugalama.

CHAPTER XX.

A FORTNIGHT'S journey in the *Eleanor* brought me to Bukumbi, the French Mission at the south of the lake, where I landed for a few hours, and was hospitably entertained at dinner by the kindly priests.

Their place was very nice, a regular seminary of young Africans. I could only give a passing glance at their arrangements, which, however, seemed excellent.

It will be interesting to learn hereafter if any of these boys are ordained, and how they bear the yoke of celibacy which the Church of Rome imposes with her orders.

At Bukumbi there was no display of European luxury. In fact, the only costly thing which they seemed to possess was the jewelled cross of their courteous Bishop. Unable as I am to reverence the system which they support, or many of the doctrines which they believe, I can at least reverence the simple devotion of their lives.

On leaving, the Bishop put into my hand a good loaf of bread—a great luxury.

A few more hours and the *Eleanor* was anchored at Muleshi's, the port for Musalala, and at about two o'clock next day I arrived at the Mission, and was warmly welcomed by my old companions, Gordon and Wise, and also not less warmly by the boys whom Mackay and I had sent here for safety. I remained at Musalala two whole days, and then started on my long 800-mile tramp to the coast.

Fourteen days' journey brought me to Uyui, our Mission station, which was at that time occupied by a young Cambridge man, who was a volunteer missionary working at his own charges. He received me kindly, and I spent some days in his house. The day that I arrived news reached us that the Arabs of Unyanyembe intended to waylay and murder a young German trader named Giesiker, and six days later we heard that the attempt on Giesiker's life had been made. The quarrel with Giesiker was not so much that he was a German, but that he was buying ivory and competing with the Arabs in their trade. Hooper, my host, at once sent messengers to Unyanyembe to offer any assistance in his power. Dr. Junker was there at the time, and also the French missionaries, so that we did not think it necessary to go ourselves. The messengers returned, bringing a letter from Brooks, a missionary of the London Missionary Society, who had been one of our companions on the voyage out from England, and who happened at this time to be at Unyanyembe. His letter ran as follows :—

"Tabora,* Sept. 30, 1886.

"DEAR MR. HOOPER,—Your mail-men arrived this morning, and it falls to me to answer your letter and

* Same as Unyanyembe.

kind offer to Mr. Giesiker. I arrived here on Monday morning, and heard of the serious affair of Giesiker from the Arabs. I went at once to his camp, and found that he had been moved to the French Mission, where I saw him. Poor fellow! he is severely wounded. It appears that Seyid bin Juma (Liwli or Governor of Unyan-yembe) had been told that Giesiker would be killed as soon as he left Tabora, and on Sunday evening, about ten o'clock, a man crept into his tent and attempted to take away the light, when all at once a volley of at least three guns was fired, killing the man who was attempting to take the light and who was probably one of the gang; another, a Mungwana, was also shot through both thighs. Poor Giesiker was shot through the left arm a little below the shoulder. Another ball, which is still in the thigh, passed between the knee and hip-joint, also left. But the feet are worst of all: the left is shot away from the ankle-joint, right under the sole, you could hardly cover it with one hand; the right is also as bad, and one ball has passed through the foot. Poor fellow, I fear very much for his life. He has a little fever now and again, is also light-headed; still, he is a strong fellow, and may possibly pull through; but it will take from eight to twelve months. I have started his caravan off with Tipotip, thinking, with others, that was the best thing to be done. It will save him much anxiety, and perhaps danger. The French missionaries are dressing him; and, should they run out of medicine, they will come to you or us. Dr. Junker is well, and left Ituro this morning with

Tipotip. Give my kind regards to Mr. Ashe, and Stokes when he comes, and not forgetting yourself,

"I remain, yours sincerely,

"A. BROOKS."

Brooks himself was murdered three years later, near Zanzibar.

I found difficulty in collecting porters, so I determined to travel as lightly as possible, and I obtained four faithful Zanzibaris, who undertook to make the journey from Uyui to Zanzibar. I had four small bundles, consisting of papers and books, blankets, clothing, food, besides a kettle, a pot, and a gunpowder flask for a water-bottle. My arms consisted of a light fowling-piece (muzzle-loading), a small carbine (also muzzle-loading), and a six-chambered revolver. Also I had a broken Bahuma spear, which had belonged to Lugalama, and which I usually carried. The men carried the other weapons. I used to have the same food as my porters, except that I had some biscuits and pots of jam which Hooper had given me. He despised such things; but I could not swallow " ugali "* without something of the kind to make it go down. In one of our camps † we had a narrow escape from fire. We were inside a " boma " (fence) made of thorn bushes, and were sleeping in straw huts. The men had lighted a big fire outside the opening of their hut. I did not think it very safe, but while I was

---

* Coarse native porridge.

† This was an old camp containing vast numbers of small straw huts which had been made by the porters of some other larger caravan.

reflecting about it I dozed off.   I had been ill at Uyui, and had not yet recovered.   I was suddenly awakened fully by seeing a blaze of fire all about me.   Instantly I jumped up and seized one or two things, and made for the opening in the boma.   It was closed with a thorny bush, which I could not remove.   Mwalimu one of my men, came and pulled it away, and I got out; but my few belongings were still in the boma. The men had just time to snatch up some of them and run.   I had run out without my boots, and I felt terribly afraid that I should lose them.   However, the men had thoughtfully rescued them.   By this time the whole great camp was on fire, and we found ourselves again within a circle of advancing flame.   Again there was a stampede, and we got the things some little distance from the burning huts.   When I counted my losses, I found that most of my books and papers had been burnt, and also a dressed antelope skin, which I had obtained from the brave young martyr, Mukassa or Musa.   Lugalama's spear was saved.   All the food of my men had been burnt; and though we were still far in the Uyui wilderness, they said, "Do not be troubled, we are black men, and can go without food for a day or two without much inconvenience."   Though their own rice was burnt, they had saved my biscuit, so when we halted I gave them some biscuits and coffee, and the next evening we reached Itura, on the far side of the "terrible garden," the Mugunda Mukali.   I was very unwell here, and could hardly crawl through the great wilderness.   However, after two or three days' journey through the scrubby forest, we came on an Arab caravan going to Unyanyembe. The Arabs visited me, and I told them I wanted to buy a donkey which they had with them. The owner of the donkey had only lately come from Muscat, and did not know whether a bill from me was worth having. However, his friend assured him that I was an Englishman and that it would be all right. So in an African wilderness, 500 miles from Zanzibar, this stranger Arab handed over to me a fine Muscat donkey with saddle and trappings in exchange for a dirty piece of paper, with an order written in English for 110 dollars. It was a heavy price, but I seldom, I think, have made a better bargain than the splendid little animal, which proved a godsend to me on my journey. I have mentioned this incident, as I think it shows that Englishmen had gained credit from the Arabs for being, at any rate, honourable in their dealings. I had no tent, and none of the usual paraphernalia of travellers on this journey; but I suffered very little from fever, and though I used to encamp without any "boma," in the wildest spots, I never was troubled by any prowling wild beasts. We always kept fires burning during the night.

In due course I reached Mpwapwa, where my friends, the Coles, most kindly received me, and it was here I first saw Dr. Pruen, whom I was to meet again on my second return journey from the Nyanza, and in company with him and his courageous wife to pass through the insurgents to Zanzibar.

After leaving these kind friends I was once more on

my way, passing again the glorious Mamboya mountains, where I was hospitably entertained by an old
friend, Roscoe, at that time in charge of the mission
station. Six days' march from here brought me to
Mkange, where I saw again the ocean. One in my
case can enter into the feelings of the retreating
ten thousand when they once more beheld the sea,
which, in their case at least, was aptly called Euxine,
and broke out with the glad cry of "Thalatta!
Thalatta!" (The sea! The sea!) I reached Sadaani
on a Sunday, and proceeded at once to buy oranges
and a mango without the faintest pang of conscience,
for I did not recollect the fact that it was Sunday
till after I had finished my meal. Whether or not
I should have abstained from the purchase had I
known the day, it is needless to enquire. In the New
Year of 1887 I saw the white cliffs of Dover once more,
and on landing in London I went straight to the rooms
of an old college friend, Rev. Robert Walker, of whose
subsequent experiences I shall have something to tell
in another chapter.

It may be of interest to state the first thing which
struck me as strange in civilized England after returning
from the heart of Africa was to find moral sentiments
displayed in the omnibuses, which, however, a little
study showed me were only advertisements of soap.
When my friend received me I had no idea that in a
little more than six months I should be setting out
with him on a second journey to the Dark Continent.
But so it was to be.

CHAPTER XXI.

SECOND JOURNEY TO THE NYANZA.

IT is needless to trouble the patient reader with another account of a journey to the Nyanza. Walker and I had a small and compact caravan of about eighty men. We had also riding donkeys, which greatly lightened the weariness of the march. The same, to me, familiar scenes were passed, but the journey was free from many of the hardships of the first undertaking. The blue hills of Mamboya were reached. The kindly hospitality of the Coles at Kisokwe was once more enjoyed; the bitter water wilderness was traversed; the Wagogo warriors again appeared in due order, and were again left far behind as we still held on our way through the "terrible garden." But we did not go by way of Uyui, where the chief had become hostile, but passing out of the Muganda Mukali we struck further east to Ikungu, and from there through another long wilderness, with low hills on our left and wide bare illimitable grassy plains on our right, stretching away into the Watatura country till we came out of this wilderness near our friend Mutinginya. Passing Tambalali and Sungwezi and Nyawa, we reached the chief's village at Usongo. At one of the villages we received a gift of a fine young ram. One of our men tied a cord to him and tried to lead him, but he refused to budge; so the man dragged him by main force, resisting at every step. The happy thought struck me of harnessing the donkey to him, which we did, and so willy-nilly he had to go; however, he lay down and suffered himself to be dragged. This was too cruel a proceeding, so we had to stop and butcher him; there was no little intercessor here, so he lost his life. It is useful to know that sheep will not travel, though goats are easily led. Just before we entered the last wilderness before Usongo, Walker and I suddenly saw an apparition, of the leanest boy we had ever beheld, walking with our men. On making inquiries who or what the poor skeleton was, we found that he was a slave who had been raided by the Arabs from Lubemba; they had treated him cruelly, having hacked off one or two of his fingers and burned him frightfully for some small offence. They had left him to die of small-pox at Itura. However, Songoro, for that was his name, managed to pull through, and took refuge with us. No one came to claim him, so we let him come on with us. He had plenty to eat, and held the desirable post of cook's assistant. I afterwards brought him to Zanzibar with me; but by that time he was the fattest of the party. The consul gave me a paper of freedom for him, so that his former cruel owner could not claim him again.

We now took a more easterly route than the one

which I had followed on the former journey, and passed through the naked Wasukuma, who were exceedingly turbulent and troublesome, especially about letting us draw water. These were the people who had killed my former Arab travelling companion, Kambi Embaya, owing to a quarrel about water.

Bishop Parker, and Blackburn, whom I mentioned as one of the members of the former expedition, had preceded us to the Nyanza, and we all met at the south of the lake at Busambiro, where Mackay had arrived some months before from Buganda with a large quantity of valuable property. A strong letter which Consul Holmwood had written from Zanzibar to Mwanga seems to have really frightened the foolish tyrant, who had allowed Mackay to leave. Thus the great controversy between Mwanga and Mackay was settled by Mwanga's consenting to Mackay's departure. The latter, however, had no idea when he left of abandoning the mission, so when he reached Musalala, where Gordon and Wise still were stationed, he represented the matter to them, and Gordon offered to go alone and place himself in the power of the young autocrat. Mackay had previously begged of the king to receive another missionary in his stead, and Mwanga had accordingly sent a "mubaka," messenger, to invite Gordon and to bring him in safety to the capital. The mission at Musalala, like that at Uyui, had been abandoned owing to the rapacity of the Wanyamwezi chiefs, who had become more insolent and importunate in their demands for cloth and other presents, and was now in the territory of Roma at Mutereza, near the village of the sub-chief Makolo, whose people were a sort of mixture of Bazinja and Wanyamwezi. We were therefore in territory which was completely under the power of Mwanga, whose warriors some few years before had raided Roma and sent him flying for his life, so that Roma now looked on Mwanga as the greatest monarch on earth. We reached the Nyanza in a time of pouring rain, and there were no houses and no proper place of shelter; although Mackay had been indefatigable, and had begun to build a long low substantial house, something like a native " tembe " only larger, but, like the tembe, it had a mud roof. At Mutereza, under Bishop Parker as president, six of us held a missionary conference, and we wrote a letter to King Mwanga in the new Bishop's name, in which, though we referred to the death of Hannington, we yet explained that we were people of peace, and that we only wished to enter his country and live there in a friendly way. This letter was duly despatched and presented by Gordon; it gave no little offence, and the king covered it with ashes, a sign of a war challenge. However, Kolugi, whom I have before mentioned, scattered them on the ground, as he saw that Gordon did not understand the action, and advised him to take no notice of the matter. In a month or two the boat returned to the south of the lake with a messenger, who was sent, not to the Bishop, but to Mackay. The messenger was instructed to return bringing on the new " Muzungu " (white man) who had arrived at Musalala with me, namely Walker, but Mwanga sent no message to me of any kind. At the same time Gordon wrote strongly urging that some one else should be sent to join him. After long consideration we decided to accede to Mwanga's request for the new "Muzungu," and so Walker, like Gordon, quite understanding the kind of host by whom he was to be entertained, was perfectly willing to proceed to Buganda. But before he left he was to have his first experience of the dark side of African life. My old companion in travel, Blackburn, had made a journey, with the view of helping Hooper, (formerly at Uyui) to open a new mission station at Nassa on Speke Gulf. Both of them suffered much from fever, and Blackburn therefore returned to Mutereza. He did not seem well, but we did not think that anything very serious was the matter. Two days later he took to his bed. At this time we were all living in huts, except the Bishop, who preferred his tent. Blackburn rapidly grew worse, and the rest of us watched by him in turns night and day, while his servant Zaburi tended him most faithfully; the end came suddenly, and was a great shock to us, since he seemed decidedly better a day or two before he died. Late on the tenth day after he took to his bed the Bishop called me, and I just reached his side in time to see him breathe his last. One of the porters in our caravan had died shortly before, and the chiefs and people said that it was "mwiko" or forbidden to bury him, since he had died

of dysentery, so we were obliged to wrap the corpse up
and have it carried away and thrown into the swamp.
We feared they might make some similar objection to
to our burying our missionary friend, and so we called
our men and had the grave dug at once. It was a time
of great sorrow to us, and deeply we felt for Blackburn's
young wife whom he had left, with a noble devotion to
duty, although he himself was in no fit condition to return
to his work. She had hoped to join him at some station
near the coast, and indeed had all her preparations
made for the journey when the sorrowful tidings of
her husband's death reached her.

Whatever may be said against missionaries and their
lack of zeal or their want of faithfulness to duty, there are
not a few unknown graves in Eastern Africa which are a
proof that, though some may have been unworthy, there
are many of all denominations who, like Blackburn, have
put duty before even life, and have bravely died at
their posts.

Our party was now reduced to four, and a deep sense
of sadness had come over us. It was arranged that the
Bishop should go and join Hooper and his companion
Deekes who had meantime arrived, at Nassa, and that
Walker should, according to the arrangement previously
made, proceed to Buganda. A few months before this
I had decided to return to Zanzibar, and had signified
this intention to the Bishop; but he and my other
companions were anxious that I should wait some
time longer, and I had acceded to their request. The

last few days had been spent in making preparations for the start of our friends, and the Sunday before Easter we had our last communion together. The Bishop seemed in very good spirits and fairly well, but he had suffered much from fever, and the attacks seemed to be more frequent. On Sunday night, 25th of March, he left us as usual. However, towards morning he was seized with what appeared to be a violent attack of ague. Mackay got a hot-water bottle and put it to his feet, and we wrapped him up well in blankets; he seemed better, and we called his boy who remained with him. We thought that it was only an ordinary fever. Next morning, however, the Bishop got up and and wandered out, and Walker met him and saw that he looked like a man walking in his sleep; he helped him back to bed, and we watched by him. In the afternoon he became terribly delirious, and Walker, who was alone with him, had to call for more help, and so two of us stayed by his side. Towards evening he grew calmer and seemed to have sunk into a troubled sleep. We arranged to remain with him by turns during the night. So Walker and I went to bed early, leaving Mackay to take the first watch. I had not been gone long when I heard some one calling me—it was one of the Bishop's black boys. As I hurriedly threw on my clothes the thought of the last summons I had received to the bedside of a sick companion stole across my mind, and with much misgiving I hastened to the bishop's room. He was now in the house which

Mackay had nearly finished, and I was shocked to see that death was written unmistakeably on his face.

Mackay had just hurried out to get some chartreuse, in hope of staving off the collapse. The Bishop was faintly breathing when I reached him, but in another moment all was over.

The bitter weeping of the faithful boy who had been watching by his master, showed me that he too had realised the sad truth. Mackay now returned and saw that another of our little band had passed away, and Walker came in at the same time, so with silent sorrow and awe we three stood and looked at the calm still face and tried to understand that the head of the mission had been taken from us. It was a pouring wet night, but it was necessary to have the grave made at once. So the Bishop's Christian porters, who had accompanied him from Freretown, were summoned to prepare their master's resting-place beside that of Blackburn. There was no time to make a coffin, but reverently we wrapped the dead in some of the beautiful bark cloths which Mackay had obtained from Buganda, and just as the first faint streak of dawn appeared in the eastern sky, we laid him in the grave. Mackay read part of the burial service in Swahili, that the Bishop's porters might understand; and as we turned sadly away, the morning song of the birds might well have seemed to be a voice from Heaven, echoing the glorious words which had been sounding in our ears :—" Blessed are the dead which die in the Lord;

even so saith the Spirit; for they rest from their labours."

A few days later and we had said farewell to Walker who left on the 1st of April in the mission-boat for Buganda. Of his grand reception there by King Mwanga I need say little, except that it somewhat resembled my own, which I have already described, only it was still more imposing, and Mwanga even rose up to meet his guest—a mark of high honour. Walker, during his brief sojurn in the country, on the whole seems to have formed a fairly favourable opinion of this young king; but Mwanga's misgovernment, his raids upon his own people, his licentious behaviour and his tyranny, became so intolerable to the Baganda that they determined to depose him.

Mwanga's monthly progresses into the provinces, his seizing the wives and daughters and cattle of his subjects, left him without a single supporter among the mass of his people; and the clever young chiefs, who were mostly reformers or readers of the Moslem and Christian faiths, became for once united and easily deposed him. And it seems that the old saying, " Whom the gods wish to destroy they first make mad," was true in Mwanga's case, for he relinquished the wise policy of attempting to play off one party against another, and to his ruin actually threw them into one another's arms. He would not admit as a factor in his policy the belief of the reformers in God, which clashed with his belief in himself. The haughty Moslems called the royal cows killed by the uncircumcised, defiled, and spurned the unholy flesh, while the Christians quietly kept away from work on Sundays. Who is this God who must be honoured before kings ? So Mwanga decreed that God must go and the worshippers of God must be swept for ever from his path. The summons went forth for " all Buganda " to come and enlarge the royal pond—Nyanza (sea) it was called out of flattery, because it was the king's ; but Mwanga will make it a Nyanza indeed. So all the chiefs are called to the work. The young king arms his favourites with Snider rifles, and some have even Winchester repeaters. A body-guard truly, but more ornamental than useful. He comes down to see the work with his boys. One is insolently set over the chiefs. Mwanga will have no one armed but his own immediate followers, and commands the workers to come unarmed. But they come armed, nominally for the protection of the king, really to intimidate him ; and so he must get rid of them. Pokino and the chancellor, who hated and despised the foreign religions, with other old chiefs, wished to return to the palmy days of the cruel Suna. The country was going to the dogs. Slaves and the young were beginning to have opinions, and dangerous doctrines of the most radical description were gradually undermining the old ideas, and every day gaining ground. Desperate diseases require desperate remedies. Mutesa had crushed Islam out and drenched it out in blood. True it had grown up again, but this time it shall not. Mukasa, the mighty god of the Nyanza, shall give his help, and shall be honoured by such a holocaust of victims in the slain believers in Allah and Katonda as has never before been heard of in the annals of Buganda.

The bloody Mujasi, head of "the Bajasi" body-guard, a bitter Moslem, is not consulted. Could he not have been used as the tool to carry out the slaughter of the Christian "Basalo Salo" body-guard, and then be broken and cast away? Sanity would answer yes, but madness, shrieking no, will sweep to a speedier revenge. All shall perish together, all shall be packed into canoes, landed on a distant island in the lake, and left to a slow and miserable death.

The day comes; the two great body-guards of Christians and Moslems are marched down to the Nyanza under their chiefs, while his personal guard of useless and insolent boys accompanies the king. The Moslems and Christians are ordered on board. Mujasi is ill and cannot go. The Christians refuse to embark unless with the king. Mwanga, with a heart full of apprehension and bitterness, baffled and angry, hastens back to his capital, where the old fox Pokino and the chancellor are waiting to hear of the success of the scheme. The only news is the ugly word flung out, " bajemye,"—they have rebelled.

To-morrow the rebels will arrive. To-day is "Sabiti," Sunday. But there will be work to-morrow—and the

morrow comes. Mujasi the murderer, before he meets
his own bloody death, must first be the instrument
used to hurl Mwanga from his throne. He comes one
way with his following, and the Christian guards
another. The Crescent and the Cross close in on
heathendom; heathendom, as usual, fights but feebly,
and flies. Mwanga, with his boy bodyguard and
a number of women, is soon hurrying away from
the scene of his former glories, to seek a refuge on
the lake. He is followed, but scornfully allowed to
go his way. Mujasi has brought Kiwewa, a quiet
man, Mutesa's eldest son. And Kiwewa duly "eats
Buganda." Thus the bloodless revolution is accomplished.

European missionaries and Moslem missionaries, i.e.
Arab slave traders, are called into the royal presence—
freedom of trade and toleration of all religions is granted.
Kagwa Apolo, formerly gashed and beaten by Mwanga,
was elevated to the "bakungu" or peerage, and became
Mukwenda, Earl of Singo, while Nyonyi Entono (the
small bird), who had been mutilated by Mwanga, was
given the highest post in the kingdom, and was now
Katikiro or Lord High Chancellor of Buganda. Samweli,
the faithful bringer-in of tribute, was made head storekeeper. Zakariya Kizito, whose letter to me I give in
the appendix, also received a high office; while Mujasi
was made Kangao, Earl of Bulemezi. Mwanga meanwhile had reached the lake, and had obtained from the
old chief Jumba five canoes, into which he crowded his

people; but I subjoin Mackay's graphic account of the young king's flight:—

> " *Usambiro, Kwa Makolo,*
> " *Oct. 23rd, 1888.*

! "Mwanga is at present at Magu, having reached that place with only one canoe and six women, and between thirty and forty boys.

"When I heard the news, I at once sent two of my most trustworthy servants to Magu, directing them to try and fetch the poor fugitive king away by night, as I feared the Arabs would betray him. I know it is a great risk to have anything to do in the way of trying to save him from being taken back a prisoner to Buganda, where he will surely be put to death, as another king is on the throne. Murderer and persecutor as he has been, I yet have not the faintest doubt but that it becomes us to do everything in our power to return him good for evil. My men reached him, and found him eager to jump at my offer, but unable to come away from the Arabs' clutches, fearing they would send after him and arrest him. He sent back here, with my men, two of his lads, begging me to go to Magu myself and endeavour to get him out of there, suggesting that one of the brethren at Nassa should come here to take my place while I conducted him (Mwanga) to the coast.

"Anticipating such a desire on his part, I had previously sent to Nassa, asking Deekes to come over here for a month. Possibly he may come, but can scarcely be here for several days yet. It will be no easy matter, but I am willing to take the poor creature as far as Usongo, where I can give him in charge of Stokes.

"From the two boys sent here by Mwanga, I have learnt the whole story of the rebellion in Buganda, and Mwanga's perilous flight to Magu.

"It appears that the king was aware for some time that his subjects meant to rebel. He learned this plainly on a trip he took recently to the border of Bunyoro, when some of his chiefs refused to obey orders. On returning to the capital he went on a boating excursion to Ntebe (at the mouth of Murchison Bay). His body-guard refused to accompany him back in the canoes, so he returned to his capital (Mengo) with only his pages. Next day he ordered the drums to beat for a public audience, but no one appeared. For a couple of days his enclosures were deserted, and after that, he heard that the Katikiro and chiefs had elected his younger brother (named Kayondo) king. By-and-by troops appeared at Mwanga's gates, so he gathered all his thousand women, and with the little boys about him (some two score or more) whom he armed with Snider rifles, which he had just purchased from Stokes's agent, made a dash by a back way to Munyonyo, on the creek. Only a few canoes were there. These he filled with as many of the women and boys as he could, and set off. Soon, however, all the canoes, except the one the king was in, deserted, and Mwanga had to coast all the way to Magu with only one canoe, paddled by his boys, he himself helping. He managed to get one fisherman from Sesse to steer. This man had once been as far as Kageye. Had Mwanga not got this man's aid, he never could have fetched this side of the lake. He was recognised at one or two places, where he had to put ashore for food, and had to fight his way to get afloat again. The only person of position who accompanied him was Kawuta, nominally head-cook, but a powerful chief. He, too, deserted after reaching Magu, but had to return there, as the canoe in which he tried to go back to Buganda was nearly swamped. Mwanga then gave Kawuta permission to go back with a few of the boys, in a small vessel belonging to a coast trader. By Kawuta he sent a letter to the Katikiro (written, of course, by the Arabs), begging to be sent for to Buganda. This he had done just before he got my message, otherwise he says he would not have requested the Arabs to send a letter. At present he has six women and thirty more boys with him. At first the Arabs treated him hospitably, but now are fleecing him of most of his Snider rifles for clothing and food. He is already heartily sick of his position in their hands, and wishes to get to the coast. Hence his sending to me an imploring message, begging me to come in person to Magu and take him anywhere I like, or slay him if I will! He will go with me to Europe if I will take him, for he has heard that the Emperor of the French found an asylum in England after being vanquished by Germany.

"I only hope that, like Nebuchadnezzar, he will get understanding to 'know that the Most High ruleth in the kingdom of men, and giveth it to whomsoever He will.' May his present affliction bring him to his knees, and teach him to break off his sins by righteousness! . . . ."

I may here take leave of Mwanga, where he appears at his best, helping in the canoe and fighting his way back to his boats like a man, and winning his way to Magu.

To return now to Buganda. The revolution was effected without bloodshed, and Mwanga's frightful tyranny passed away like an unsubstantial dream. And a time of marvellous peace dawned on the unhappy kingdom; but it was only like a burst of sunlight in a stormy sky, and soon new troubles arose. The Christians had obtained the lion's share of the power and influence because they were the more powerful party, while the new Kangao Mujasi and his following viewed with ill-concealed envy the good fortune of their opponents. This did not escape the notice of the Arab slave traders, who formed a plot with Mujasi to murder the Christian chiefs as they came from the king's reception. The plot proved a complete success. Mujasi, aided by the Arabs, opened a murderous volley on the Christian chiefs, as they streamed out from the king's presence. Young Gabunga, the admiral, my faithful friend, was shot dead; others also fell, a scene of wild confusion ensued, the Christians had not time to gather in force and were driven away. They left the capital in a compact body, and a new distribution of chieftainships took place. Mujasi now became Mukwenda, Earl of Singo. Bugalla, whose story I have told on p. 129, became Kymbugwe, or keeper of the palace. The Cross had now yielded for a time before the Crescent, and the triumphant Moslems determined to drive the missionaries, both English and French, out of the country. Walker, Gordon, and Monseigneur Lavinhàc, Pères Lourdel and Denoit, and a lay brother—six Europeans in all—were summoned into the presence of the chiefs. The priests had received some warning of what they might expect, and had come provided with a few necessaries, such as food and blankets carried by some boys. Walker and Gordon, however, went just as they were. On reaching Bugala's enclosure they were seized and thrust into a dirty hut, strongly guarded, where they were kept seven days. The mission-houses were meanwhile sacked, and everything they contained was either stolen or destroyed. On the eighth day the prisoners were marched down to the lake and allowed to go on board the mission-boat with a number of their boys. The Frenchmen were allowed to take some loads of cowrie shells and about twenty persons, mostly boys, with them. They generously shared all their things with their English brothers in adversity. And so this strange party found a fitting refuge together in the "Eleanor" or Mirembe, which was her native name, the word "mirembe." meaning peace. Walker was robbed of his coat and hat, and even his trousers, before being allowed to start on the long and perilous voyage. One of the kindly Frenchmen, however, gave him a pair of corduroy trousers and a blanket, and with one of their party thus arrayed, they pushed off into the lake with light hearts and a sense of the joy of freedom after their wearisome imprisonment. But their adventures were not yet over. I cannot forbear giving Walker's account of the circumstances of their shipwreck later on. He says:—

"After rowing for some hours, and being well out of sight of the starting-place, we determined to go to some island and cook food, and arrange the boat better. We landed, made fires, cooked rice and wheat. A heavy shower came on, and most of us were rather damp. It was a nice island with hippopotamuses playing about in the water near shore. At sunset we went to the boat and began to row; we had not gone far when a cry was raised of "kiboko" (hippo). We had gone on to the top of one of them. A rush of water showed us that we had a hole in the bottom of the boat. Gordon told the men to bail the water out. I repeated the remark. The bishop (Lavinhàc) came to me and said something about dying. I was getting over the rail at the side of the boat, so as to be more free in case of its sinking. I got off the boat and sat in the water, and the boat turned over away from the place where I was swimming. I made for the shore, about 150 yards off. As I looked back I saw the captain, many of the sailors, Gordon, and two of the Frenchmen, following me. All the rest were struggling in the water. I saw the boat was still floating on its side (not quite wrong way up), and that many had scrambled on to it. I gained the shore, and was able to give a hand over the rough stones to the much exhausted Père Lourdel, who had no boots on. In course of time Gordon and the bishop came ashore and all the sailors. One Zanzibar man who was unable to swim, the other two Frenchmen and a crowd of boys and girls were drifting nearer to the shore on the inverted boat. Every moment I expected the boat would disappear. A drum came ashore, which I beat vigorously. A canoe appeared at a distance, but would not come near. The captain and other sailors then swam to the wreck and brought off some of the smaller children. Another canoe appeared and came to where I stood beating the drum, the man took the sticks from me and gave his peculiar call for help; soon another canoe came on the scene, and one by one the canoes brought the people ashore. Five of the Frenchmen's men were missing. It was sad to think that five of our companions in trouble were lost."

They managed at length, with the generous help of some natives, to get the boat ashore, and then came the question of repairing her. He goes on :—

"The fourth of the Frenchmen is a sort of cook or carpenter. He looked at the boat and said it could be mended, but when he found there were no tools he gave up the job. I therefore undertook to patch the boat with the spokeshave. I chopped a piece of board in two, which I got out of the bottom of the boat; one piece I fixed, with the captain's help, inside the boat over the larger hole, and fastened the ends down with wedges driven under the ribs. Then we got some rope and pulled it to pieces. Most fortunately the Frenchmen had a pail of dripping; this we worked up into the tow and drove it in all round and under our board. Then we filled up the hole with large pads of this tow and dripping from the outside, and nailed and screwed pieces of board over them. The leeches in the water bit my legs. At about midday of the third day at the island, the boat was pronounced to be ready for sea. I confess I felt bad as we rowed away from shore. Miles away from land, thirty-four souls on board, and only a pad of tow and dripping to keep the water out. The good hand of the Lord was upon us; we came on slowly day by day, buying food with the Frenchmen's shells, sleeping in grass-built huts at night, or on the sandy shore by large fires. What was wetted by the rain was soon dried by the sun. After seventeen days we came to the Frenchmen's house at midnight (at Bukumbi). They gave us a good supper and bed, and the next day, at 5 P.M., we arrived at Mackay's."

Here I must leave these brave adventurers to rest after their perilous voyage, and return once more to Buganda, where another revolution soon took place. I give the account of it in Mackay's own words; the news was brought to him by a dozen of our former pupils, who had effected their escape from Buganda in a canoe. He writes as follows :—

"It appears that soon after the departure of our brethren from Buganda, the authorities expressed their regret at having allowed the white men to go in safety, as it was feared they would join Mwanga on this side (*i.e.* south of Nyanza at Magu), and aided by the Christian chiefs who had fled (although in another direction), return and fight Kiwewa. Poor Kiwewa was not, however, long allowed to enjoy his exaltation to the throne. His head chiefs, who called themselves Mohammedans, in company with the Arabs, sorely pressed the king to be circumcised. Meantime the king was being advised by the old Katikiro (chancellor), then retired and living near the sepulchre of Mutesa, not to yield to the demand of the Arab party, as his father Mutesa had not been circumcised. Kiwewa therefore determined to try and rid himself of his new Katikiro, Kimbugwe (Bugala) and Mukwenda (formerly Mujasi), and others who were pressing him to yield to their request that he should become a pronounced Mussulman. The king tried to poison them, but the scheme failed. Next he ordered their attendance one day at a private audience, when he said he would consent to be circumcised. At this audience the king's executioners suddenly seized the Katikiro, Kimbugwe, and Mukwenda (Mujasi) ; Kiwewa seizing a spear and killing the two last; but as he was about to slay his chief minister, a gun was fired at him by a lad of the Katikiro's, whereupon the king fled, and the chief minister got himself released. The Katikiro at once selected another prince, named Kalema, one of Mutesa's eldest sons, who some years ago murdered his brother Ma'anda, and calling the Arabs to his aid, circumcised him and set him on the throne now vacated by Kiwewa. The latter fled to Nabulagala and took refuge at the grave of his father. The Arabs, however, attacked that place and drove him from it, plundering and burning the houses of the old Katikiro, in the hope probably of trying to recover their debts. Meantime they act as Kalema's body-guard, while Kiwewa has fled to Singo, the part of Buganda nearest Bunyoro, and has there been joined by the old Katikiro, Kolugi, and many others who were Mwanga's principal chiefs. I believe that Kiwewa has sent to recall the the Christian chiefs and soldiers, who had fled to Busàgara and Bunyoro; and should these consent to come to his aid, we may soon hear of the overthrow of Kalema and his Arab guard, and the re-establishment of Kiwewa on the throne. These events, coupled ·with the difficulties on Lake Nyassa, on the Upper Congo, and on the Nile, render the question now paramount, *Is Arab or European influence henceforth to prevail in Central Africa?* The answer to this question rests with Christian Europe. God grant that the suicidal policy of ABANDON, adopted in the Soudan, may not now be followed in East Africa."

And so the curtain falls. Mujasi, the murderer, murdered; the haughty chancellor humbled; Mwanga a fugitive, begging the Christian missionary to slay him if he will. All this within four short years. Surely innocent blood cries from the ground; and an unseen hand righteously metes out punishment to evil-doers.

T

CHAPTER XXII.

SECOND JOURNEY TO THE COAST.

WHILE the above stirring events were brewing in
Buganda, I was far on my way to Zanzibar, having at
the end of July, 1888, taken a sorrowful farewell of my
best of friends Mackay, who had spared no pains to
make my little caravan complete in every respect. We
were rather more than a dozen, all told. My arms consisted of a Winchester repeating rifle, a revolver, and a
Snider rifle, and three muzzle-loading guns. I had a fine
big Unyamwezi donkey, of which, when I reached the
neighbourhood of the Masai, those ignoble savages robbed
me and left me to proceed on foot. However, I had the
help of the donkey for the first five hundred miles of the
march, which was an important consideration. I was by
this time quite an old traveller, and I had in the boy
Mwana awulira, whom I have before mentioned, an excellent interpreter, for he knew four African languages.
He was also armour-bearer, as he carried my rifle, and
combined this function with that of cook and general
servant. Affectionate and as honest as the day, he
was seldom tired and never out of temper. Add to this
that he was my nurse when I was ill, and when I

became blind my leader, it will be seen that if ransoming a slave be an act of charity, in this case I received an ample reward. I was far from well on the march, and was laid up six days at one village with bad fever. However, I struggled on to Ugogo, where I was attacked with ophthalmia. The prostration caused by frequent fevers had made me liable to this terrible complaint and to violent and prolonged toothache. The light caused me so much agony that I had to completely blindfold myself, and so in utter darkness for seven days I made the journey through Ugogo. Mwana awulira, the obedient child, did everything for me, and indeed all my followers were as kind as could be. They were mostly Wanyamwezi, and in spite of certain things which I could not but dislike about these people, they showed so many fine qualities that they won my sincerest admiration. Patience, fortitude, strong affection, dogged perseverance, were their better characteristics.

And so, in spite of the fact that I was blind and had toothache, I had a pleasant journey. As I neared Kisokwe, where I knew I should meet with a hearty welcome from the Coles, I found that constant want of sleep at night had so affected me that I could hardly walk straight; I seemed to be wandering in a circle and winding among awful abysses, down which I expected to fall. Riding the donkey made things worse. Sometimes I believed that I was walking round towards the right hand, at others to the left. I can hardly describe my sensation of relief when I heard the familiar voice of my kind-hearted host giving me a warm Irish welcome. He and his wife soon made me forget my past troubles, and among other kindnesses which he conferred, he drew my offending tooth.

Next day Dr. Pruen, the medical missionary from Kikombo, a new Mission station near Kisokwe, came over and examined my eyes. He pronounced the case a serious one, and said there was some danger of my losing my sight. He most kindly urged me to go back with him, saying he would like to have me near him, so that he could give me more frequent attention. I therefore returned to Kikombo with him, where for ten days I was most hospitably entertained by him and his wife. Soon after my arrival there, Dr. Pruen received a summons from Freretown to proceed at once to the coast, so the next few days were spent in packing. I sat most of the day with a shade over my eyes, and could do little more to help than by occasionally rocking the cradle; for six weeks before a fine baby, little Stella, had made her appearance in this naughty and trouble-some world. Under any circumstances the journey for a young mother and six weeks old child would have been a trying and dangerous undertaking; but ere we had half crossed the rocky mountains which led to Mamboya we received for the first time tidings of the terrible doings at Zanzibar, of the bombardment of Bagamoyo by the Germans, and the slaughter of many insurgents; this made things infinitely worse, and had not Mrs. Pruen been an exceptionally courageous woman I know not

how we should have ever made the journey. The advice
we received from Zanzibar was that we had better
remain where we were, but at Kikombo there were hardly
any stores, and at Mamboya there were no houses, and
the rains were fast approaching. We decided that it
was better to face the uncertain risk of the insurgents
than the more certain peril of a wet season under
insufficient shelter. We therefore sent letters to the
coast at once asking that we might be informed if there
was serious danger, and then went on quietly to
Mamboya. The Pruens made their camp in the valley—
they feared the cold of the mountain for the little one—
while I took up my abode with my old friend Roscoe
and his wife.

A fortnight passed and yet our messengers did not
return, so notwithstanding my friends' hospitable invitation to remain with them, and in spite of their
warnings of my indiscretion, I determined to go on and
see for myself how matters stood. So bidding my companions farewell, I started again on the journey. I
thought it would be better for me to be in front, as I
should be able to send news back to the Pruens if there
was really serious danger. Four days later, after
crossing the beautiful rocky river of Mto ya mawe, I
made my forenoon halt. I observed numbers of natives
with spears on the hill at the base of which the river
flows. However, they made no impression on my
mind, as I was intent on cooking. I was camped in a
small village just below that where the warriors were

gathered. The people at first were inclined to be un-friendly; but when I talked to them they thawed, and all went merry as a marriage bell. We soon left and went our way, but we had not gone far when messengers from Zanzibar came up; they were going to the Arab soldiers stationed on the other side of the river, and they so frightened my little band with the tidings which they brought that my men came and begged me not to go on until I had reliable news. The messengers told us, moreover, that our mail-men had been attacked near Zanzibar, and that one of them had been killed, because they were the white men's servants. We went on another mile or so and halted at Kwe Mazengo, a pretty village in the Nguru Hills. Next morning I sent off three of my men, armed with a couple of guns, carrying a letter to Bwana Heri, chief of Sadaani, and another to the British Consul at Zanzibar. I told my messengers I would remain till they returned; I was not sorry to wait here, for my boy Mwana awulira had become very ill with pleurisy or inflammation of the lungs, and could hardly crawl.

This was at the end of October 1888. The third day of my sojourn, a lad whom Dr. Pruen had dismissed arrived and told me that the Pruens had left Mamboya and were only a few marches behind. So I sent one of my men back to tell how I was detained at Kwa Mazengo waiting for news. A day or two later Pruen's caravan came in. He had also heard the story which my men had told me, that the warriors at the former village whom I had seen had been holding a council with the intention of killing me ; but eventually decided to leave me alone. A night or two after my arrival at Kwa Mazengo, some of the youths of the village were sitting out in the moonlight, and I heard them talking in an insolent manner about white men. I went out and said, " If you have anything to say, come and say it here." They slunk into their houses, but in a few days I had made great friends with most of the village. Day after day passed and our men did not return, and frequent reports kept coming in of massacres of Europeans. Dr. Pruen's porters were greatly frightened, and told him plainly that if the Arabs made an attack, they could not help us ; but they would defend us against the "Washenzi" natives, whom we did not fear. During the whole time I feared our own Moslem porters more than all the natives put together, and these men were daily becoming more insolent as fresh reports of disasters to Europeans kept coming in. Our case was a serious one, especially as our cloth was running short. There was a French Roman Catholic Mission some hours' distance, so we wrote to the priests asking if they could let us have a small supply ; and they most generously sent us two pieces of thirty yards each, a great boon, as well as some fruits and vegetables from their garden. We waited till the 8th of November, and then determined to return to Mamboya. When we had come within one long march on our return journey to Mamboya our letters came in from the coast ; this showed us that communication was still open. We had, before leaving Kwa Mazengo, at Mrs. Pruen's suggestion, written a tiny letter, which was put in a needle-case as an envelope, and which we sent off secretly by two trusty messengers, one of whom concealed the minute missive about his person. We had briefly explained our position, our shortness of cloth, and the difficulties with the porters. The letters now received showed that our messengers had not arrived at Zanzibar, as there was no reference to them; but Bwana Heri had sent one of his slaves to take our mail-men through the insurgents, and he had succeeded in doing so. The question now was whether, if we decided to make the attempt to reach the coast, he could succeed in passing us through as well. We were in a dilemma: discomfort and starvation were frowning behind us at Mamboya, fighting and tumult were looming before us at the coast.

Mrs. Pruen had always been in favour of an advance, and with many misgivings and questionings I went across to their tent the day that our letters arrived to say that I thought on the whole that this was the best thing we could do. The chief point in favour of making for the coast was that our porters were all willing and ready for the journey, which they had previously refused. So the next day we were once more walking towards the sunrise. We made long forced marches; Mrs. Pruen was carried in the Bath-chair which Mrs. Hore has made famous in her interesting book 'To the Tanganyika in a Bath-chair'; it had been taken off the wheels, and was carried slung on a pole resting on the shoulders of two men.

We went on without adventure till we reached a village some three marches from the coast. Here, while making a halt, suddenly we heard a great firing of guns outside the stockade, and up trotted the young half-bred Arab Abdallah on a fine Muscat donkey, followed by about twenty men. This was the fruit of Mrs. Pruen's needle-case letter. The messengers had taken it in safety to our energetic friend and agent, Mr. Muxworthy, at Zanzibar, who had handed it on to the Consul-General, Col. Euan-Smith. The latter went at once to the Sultan and prevailed upon him to send a peremptory order to the turbulent Abdallah, son of Bwana Heri, to go himself in person and escort us to the coast, which after some demur he proceeded to do. As we passed from village to village we could not but observe the scowling looks which greeted us ; but by dint of talking and laughing with the people in a friendly way, the angry faces soon relaxed into smiles.

On Sunday, Oct. 18, we once more beheld the sea from Mkange. We were now at the most dangerous part of our journey, at the place where a missionary of the London Missionary Society, Mr. Brooks, lost his life a few weeks later. We had heard some time before that he was on his way to the coast. When he afterwards reached Mkange he acted just as I had done at Kwa Mazengo: sent some men on with a letter to Bwana Heri, chief at Sadaani, and awaited their return.

Some men came from Bwana Heri and walked into Brooks's camp when he was just on the point of returning towards Mamboya. One of these men came up and saluted him, and shook hands with him, saying, "Jambo Bwana?" "How do you do, sir?" at the same time another insurgent shot him dead from behind. He was the last of eleven English missionaries with whom I had been personally associated in some way or other who have lost their lives in Africa.

Before making our last march we received the unpleasant intelligence that the *Henry Wright*, the Mission steamer, had appeared off Sadaani; but that her boat had been fired on by the insurgents, and that the vessel had steamed back to Zanzibar.

Early on Monday morning, November 19th, 1888, we reached Sadaani; and as we entered the miserable place we saw every sign of preparation for fighting. The principal Arabs had sent their households inland for some miles, and nearly all the houses were stripped of their roofs. As we came into the town we discerned the portly figure of Bwana Heri coming to meet us with one or two other Arabs and large numbers of Indians who saluted us warmly. The chief greeted us with cold but studied politeness. The scowling mob through which we passed were silent. We were conducted to a filthy house, where we spent a long, uncomfortable day. Our porters were in great terror, and would not go anywhere far from where we were, except Mwana awulira, my faithful boy, who did not understand politics, and walked with me through the town and down to the sea-shore, where he assured himself that the Nyanza here was really salt. We bought some eggs and then returned, but the hours dragged on wearily. We had to wait till midnight before we could go on board the miserable dhow which Bwana Heri had allowed us to hire. We tried in vain to sleep; I was lying on my bed outside in the verandah of the house, and could hear a constant stream of remarks, often with ugly words occurring in juxtaposition to the hated name Mzungu (white man). Before the time fixed for starting we made our way down to the sea by the soft light of the moon, and climbed into the dhow; she was lying over on her side, as the tide had not yet come in.

This was better than the stifling house and the half-understood insults of the insurgents, although we were in an extraordinarily uncomfortable position on the little poop deck, which was like the side of a house. Here we were reclining on the hard boards, watching with some uneasiness the Arab sentries armed with guns patrolling the beach. At last the whispering tide stole in and flowed around us, then gently rocked us, then lifted us up, and we were afloat. And soon the great lateen sail was hoisted, and we swept out to sea. But the faithless breeze failed as the light of day increased, and the cool of the morning gave place to the terrible blaze of the noontide sun; and so we lay "as idle as a painted ship upon a painted ocean."

Again the fickle breeze dallied with the sail and we

made some tardy progress. At last we sighted a ship approaching us, coming nearer and nearer—

" Hither to work us weal;
Without a breeze, without a tide, she steadies with upright keel."

It was the *Henry Wright* steamer, and so finally, at about 3 o'clock in the afternoon, after having been fifteen hours on the dhow, we went on board, and were soon clasping the hand of the kindly Scot, Captain Wilson, who commanded her.

I need not try and describe our feelings as the long strain of anxiety was suddenly removed; but I can describe how we revelled in toast and tea, and how our entertainer would insist on opening a bottle of champagne for our delectation. Strange it was to hear the steady thud of the engines as the little steamer flew through the water, and sadly I saw the Dark Continent die down on the horizon as Zanzibar came more clearly into view.

We were most kindly received by Colonel Euan-Smith, the able and courteous Consul-General. We could not but feel that his wise and prompt action had been the chief cause of our getting safely through the insurgents. The reaction prostrated us all with severe fever, and we met with the greatest attention from members of the Universities Mission, and I am sure that none of us will ever forget the kindness of the trained nurse who is one of the Mission staff. After more than a fortnight at Zanzibar I left for home, and reached England on Christmas Day, 1888.

CHAPTER XXIII.

MANNERS AND CUSTOMS OF THE BAGANDA.

WITH regard to the life of the Baganda and their manners and customs, I feel that I really know very little, yet even this little would fill many chapters if I were to write at any length.

I have already stated that the nation is divided into Ebyika* or clans, each of which is distinguished by its animal crest or *totem*, which is sacred to members of the family and may not be eaten by them. Yet, although the clannish feeling is so strong, marriage between two persons of the same "kyika" is not permitted. Indeed matrimony in Buganda is not generally an affair of much romance, but rather a question of driving a bargain. The parents receive in return for their daughter, purchase money or "kasimu," which usually consists of cows or cowrie shells or other barter goods; and the bridegroom also provides quantities of banana cider and goats' flesh for the wedding feast. If the kasimu has been duly paid, there is no further difficulty, and after the feast the bridegroom takes his wife to his own home. The rich and powerful are not, so far as I

---

* This is the plural of the word "kyika," a clan.

am aware, obliged to pay any kasimu.   Sub-chiefs and peasants are only too happy to give their "bawala" (daughters) for nothing to a powerful patron, and woe betide them if they neglect to do so.   The easiest way however, for an ordinary man to obtain a wife is by simply purchasing a slave, who is then her husband's absolute property, and has not the privilege of "kunoba," that is of returning to her parents, as a free woman has. The latter, if she is ill-treated by her husband, can leave him, and if the case is proved against him, the parents can give her to another man.   If the woman is in fault, the husband can demand her again, and generally succeeds in obtaining her the second time by giving some small present to her parents.   Should they, however, refuse to give her up, he can then claim the kasimu which he paid for her.

In case of the birth of children, the former owners or parents of the mother seem, in certain cases, to have some right in, or claim upon the child ; for I recollect a man begging me for cloth under the following circumstances : His wife had borne him a child, which had died, and the father was compelled to pay to the parents or former owners of his wife the price of a slave, which he was endeavouring to make up.   This was by way of compensation for the child who was dead.

The system of polygamy, so largely practised in Buganda, naturally lessens the affection of a father for his child, and the relationship between them is rather that of master and slave than of parent and child.   The clan system also has a tendency to make relationship rather general than particular, and hence a child calls all its father's brothers " father," and all its mother's sisters " mother."

Babies in Buganda, as in most African countries, are carried on the back, low down, and are secured by the bark-cloth robe worn by the mother. A Muganda mother takes no little pride in her child, and I have watched with some amusement a novel way of washing a baby which is usually practised. The mother fills her mouth with water, which she blows and squirts over the child until the operation is satisfactorily performed. On passing out of the stage of childhood no particular rite or ceremony is observed in the case of young people in Buganda, so far as I am aware. The Wagogo and Wasagara, however, circumcise the boys at this stage, and perform, I believe, some analogous rite in the case of girls, who after this time are shut up within doors and never allowed out until married. In the Unyamwezi and Useguha countries, chipping the two upper front teeth is the sign that childhood's years are ended. The Wanyamwezi make a narrow angular gap, while the Waseguha* make a wider gap. I observed some Waseguha girls wearing pounds and pounds weight of beads round their waists, and was informed that it was because they were newly married brides. They borrow from friends as many beads as they are able,

* In the Swahili language, the first syllable " Wa" signifies the people ; " u " the country.

in order to make a fine show, though, strange to say, the beads are worn under their cotton cloth wrap. In Unyamwezi it is customary for both sexes to wear under their clothing a cincture of beads, which they never remove.

The Baganda people do not mutilate themselves in any way, although tatooing is usual among women who have been brought in from the surrounding tribes. Cicatrices from burning are common marks; and the Bahuma tribe-mark is, I believe, branded upon the hand. Burning among the Banyoro seems to be a common remedy in sickness; it is used, I suppose, on the principle of a blister.

Girls in Buganda become wives at a disgracefully early age, and long before they are properly developed. The practice of taking child wives is common in most African tribes, and this may possibly be one of the causes of the few children which African women bear.

Young children—boys, at any rate—are not given any name except the general appellation of "Ka-saja" (wee man). "Ka" in Buganda is the diminutive prefix. A little Mu-huma or Mu-yima slave-boy is called Ka-yima, though a little Mu-soga or Mu-nyoro slave is not called Ka-soga or Ka-nyoro, as might have been expected, but some other ordinary name. I have been told a curious fact about Bahuma children, that they are far more stupid at remembering their parents and early life than are slaves from other countries; no doubt because they are a much cleverer and brighter people,

NAKAYIMA.

To face p. 289.

and so take longer to become developed, either mentally or physically.

A Muyima slave-boy is often called Na-ka-yima. "Na" is a feminine prefix, and is no doubt added because of the girlish faces which the boys of this tribe usually have.* Some of the names of women are simply men's names with the feminine syllable "Na" prefixed, such as Na-Mukasa, Na-Kibuka. Mukasa and Kibuka are divinities or demi-gods.

The name of the semi-divine founder of the race, Kintu (a thing), is also a very favourite one for men. Other names are compounded of two or more words, such as "Mudu awulira" (The slave who hears); "Kalenzi genda" (Go, little boy); "Musaja alide ki?" (What has the fellow eaten?) Names of animals are also often borne, as "Ngiri" (peccary); "Embwa" (dog); and one of the princesses was called "Nawati emporogoma," the latter word meaning lion. The name Kidza is common to both sexes. In Unyamwezi, such names as "Limi" (sun), "Sonda" (stars), "Lushinge" (needle), and "Bunduchi" (gun), are common, though I have never heard people so called in Buganda. I knew a man from the province of Budu, however, who was named Kazoba, which means, I believe, either the sun or the supreme being, or possibly both.

---

* Albinos, or persons who are a ghastly pinky-white colour, owing to a lack of pigment in the skin, have the feminine appellation of Na-magoye. They are more usually of the female sex, though not invariably so.

The Baganda swear by the name of some ancient Kabaka (king), or by the present ruler. Should any person of position suddenly address a Muganda, he should politely reply, "Kabaka," or simply the king's name, *e.g.* "Mutesa," or "Mwanga." In reply to the call of an equal, the reply is, "Owange," mine; to a superior, "Wampa sebo," You gave to me, sir."

A peasant, when he meets a chief, bends low or kneels, and says, "Otyanno sebo?" "How do you do, sir?" the reply to which is, "Ndi wano," "I am here." In paying a visit, you may say, "Oli awo?" "Are you there?"—a form of salutation not unknown, I believe, in the Emerald Isle. An equal meeting an equal merely says, "Otiya?" "How are you?" or "Kulungi?" "Is it well?" the reply to which is, "Aa! gwotya?" "No, no, you, how are you?"—meaning politely, No, don't ask for me, let me ask for you. It is etiquette for an inferior first to salute one socially above him.

Two intimate friends, when they meet, will embrace one another, "lamusa," a word used generally for any salutation, but properly it is the action of friends embracing and laying their heads alternately on one another's right and left shoulders two or three times. Kissing is not practised among any African tribes that I have seen. The Baganda, indeed, have a word for it, as they have for nearly every conceivable thing, but it is considered very improper.

It is usual to send a slave to salute a friend when he passes on the road. The slave comes up and bows low or

kneels, and says, " Mwami antumye kukulaba," " Master
has sent me to see you." Generally some token accompanies the message; usually a few coffee-berries wrapped
in a small square of bark-cloth; this is called a
" Kirabbo."

It is an invariable custom for persons of quality
when they walk abroad to be followed by a number
of retainers or slaves; even the poorest peasant will at
least have one little slave-boy to grace his presence.
People on the roads in the morning are generally all
walking in the direction of the king's enclosure; but in
an afternoon they are more often going to pay calls. On
these occasions, coffee-berries in a neat little open basket
are always produced for the visitors, and often a present
of a goat or a bunch of plantains or some other fruit or
vegetable is given. Coffee-berries are called " Mwanyi,"
and this word has now come to mean a present of any
kind. The coffee in Buganda is always chewed, the
husk being rejected. It is a much smaller berry than
the Arabian kind, but it has not such an agreeable
flavour.

If a meal is served during the visit, a guest is always
asked to partake, and the afternoon is usually spent in
smoking and drinking banana cider or playing " Mweso,"
the game I have referred to elsewhere. " Mweso "
seems to be the only indoor amusement the Baganda
have, though the Egyptian runaways have introduced a
gambling game called " kukuba ensimbi " (throwing
shells), which is played with cowries. It is a game

u 2

which exercises a great fascination over its votaries, who often lose everything they have before they leave off. Outdoor games are not unknown; wrestling, "kumega," is a very favourite pastime, as also "kubiriga," or throwing short sticks on a bare piece of ground and causing them to turn over and over; the sticks are called "embirigo." I have never seen the Baganda jumping or running races for amusement. They can run quickly, however, and the king's messengers always go at full speed.

Walking is the almost invariable method of locomotion, though a sick man is borne upon a stretcher or framework of branches, called "lunyo," and the king or other royal personage is carried on a man's shoulders. A missionary has described his surprise when he saw approaching him what appeared to be a gigantic man; but, on coming nearer, he discovered that it was only a "mumbeja" (princess) on the shoulders of a tall slave. Riding is unknown in Buganda, and is considered indecorous. Lads, however, will sometimes mount a cow and set her off at full gallop; but no practical use is ever made of any beast of burden. Human beings here, as in so many other parts of Africa, perform this function, and every morning there may be seen coming into the capital long strings of women and slaves, carrying bunches of plantains or bundles of other vegetables upon their heads. These they are bringing in from the country places, which every person of rank or importance possesses. This food is for the maintenance of the vast gathering of people who are always in attendance at or near the royal enclosure. Women of the slave class travel unattended, unlike the ladies of a chief's harem, who are always in charge of a young boy. These women, in the absence of their lord, are left pretty much to themselves, and are generally on the look-out to be unfaithful. If discovered, then the most frightful punishments are inflicted upon the guilty persons, such as burning to death, or frightful semi-roasting and various mutilations;* and yet, in spite of these drastic measures, offences of this kind appear to be utterly unchecked.

The ordinary punishments in Buganda are death by fire, being hacked to pieces by reed splinters, fine, imprisonment in the stocks "mvuba," or in the slave fork "kaligo," also mutilation. It is most common to see people deprived of an eye, or in some cases of both eyes; persons lacking their ears are also frequently met with. I used to wonder why one of our converts always wore his "kiremba" (turban) so low down on his head, and I discovered it was to hide the loss of his ears. Other hideous mutilations, but less often practised, are cutting off the lips and nose. Sometimes a hand or both hands or arms are cut off, but this very often proves fatal.

* The evil counsel given by the Arabs to Mutesa with reference to the guardianship of his harem was followed frequently by Mwanga, as a punishment for Christian converts, one or two of whom died under the operation.

I have alluded to the way in which law is administered in Buganda. The people are very litigious and go to law about trifles. When a case is gained, the judgment is carried out by the successful suitor, who obtains a "mubaka" (messenger or officer) from the magistrate who has tried the case. We had one or two cases of "musango," or judgment, which were tried, and which, to the credit of the natives as well as of ourselves, we generally gained. One of these cases was tried before a small officer, Bilali, chief of the market, and was as follows :—Our lads discovered two girls and a boy robbing our garden, and succeeded in capturing them. We put our prisoners in chains, and the next day obtained judgment against them, which was that we might keep one of them, and let the other two go free. We selected the boy, but were not sorry when he ran away the next day, for we did not want him, but only wished to deter others from . entering our premises. The decision which we obtained may seem severe, but the law is very stringent in such cases, and there is no penalty for killing a thief who enters an enclosure at night. Indeed, it is against the law for any one to be found even on the high-roads after dark, as it is supposed that he can be out for no good purpose, and the king's executioners go out periodically at night and kill all and sundry whom they find on the roads.

Robbery is not thought shameful, although it is so rigorously punished. The haughty chancellor, for example, would receive articles which his own pages purloined from our premises and presented to him to curry favour. In the same way lying is considered clever rather than disgraceful, and the sin consists in being discovered. Falsehood, though not unfortunately a vice confined to Africans, is one in which they have a bad eminence. I have known a few noble exceptions, but they are very rare.

To turn now to war, which is the chief occupation of the Baganda people. They are essentially a nation of warriors, and are wonderfully organised under captains, or "Batongole," over tens and fifties and hundreds and thousands and so forth up to the "Mugabe" or generalissimo. Before going on the warpath, the various chiefs and officers repair with their immediate followers to the royal enclosure to swear fidelity and obedience, and to receive their commissions from the king. The warriors pass in order before the monarch, making demonstrations of loyalty and allegiance by brandishing and shaking sticks as if they were spears. I have never seen the ceremonies performed on such an occasion; but when the great royal drum has boomed out its war-signal, and when the general has been chosen, the various chiefs appointed to take part in the raid, return home, beat their own drums and gather their retainers, and then set off for the rendezvous appointed.

With regard to the number of available Baganda warriors, this, of course, depends upon the population of the country. Mr. Wilson, in his book, puts the latter down as five millions, although to reach this moderate number I think he had to take fifteen millions off the first estimate of the missionaries; but even five millions appears to me to be far too high. A visit to Scotland perhaps might help to keep down the exaggerated notion of such myriads of people. On my second journey to the Nyanza, my new companion used to ask me, "Where are the people?" and I had to reply, "Wait till we reach Ugogo and you will see." And yet even Ugogo is only very thinly populated. Some of the Wanyamwezi and Wasukuma districts are pretty thickly peopled; but in Buganda, except about 'the king's capital, the population is very sparse.*

I very much question, therefore, if the whole population of Buganda proper amounts to as much as one million of souls; and I doubt if by the mightiest effort more than forty thousand warriors could be massed at any given point. However, I offer this estimate, and indeed all my statements, with the humble admission that my knowledge is very partial and imperfect.

The Baganda chiefs always travel with their harems when on the warpath, since they cannot trust any one to ook after them during their absence, on Juvenal's prin-

---

* I asked Mr. Stanley how he came to make so high an estimate of Mutesa's fighting men as 150,000. He, however, explained that he had included the warriors of the surrounding tributary nations; but I do not think these would be available. I can bear witness to the accuracy of the great traveller, and to his wonderful power of laying hold on salient points. I have often been surprised at the amount of exact information he obtained during his brief visit to Buganda in 1875.

ciple of " Quis custodiet," and so there is always a vast
following of women and slaves in a Buganda camp.
The whole of the country *en route* is eaten up as by
an army of locusts, and the unhappy people of the
provinces through which the home army passes on a
foreign raid endure almost as much hardship as the
people who are raided. The suffering and loss of life
on the march is terrible; for the Muganda general, as
a rule, lacks the first quality of a leader, that of caring
for the health and comfort of his soldiers. The warriors
are armed with two long throwing spears, which they
can hurl very dexterously, while for defence they carry
wooden shields, beautifully covered both inside and out
with fine woven or plaited cane work. The shield is
pointed at the top and bottom and has a conical wooden
boss. The Baganda do not know the use of the bow,
and are terribly afraid of arrows. Before going to
battle, the soldiers smear their faces with white china
clay, to give themselves a horrible and ghastly appearance; they use besides a red compound called " girenge,"
with which they also colour their canoes. Their spears
are much longer and more formidable than those of the
Bahuma or Wanyamwezi. These latter however are
armed besides with bows and arrows, but they do not
use shields.

It is worth mentioning how after a Baganda army
had been annihilated by the naked Bakede, who only
use the assegai or light throwing spear, of which they
carry several, the Baganda set to work to make spears

like those of the Bakede, that they might in future encounter their antagonists on more equal terms. I do not know if the new weapons were ever tried, but I rather think not.

At the present time, however, the number of guns in the country is rapidly increasing; iron is used for making bullets, as lead is very scarce. Many breech-loading rifles have also been introduced into the country, including not a few of the Winchester repeating type. The Bakede people despise guns, and in the hands of the Baganda, who, as a rule, neither take aim nor fire from the shoulder, they have not found them very formidable weapons. The Wasukuma, also, as well as the Bakede, have a contempt for such innovations as clothing and firearms.

But although the Baganda are essentially a fighting people, they have made considerable progress in the arts of peace. In building, although they never use clay or wattles, and though their houses are only vast beehive-like structures of grass supported upon wooden poles, yet for neatness and finish they excel those of any other tribe in East Africa. Like the philosopher of Laputa, the Baganda begin from the roof. First a small ring of fine grass is formed, outside of which are tied a number of stalks which stick out all round like the ribs of an umbrella, sloping downwards. Under the first ring, and lower down, another wider ring of grass is formed; more reeds are added, and more rings lower and lower and wider and wider, until the rings become so wide that stiff tiger grass can be substituted for the finer grass. The whole structure is supported on low posts; but as lower rings are added nearer the ground, the frame is raised upon higher poles to make room. This goes on until a height is attained in the largest buildings of seventy or eighty feet. The supporting trees run in four rows. When this great reed-built dome is completed, a doorway is cut out and a large bonnet-like projection is built over it—this serves as a kind of porch; a low clay ridge runs all round, over which one has to step to enter. The door, as I have mentioned in another place, always looks up-hill. When the reed-work dome is ready, the thatch is put on, beginning from the ground. The straw is tied up in small bundles before being placed in position; the amount of material used in the operation is almost incredible. I think that I am not wrong in stating that Mackay, when he was putting the lightning conductor upon Mutesa's great grave-house, found a depth of something like twenty feet of grass upon the roof.

Inside, the floor is always covered with a fine, fragrant kind of dry grass, which, when first put down, is very nice; but when it has become foul, the occupants of the dwelling do not change it, but simply put new grass over the old. The inmates make a practice of washing their hands by pouring water over them; and as they use no receptacle to catch the water, it falls on the grass and then causes it to decay; and even if this were all, it would be quite enough to make the house very unwholesome. Cleanliness, indeed, may be pleaded as an excuse ; but other shockingly unsanitary arrangements are tolerated still more productive of disease ; and such things, coupled with the large numbers of people often crowded together in one sleeping-place, are, I imagine, mainly responsible for the terrible black plague, or "Kaumpuli," which is so common and so fatal in Buganda.

The sleeping-places are curtained off with bark cloth, and bedsteads are generally used. These consist of a framework of branches supported on stakes driven into the ground. Plenty of fine grass serves as a mattress, over which a nice mat is placed ; the coverlet is a large square of bark cloth. Like all Africans, the Baganda sleep with their heads under the bedclothes. In a Buganda household, each individual, strange to say, has a separate bed—the "kiriri," or bedstead, just described, being a small narrow structure. The natives have, however, now learned to make "ebitanda," or broad bedsteads, which are coming into common use.

The bark-cloth mentioned above is one of the chief staples of wealth in the country, and is largely manufactured by slaves and the poorer class of peasants. It is made from the bark of a kind of fig-tree, which is cut from the trunk in large felt-like matted pieces. The wound on the tree is bound up with plaintain fibre, when a new bark forms. After removal, the bark is damped and repeatedly hammered on smooth logs with wooden mallets like those used by stonemasons. This process is continued until it is beaten out into a fine wide felt cloth, very strong the way the fibre runs, but easily pulled into holes crossways. In the last beating a hammer is used on which lines are cut, and these, striking the cloth, mark it and give it the appearance of being ribbed. The sap in the bark is at first a milky white; but exposure to the air causes oxidation, which turns it to a deep orange tint. Any flaws or holes in the cloth are beautifully stitched up with native needles and fine fibre thread; the eye of the needle is made by flattening one end of the wire and by bending it over and then the joining is dressed on a stone or touched with a file, so that the needle may run smoothly through the cloth. A coarser kind of bark-cloth, called " kitentegere," is used for bedclothes and bedding. The finest quality, called " sango," is very valuable, and is coloured a deep red with " girenge " before-mentioned. Women usually fumigate their cloths with a scented wood named " mugavu."

Fires are continually burning in Buganda houses, and all cooking operations are carried on indoors. This is no doubt one cause of the conflagrations which are so constantly occurring. The fireplace is a square in the middle of the house marked off by four logs, which serve to protect the grass carpet from the flames. The " entamu " (cooking pot), rests on three stones, which are termed " masiga." The entamu is a large, round, openmouthed clay cauldron, and, like most African pottery, it is insufficiently burned, and therefore very brittle.

The natives excel in making pipes, which they mould most tastefully, and on which they prick out patterns in white, the rest of the pipe being coloured a jetty black. I have seen some excellent imitations in clay work of a small European bottle. The native drinking cups, " ebibia," and large water-jars, " ensuwa," display also no little skill.

I have spoken of cooking-pots, and this naturally leads to the useful subject of cookery, which is an important adjunct of African civilisation. In this art, as in so many others, the Baganda excel most African tribes. The King and Katikiro have quite an elaborate *ménu*, including fish and the large edible rat, " musu," and vegetables and fruits of various kinds, beef and goats' flesh as a matter of course. But the ordinary food of all classes is the banana or plantain.

In Buganda, as in other countries, certain foods are " muzizo," or forbidden. On what system certain animals are rejected in the various tribes I do not know. The Baganda, for example, reject the hippopotamus and crocodile, while their co-subjects, the islanders on the Sesse group, eat both greedily, and will give as much as a couple of goats for a fine fat crocodile's tail. The Wanyamwezi, like the Sesse islanders, will eat hippopotamus, and also animals which have died a natural death. The Bahuma will only eat their own cows when they have died. The Baganda reject all animals which have died of themselves, but will eat the entrails of cows and goats, which the Bahuma will not. The latter refuse sheep and fowls and eggs, which the Baganda women also refuse, but curiously enough, Baganda men have no such scruple. East African tribes do not appear to eat birds as a rule, with the exception of guinea fowl. The Wanyamwezi, however, when travelling in caravans, break this custom and eat fowls, although in their own villages to do so is "mwiko" or forbidden. The plantains, like all other products of the ground, are entirely cultivated by women, by whom also they are cooked. A woman may not cook the food of any man except her own husband; indeed the word "kufumbira," to cook for a person, means to marry him, and the passive voice of the verb "to cook for," is always used of a woman and means to be married. The word to "marry," when applied to a man, is "kuwasa;" thus an entirely different word is used for each sex.

When the woman has cut her bunch of green plantains, she proceeds to peel them with a curved knife, and the peelings are either given to the goat or they may be used for making soap. When the fruit is peeled, the "mufumbiro," or cook, takes a broad plantain leaf, from which she has stripped off the midrib, and which she has softened and made pliant by holding over the fire. She then wraps the plantains up in the leaf and neatly ties it at the top as a cloth is tied over a pudding. She arranges her fire, and places the large cooking-pot on the three stones already referred to. At the bottom of the pot she spreads some withered leaves, and on these she places the plantains which are to be cooked. She then covers them up with more withered leaves until the cooking-pot is quite filled. She now pours in a little water; so that the food is steamed by this method, and from time to time she adds a small quantity of water until it is quite cooked. Then she takes it out, works it up into a mass with a kind of pot-stick, and then dishes it up in a beautiful open basket; she covers the food with fresh plantain leaves, over which another basket is placed. A certain red kind of ripe plantains, called " gonja," are also often cooked by simply putting the fruit in their skins among the withered leaves in the pot. And it is customary also to roast them in the ashes when not too ripe. Indian corn, " kasoli," is roasted or boiled, but never ground, as the Baganda do not use meal of any sort. They make, however, a kind of savoury cake, called " nyaggo," of sem-sem seeds, " entungo," which are full of a strongly flavoured oil.

The common people have but little variety in their food; but meat and fish is sometimes obtained, and is cooked by placing in the leaf as prepared for plantains and by adding a little water. " Enkeje," a small, strongly-flavoured fish something like anchovy, is largely used as " kyokulira," or what an Irish peasant would call " kitchen," when he has some such luxury as a salt herring to make his potatoes go down. The Swahili people call it " mchuzi " or gravy. A good deal of fish is consumed in Buganda, but is generally smoked and dried, since it is difficult to convey it from the lake in the hot sun without its being spoilt. I have never seen milk used as " kyokulira," though it is the usual relish in Unyamwezi and Ugogo. And the butter which the Baganda obtain from the Bahuma or Bayima herdsmen, they prefer to use for anointing their bodies rather than for eating.

When going on a raid or canoe voyage, it is customary to carry a small quantity of dried plantains or " mutere; " this is prepared by cutting the green fruit into thin strips and drying it in the sun. A small variety of tomato, " njage," is much used in cooking. Onions have been introduced by the Arabs, but are not largely cultivated. Beans " bijanjaro," sweet potatoes " du-monde," yams " kandi," casava " dumonde yo muti " (*lit.* potatoes of wood), green leaves of various kinds called " mvwa," and innumerable other vegetables are common. In fact, Buganda may well be called a vegetarian's paradise.

The people eat, as a rule, twice in the day. The first meal or breakfast at about eleven, and the evening meal or supper at sunset. Like most Africans, they are very ready to share their food with others, and indeed are generous in all things; perhaps their poverty helps to keep down avarice. Before eating, the Baganda are most careful to wash their hands. An attendant or slave pours water over their fingers, or else a kind of sponge is used formed of the succulent stem of the banana tree. This is given, dripping with its sap, to each person, who cleans his

X

hands with it. Pounding the stem to make these sponge-like napkins is the work of some aged crone who is useless for much else. The food is usually served under the bonnet-like porch before the door, the company sitting the while round the " diro," a space on the ground covered with green plantain leaves, which serve as a tablecloth. The children and slaves and others sit outside and receive small pieces of the " meré," or mashed plantains, after their elders have been helped. When the cover has been removed from the basket containing the meré, the person appointed " mugabi," or server, takes a small piece of plantain leaf to protect his or her fingers, and scoops out a portion of the smoking mass. This is then worked up into a sort of ball varying in size according to the amount of food provided, and handed round to the company who are going to partake. When they have beef or goat's flesh, it is cut up into small pieces with sharp reed splinters. Fruit is not usually eaten at meal times, though there are several kinds in the country; some indigenous and others which have been introduced by the Arabs. Among the former are the " empafu," a small black fruit like a damson in appearance, but it has an oily and faintly sweet taste (before being eaten it is placed in hot water for a few minutes) ; also the " ensali," a small and very acid fruit, something like a cherry. Among the latter, the " pera " (guava), the " papala " or " papai " or " papaw," a large luscious fruit, and also " koma manga," a poor kind of pomegranate, which has, however, useful medicinal properties.

When dinner is over, hands are again washed and tooth-brushes put into requisition before the great "kita" (bottle gourd) of "mwenge," or banana cider, is produced. Before proceeding to describe the manufacture of "mwenge," I may mention that the use of tooth-brushes is known from the west to the east of Africa; these consist of a short stick of fibrous wood, which is chewed until the fibres at the end become loose and represent bristles. The end of the little stick is continually rubbed over the teeth, and, no doubt, tends to keep them sound. I never saw the Bahuma using these brushes; and they have, as a rule, very poor teeth. The Wanyamwezi, who have splendid teeth, never have the brushes out of their mouths.

Let me now say something about "mwenge," the national beverage of Buganda. It is kept in the great bottle gourds mentioned above, and is usually drunk out of exquisitely fine gourd cups, called "endeku," which are of all sizes and capacity, the taller holding more than a quart, and some of the smaller not more than a tea-cupful. Some of the useful decanter-shaped "endeku" hold three or four quarts, but they vary much in size. Banana cider is used in the countries to the south of Buganda, and is called "marwa" in those regions; but the word "marwa" is used also in Buganda. The cider is made in a large wooden trough called a "lyato" (canoe). The bananas are cut and placed in pits until over-ripe. They are quite different from the plantain used for cooking, which is larger and longer.

x 2

These "memvu," or cider bananas, are the small kind so often seen in England. When they are quite yellow, the skins are removed and the fruit is thrown into the "lyato," in which is also placed a quantity of fine dried grass of a particular kind. The bananas are now worked up by hand and pressed and squeezed through the grass till they become a thick creamy liquid. Water is then added, and the result is an intensely sweet and vapid liquor called "mubisi." This may be drunk by strict Mahometans and teetotal Europeans, but at best it is a bilious and unwholesome beverage. A malt is added to the "mubisi" in the shape of a fine small grain, a kind of millet called "mwemba;" the liquor is then strained off and left for twenty-four hours, when it is ready for use. If kept too long, it soon becomes sour; but when fresh it is a very refreshing and hardly intoxicating drink, unless taken in very large quantities, which unfortunately is usually the case. The Arabs used to distil a spirit from this "mwenge," of which they were very fond; but I do not think that the Baganda cared for it as a rule. At any rate, I never heard that they made it themselves. In Unyamwezi, Ugogo, and the districts near the coast, the native beer is made from grain, and is not nearly so nice as the banana cider of the Lake region. I remember arriving at an Unyamwezi village one morning, just as the elders were about to hold a beer drinking. They came out and solemnly seated themselves in a circle under a spreading tree; a huge cauldron of "pombe," or beer, was brought out and ladled into gourds and cups made of basket work from which not a drop of the liquor escaped. These were silently passed from hand to hand until the cauldron was emptied. But beer drinking is more generally, I imagine, an evening relaxation. At an Useguha village, about a hundred miles from Zanzibar, where I spent ten days, half the inhabitants would go off now and then to a neighbouring village for a grand carouse, and with the musical accompaniment of the incessant beating of drums and the singing of the revellers, the flowing bowl was passed from hand to hand. I never saw these people more than a little merry or maudlin; but it is far otherwise at the coast towns, where European and other foreign liquors of uncertain ingredients are freely sold, and often induce a dangerous temporary insanity.

But to return to Buganda. Some of the manufactures of the country prove that these people possess a large share of the acquisitive faculty, and they may be termed with some degree of justice the Japanese of Africa.

The metal work is carried on in straw-built huts, and the stone anvil, bent green stick used as tongs, and goatskin bellows, have a general resemblance to the Unyamwezi implements already described; but the Baganda substitute a hammer of iron for the stone hammers of Unyamwezi. It has no handle, and is in shape something like a thick heavy marlinspike. Some of the brass and copper work is very beautiful. The royal copper and brass spears, and the necklets marked in patterns to distinguish the different " bitongole " or offices of the wearers, are beautifully finished ; as also are the anklets of the same metals, only worn by royalty or the despised though kingly tribe of the Bahuma. I recollect having given Samweli a pair of old boots, and he was most careful to blacken the brass eyeholes. I could not understand why he was at such pains to do this, till he explained that only royalty might wear brass upon their feet, although, strange to say, any one may wear bracelets of these royal metals upon their arms. The small bells, " bijugo," which hang round the royal drums, are also nicely finished. The chief manufactures in iron are the long war-spears, also knives and small hatchets, also cow-bells, " ebide," or " endege." The knives are always curved, and are fixed into wooden handles, the hole being bored with a red-hot iron. The principle is much the same as that of an English dinner-knife, except that no rivets are used. The axes too are stuck through a wooden handle; adzes are also used—in fact, I am not sure that the adze is not the Buganda national implement rather than the axe ; axes or small hatchets are met with, but whether, like the " muhoro " or " Buziba " bill-hook so common in Buganda, they are of foreign manufacture, I do not know. At any rate, they are very small and light, but it is astonishing to see the work which they accomplish *non vi sed sæpe cædendo* by the continual and rapidly repeated strokes. The Buganda hoes, unlike the axes and hatchets and the hoes of the

Wanyamwezi, are not wedged through a hole in the wooden handle, but are tied on to the root of a stick, or a branch which happens to be at an acute angle to a stick.

Pig-iron is introduced from Bunyoro to the north, and so far as I know, iron is neither found nor smelted in Buganda. Files in numbers and a bow-brace for boring have been introduced by the Arabs. The art of brazing and tinning has also been brought from Zanzibar, and some of the Baganda smiths have acquired it.

The manufacture of a very different though largely-used article has also been introduced from the Soudan, I refer to the soap which the Baganda make; it is dirty-looking, dark-coloured, and soft, yet it effects its purpose very well. The peelings of plantains are burned, and the ashes placed in a plantain leaf folded like a funnel; this is filled with water, which drips down and is caught in some vessel underneath. Then fat is procured and boiled down, and the liquid ley is added. People are often badly scalded during the operation, I suppose while pouring the watery liquid into the melted fat. The Baganda also manufacture candles. The usual light is simply a fire, or, in the case of royalty, split reeds called " mimuli," which the pages hold.

Though many foreign articles of barter have been introduced, and though cotton cloth and coloured calicoes are very common, still some of the beautiful native wearing apparel holds its own. Foremost of all are the exquisite skins which are so largely worn. The leopard is the royal animal, and the king alone has the privilege of sitting on a leopard skin. It would be high treason for any other person to do so. Chiefs, however, on certain occasions, may wear them, but only in a particular way. Other skins, however, are very much affected—dressed cow-skins and goat-skins. The beautiful skins of antelopes are also frequently used. The goat-skins are often dressed so as to resemble fine chamois leather, and one or two sewn together make a very handsome robe ; but the most beautiful of all is a number of small skins exquisitely sewn together into the shape of one. It is a curious fact that the guild of *thatchers* always wear goat-skins while following their peculiar trade.

Other articles manufactured of leather are shoes and belts ; the former are always made of buffalo hide, and are fastened to the foot with a loop through which the great toe passes, and another loop of fur across the instep. The shoes are tray-shaped, and inside are marked out into patterns, and coloured red and white and black. The belts are of dressed leather, and are now being made in imitation of those brought from Zanzibar.

I have already alluded to the " enseke," or beautiful grass-woven bent drinking tubes. The various grasses are dyed and are plaited or woven over a bent hollow stick, through which the banana cider is drunk. Baskets are also beautifully made of grass. A particular kind of grass is taken and bound together by winding fine grass or

fibre round and round it so as to form a long rope or
cord about as thick as a finger; but the diameter varies
according to the size of the basket; it is then coiled
round and round, somewhat as a straw hat is made in
Europe, and the coils are sewn together with strong
fibre, the holes being bored by a kind of skewer. The
baskets are shallow as a rule, and are made with covers.
A coarser and commoner kind, also deeper, are made for
rougher usage.

The Baganda are very tasteful and skilful in bead-
work, which is always done by women; the gold and
silver embroidery is, however, always worked by men.
The Baganda make small ornamental articles of beads;
but the two most usual ornaments are a bead necklet,
worn by both sexes; and for females only, a girdle or
cincture made of grass, worked over with the minutest
beads in beautiful patterns. This cincture or hoop
probably has something like cane inside it to make it
like a spring; it is put on as those bracelets among
us which open a little at the ends; the cincture
thickens out into two knobs, and is the only dress
which girls up to a marriageable age have. The purpose
for which it may be possibly intended is actually attained in Unyamwezi by the small bead apron also beautifully worked in patterns, which is so very common,
though the poorest girls are obliged in that country to
content themselves with a small square of cloth instead.
Women of the higher classes wear most delicately made
ivory bracelets. I have never seen them being made,

but they must require most skilful workmanship. It is a curious circumstance that, in cutting ivory, the Baganda use a kind of saw, yet it has never struck them that wood might be cut in the same way.

The Baganda, in making their canoes, can chop only two boards out of a whole tree, which is an enormous loss of time and material. Like all other equatorial tribes, they know nothing of carpentery or the use of nails, but tie everything together. For example, in their canoes, a red-hot iron is used for boring holes on each side of the long log which has been chopped out for the keel, and corresponding holes for the " embawo " or boards, which are tied to the keel on both sides. These boards are at an angle sloping outwards; and then, along the edge of these, more holes are bored, and then another board on each side is tied on vertically. The boards are kept in position by thwarts, which are conveniently sized branches cut to the proper length. The canoes are caulked with plantain fibre, and coloured red with the " girenge " before mentioned.

To turn now to the religion of the Baganda, I feel that I am on doubtful and uncertain ground. It may naturally be thought that those who wish to substitute a new teaching for an old, and to overthrow an existing religion, ought to be thoroughly acquainted with the system which they desire to destroy. And no doubt our ignorance of *Lubareism* would have proved a great hindrance to our teaching had not that religion been already undermined, and by the more enlightened

almost cast off before we came into the country. No
doubt the presence of the Arabs had had much to do
with this loosening of the hold of the religion of Lubare
on the minds of those who lived in the neighbourhood
of the king's capital. But people who have lost their
religion are like those who have lost their clothing, and
are apt to pick up the first substitute that offers.
Glorious and blessed Humanity, as seen in Central
Africa, did not apparently present many attractions to
the Baganda, and so they listened with surprising
attention to our poor preaching of Christ. They trusted
themselves implicitly to our teaching; but those who
had been formerly followers of Lubare seemed ashamed
of the fact, and did not allude to it very much. While
others who still held to the old cult were very reticent
in speaking of what they supposed we despised. And
hence we had not many opportunities of carefully
studying the religion. We soon became known as the
people of "Katonda" or the Creator, and the name
"Bantu ba Katonda," people of God, was sometimes
applied to those who followed our teaching. It is worth
noticing that some of the converts had not in the least
realised the time which has elapsed since the appearance
of Christ on earth, and it is quite possible that the nearer
point from which they would view His story might give
them a clearer and more vivid conception of the Gospel
narrative. I have often spoken to serious and intelligent people in Buganda on the question of the immortality of the soul, or rather of the possession of a soul.

They seemed to have no definite ideas on the subject, but all allowed they believed that there was nothing after death, and that they should die as a cow or a dog. The only fact from which their belief in a soul might be inferred is that they have a word for a departed spirit, "muzimu," and the strongest belief that the soul of a departed king can come back and enter into certain persons, who are said to "samira," be possessed of, the spirit of such and such a departed king. The word "samira," translated "possessed of," is not, however, passive, but has more the force of the Greek middle. The active form of the word would be "sama." That the person who *samiras* has control over the spirit seems to be the prevalent idea, and Mutesa begged that after his death no one should "samira" him. A person who "samiras," works himself up into a state of ecstasy or madness until the afflatus has subsided.

The negative condition of mind with reference to the question of the existence of a soul is not without its interesting side; for the Baganda lack that rooted notion of their own natural immortality which is so common in Europe. To a religious Englishman, Christ is only the door of admission to a higher and more blessed state of an immortality which is inherently his own. To a Muganda convert, Christ is immortality itself.

The Baganda have a vague idea of a sublime creator, "Katonda," of whom nothing is known and from whom nothing is hoped or feared. They have the word "kutonda," to create, quite distinct from the word "kukola," to make. Next in order is Lubarè, the upper air and the waters, including the deities and divinities who inhabit them. Of these the chief appears to be Mukasa, the Neptune of the Nyanja, who holds the lives of adventurous mariners in his hand, and whom the pious sailor ever propitiates with offerings of bananas or some other fruit which he throws into the lake as he prays for a prosperous voyage. Lubarè is also the dispenser of wealth and the giver of children, though which individuals must be sought for these blessings I do not know. "Musoke" is the rainbow; "Musisi" the earthquake; "Kiwanuka" the thunderer; "Nende" and "Kibuka" are others; but among the demi-gods and heroes the divine "Kintu" stands out starry and mysterious amid the night of his dark surroundings. Others have given the beautiful legend of the gentle Kintu's disappearance, because his children hated one another and hated him, and have told how the hope lived on that some day he would return to bless his wayward descendants.

Diseases seem to be looked upon as gods or evil spirits, and "kaumpuli," the plague, and "kawali," small-pox, are spoken of as persons. He has seized him, *i.e.* small-pox has seized him. But, strange to say, the word for a departed spirit is neuter, "muzimu." So, speaking of the spirit, the expression "it has seized him," is used. The belief that disease and death are caused by witchcraft is very strong among all African tribes, nor are the Baganda any exception. But

though the word "roga," to bewitch, is used generally
in a bad sense, it means also to cure or to heal, *e.g.*,
"roga endwade," to heal disease; "roga enjala," to
satisfy hunger; "roga enyonta," to quench thirst.   But
the Baganda do not depend entirely upon incantations
or charms or witchcraft for either the production or
cure of disease.   Poison* is frequently resorted to for
the former purpose, and for the latter purpose I have
seen various native remedies, *e.g.* a mass of chopped
green leaves and charcoal, applied to a purulent sore.
They have also a medicine for fever.   The Waseguha
know the medicinal effect of drinking castor-oil; but
they manufacture it chiefly for anointing their bodies.
Though the castor-oil tree grows profusely in Buganda,
the people make no use of it.   Africans are great
believers in " blood letting," and the method employed
in Buganda is cupping, "kulumika."   A horn which has
been bored out at the thin end so as to admit the passage
of air, is pressed tightly over the punctured vein, the air
is exhausted by sucking at the thin end, when the hole
is immediately filled up with a piece of " bubane "†
(gum or incense) or other substance, when the required
amount of blood can be drawn.   The doctors who
perform this operation are called " Basawo," and must
be distinguished from the " Bamandwa " or sorcerers,

---

* One deadly poison is extracted from a corpse.

† "Bubane" is a rich odoriferous incense which exudes from the
gigantic "mwafu" tree, the fruit of which is called " empafu."   It
is mentioned by Cameron and other travellers.

whose gifts are altogether of a supernatural order, and include the power of catching thieves and of performing other valuable and useful functions: if they do not always catch the right person, they catch somebody, so that justice is vindicated. These jugglers seem to have a sort of prescriptive right to murder and rob persons of the lower class, and are consequently held in the most abject veneration. They possess large grants of land, and are a wealthy and important caste. They seem, generally speaking, half-witted, yet are crafty and cunning. They adopt a horrible and unnatural high falsetto tone in speaking, and are loaded with "ma-yembe," magic horns, and curiously shaped implements covered with cowrie shells for purposes of their profession. In Unyamwezi, there is also a caste of wizards who are called "Baganga," for the Wanyamwezi are also devoted believers in witchcraft. The young chief Sonda, to whom I gave the surplice when at Musalala, died of small-pox on the war-path. However, this was put down to witchcraft, and a poor old woman, who lived in his village some hundred miles from where he died, was put to death for having "*rogad,*" bewitched, him. The threat to bewitch any one is considered most evil; and I recollect Mackay's telling me of a coast trader who, in order to overawe some of the natives of a village through which he passed, threatened to "*roga,*" or bewitch, them. He was immediately knocked down and murdered before he had time to carry out his dreaded purpose.

Among most African tribes, small miniature sacred huts are found; but in Buganda, large houses, called "Masabo" or "Bigwa" temples, occur constantly. Inside a "Sabo" is the "Mwaliro," a raised platform on which offerings are laid. These consist chiefly of plantains and beer; live goats are also presented, but there are, properly speaking, no sacrifices of animals. The only sacrifice I know of is the terrible holocaust of human victims called a "Kiwendo," and that awful tragedy of the burning of the thirty Christians was commonly so-called. But though they do not sacrifice goats, they send one out in a way which reminds one strongly of the Jewish scape-goat. The animal is sent away to wander where it will, and is distinguished by wearing a collar of cowrie shells. It is devoted to Lubarè, and no one will molest or kill it. What the meaning of this custom is I do not know. But though there are so many "masabo," or temples, I do not think that the people prostrate themselves within them. The king is the only object of worship and adoration, and when entering his presence, the usual salutation is "Osinze," "Thou art most high." He is also styled "Sa-basaja," controller of men.* The words for worship and adoration are numerous, such as "kusinza," to adore; "kusima," to praise; "kweanza," to thank;

* The syllable *sa* or *se* means head of or ruler, and occurs in the words "Sa-badu," head of the slaves; "Se-batimba," head of the upholsterers; "Sabakaki," chief of the great door (wankaki); "Se-bwato," head of the great canoe, &c.

"kuvunamira," to fall down to; "kufukamirira," to kneel to; "kwekulukunya," to grovel in the dust before; but the word for the worship of Lubarè is "kuwonga," which would be better translated by some English equivalent of the Latin *colere*, since the worshippers do not prostrate themselves, at least so far as my information goes.

To glance now at the people themselves. Of what race are they? They have much of the negro element about them, but they are not pure negroes. Many of them have the woolly hair and thick lips and often bridgeless noses; but many, too, have regular, almost European features, owing to their large admixture with Bahuma blood. Native Baganda vary in shade between a light and dark chocolate colour. The Bahuma, as I have elsewhere stated, are a light copper colour, and are the finest race with which the Baganda are mixed. Vast numbers of slaves of both sexes are introduced from Bunyoro, and the upper classes of that country are strongly marked with Bahuma characteristics, so that this helps to improve the Baganda stock. The next largest raiding-field for wives and slaves is Busoga on the east. The people of this country are darker than the Baganda, but are a bright intelligent race, not at all of the ideal negro type, which is confined, I imagine, to the upper Sudan and further towards the west coast. To the west of Buganda are the Basàgara, a splendid race of herdsmen, very tall and very handsome. These are the same as the Bahuma in Buganda, but of purer descent. Ankori

Y

and Koki are two semi-independent states bordering
on the west of Buganda, the people of which are prin-
cipally of the Bahuma type.   South of the province of
Budu in Buganda are the Baziba, Bazongora, and
Bajangero, dark of colour, and in this respect like the
subject race of Karagwe, who are called Banyambo.   The
upper classes of Karagwe or Banakaragwe are of the
Bahuma tribe.   But all these peoples are much mixed.
The language spoken by them is apparently that of the
Bahuma, a few words of which I have given in the
Appendix.   Further west of Karagwe lies the great
kingdom of Ruanda.   The Banaruanda are a tall and dark
race who are much feared by the Baganda; it is said
that they are governed by a queen, but information about
them is very scanty.   Stanley, in his recent letters,
mentions Mazamboni, the ruler of the district south
and west of the Albert Lake, but I never heard of him,
although the words used by his people, " kunwana," to
make friends, and " kuruwana," to make war, are two
words of the Bahuma language.

Here I need not touch upon the language at any
length as I give one or two specimens of it in the
Appendix.   Like all languages of the Bantu class, the
changes are sometimes made before and not after the
root, for example, the root of the word to give is *wa;* he
gives, *a wa;* he will give, *a li wa;* he will give it (the
knife), *a li ka wa;* he will give it him, *a li ka mu wa.*
Sometimes again the inflections are placed after the
root, as in the word *ku gula,* to buy; *gulira,* buy for

(some one else); *gulibwa*, be bought; *gulirwa*, be bought for (some one else). The peculiar inflection *ir* in the verb takes the place of a preposition; other prepositions are either separate words or prefixes.

In some cases abstract nouns are used adverbially; *agenda bubi*, he goes badness, *i.e.* he goes badly; *akola bugayavu*, he works laziness, *i.e.* he works lazily. There are a good many other distinct adverbs. The language is without aspirates, and gutteral sounds are seldom found. Adjectives are formed by taking the first syllable of the noun which they qualify and adding it to the root of the word. *Bi* is the root word meaning bad, *muti* is a tree, and *muti mubi* is a bad tree; *kalenzi* is a little boy, *kalenzi kabi* a bad little boy; *kigambo* is a word, *kigambo kibi* is a bad word. Diminutives are expressed by the prefix *ka* added to the root of the word. The word for a girl is *muwala*, *kawala* is a little girl; *musaja* is a man (male), *kasaja*, a little boy.

Plurals are formed according to the class to which the words belongs, *e.g. muntu*, man, *bantu*, men; *muti*, tree, *miti*, trees; *kigambo*, word, *bigambo*, words; *fumo*, spear, *mafumo*, spears.

The subject of the language to me is a very tempting one, but is probably not so interesting to my readers, so I must content myself with the few facts stated above. I may add, however, that curiously the pronouns in Buganda show no distinction between masculine and feminine, as there are only two genders, the masculofeminine and neuter. There was no written language before the arrival of Europeans.

The Baganda have a large number of riddles, proverbs, and fables.

Let me give one of each. The following is a riddle :—

"Omuntu alina omukazi atafluma mu nju," A man has a wife who does not go out of the house. The answer is " Olugi," a door.

This a proverb :—" Akwata empola atuka wala," He who goes gently reaches afar.

The following is one of the many Luganda fables :—

THE HARE AND THE LEOPARD.*

The hare and the leopard made blood brotherhood and went and lived in the same house. They set off to go and steal some goats. The leopard soon succeeded in securing one, but the hare went and waited in the long grass ; and while he was waiting, he saw the leopard coming with the goat, so he took a stick and beat on the ground, which so terrified the leopard that he threw down the goat and ran. The hare then took up the goat and brought it home, where he found the leopard, who had arrived some time before. Quoth the hare, as soon as he saw the leopard, " I have brought this goat." The leopard said, " For my part, I have been a long way to steal ; but, oh, my friend, the owners of the flock have given me a frightful cudgelling." " Well,

* In the Appendix the Luganda version is given, and a more literal translation.

never mind," answered the hare, "let us flay and eat
this one." So they finished their meal and went to sleep.
The next morning the hare said, "I am going to steal
in this direction." "And I," said the leopard, "will
go in that." The hare, however, did not go where he
said, but watched his companion, who soon secured a
fat goat, with which he was making his way home.
The hare ensconced himself in a thicket, and when the
leopard passed, he again beat on the ground with a stick,
and the leopard, as before, was terribly frightened, and
threw down the goat and ran. The hare now took up
the goat and brought it, but the leopard had hidden himself in the long grass and saw the hare coming with the
goat, and he understood the trick; so he sprang out and
seized the hare and tied him up and led him away with
a cord, and he came and threw him into a hole (ant
hole), and called a raven and said to her, "Guard the
prisoner while I go and fetch fire, that I may come and
burn him." When he was gone, the hare said to the
raven, "I have found some delicious ants; catch them,"
but he took earth and scattered it into her eyes. The
raven wiped her eyes, and when the earth was cleared
away, she found that the hare had escaped. She was
now very frightened, so she went and gathered some
"entengo" (colocinth apples?), and brought them and
put them into the hole. Presently the leopard arrived
with the fire, and said, "Where is the prisoner?" The
raven replied and said, "He is in the hole." The
leopard then proceeded to kindle a fire and to heap on

firewood, and the things which the raven had put into the hole exploded—ba, pu! So she said to the leopard "Do you hear the prisoner how he is exploding?" whereupon the raven escaped. The leopard now scraped away the fire and found that the hare was not in the hole.

The preceding is one of the shortest stories, most of which are fairly presentable, though some are rather wanting in delicacy. The hare is always the clever person and invariably comes off best. The Baganda fables are all, so to speak, indigenous, while the Swahili tales of Zanzibar have a strong flavour of the Arabian nights. In one of these stories, collected by the late Bishop Steere, there is a wonderful lamp, which, when lighted with the wick a certain height, produced two men, who brought gold *ad libitum* to the owner of the lamp; but if the wick were too high or too low, I know not which, the genii of the lamp brought clubs with which they belaboured its unfortunate possessor the whole night long. There is a startling resemblance here to the old Irish legend of "Bottle Hill." The story runs that a certain poor man, being unable to pay his rent, took his last cow in order to sell her at the neighbouring fair. On the way, when crossing a bridge, he encountered a strange-looking individual, who offered to buy the animal, and as payment produced an empty bottle, which he assured her owner would be greatly to his advantage. Pat believed the stranger and took the bottle which, like the Swahili lamp, produced the gold-bringing genii. However, Pat was weak enough to sell the bottle which "laid the golden eggs," and was again obliged to part with his last cow for the "rint." He sadly took his way, hoping against hope to meet the stranger, and just as he reached the bridge before mentioned, there, sure enough, was the mysterious personage who had sold the gold-bearing bottle. Trembling with eagerness, Pat addressed the stranger, "Maybe thin, yer honour hasn't another bottle?" "Faix thin, I have," said the stranger. "Och, thin take the cow," replied Pat. "And take the bottle," answered the stranger, producing an empty bottle, similar in every respect to the first. Full of eager joy, Pat hurried home and used the prescribed formula of "Bottle, do your duty," when again, like its Swahili counterpart, out came the genii with the clubs and cudgelled poor Pat, and Biddy his wife, till their bones ached. Pat, however, succeeded in getting back his first bottle by coercing his landlord, to whom he had sold it, by the clubs of the giants in bottle number two. When the hero of the story died, both bottles were broken at his wake, and so ends the veracious narrative.

As I said at the beginning of this chapter, there are so many points of interest that it is difficult to make a selection; but I may say something of the musical instruments of the Baganda. These are of three kinds: those which are blown—for example, reed flutes, pan pipes, horns, and the long necks of bottle gourds, which form trumpets.

Secondly, those which have strings, as the Buganda and Busoga banjo, though the Busoga instrument is shaped like a lyre. The Unyamwezi instrument of this type is simply a bow with an empty gourd tied on to the middle to act as a sounding-board.

And, thirdly, those which are struck, including the " madinda," a kind of harmonicon, and all kinds of drums. The harmonicon is a scale, formed by placing a row of flat pieces of board transversely on two parallel logs. The cross-pieces are cut and chipped till they give out the correct tone in the scale; they are played by being struck with sticks, and there may be either one or two performers. The effect is decidedly pleasing. I noticed a curious musical instrument in Useguha; this was a section of bamboo cut something like an organ pipe, and which, when struck vertically upon the hard ground, produced a musical note. These bamboos could be graduated according to the thickness of the reed.

But drums are by far the most important instruments which Africans use. They are made of all sizes, from the great war-drums down to the little hand-drums beaten by women. The same shape is adhered to all over East Africa, at least so far as I have seen. The drums are manufactured by taking a section of a tree, which is hollowed out and shaped like the upper part of an egg-cup; there is a narrow base below, on which the drum might stand, but they are always slung; over the open mouth of this hollow wooden shell a piece of hide is tightly stretched. Another piece is also stretched under the narrow wooden base, and the upper and lower hides are laced together with cords of narrow twisted thong. Drums are beaten upon all special occasions; war, of course, being the most important, and beer-drinking and feasting the next in order. I remember being in an Unyamwezi village when an all-night drumming service was held, accompanied by religious ceremonies. This was in preparation for a hostile expedition on the morrow; all who took part in the function had little beauty patches of white clay plastered here and there over their faces and persons. This is a sure sign of hostile intention among the Wanyamwezi.

I cannot leave the subject of music without adverting to African song. The Wanyamwezi in this respect are the most musical tribe I have met with. Native melodies are, as a rule, in minor keys and very monotonous. The iteration seems to have a soothing and pleasing effect upon the singers. Our little boys, for example, would rather sing over and over again the line, "Bona bona, bakusinza" ("All the people bow before Thee"), than go through the whole hymn. The Baganda have many songs, but most of them, I believe, unfit for repetition. One favourite childish air is called "Nakatanza." I can remember a number of our boys sitting round me in the twilight while an elder lad played this tune on the flute, another singing the words; the chorus seemed to be this word "Nakatanza" coming in again and again. It sounded very sweet and strange.

Speaking of reiteration, I remember being struck with the same feature in a Mahometan service which I witnessed for the first time at Sadaani. The worshippers —all men—came out in the moonlight to an open space in the town, having previously performed their lustrations. They were dressed in the ordinary Arab "kansu"—the long snowy cotton gown; they formed a large circle, and one, a kind of reader or reciter, stood in the middle. He repeated some words or verses to which the other worshippers responded. After a while they all took up one verse, reiterating the words over and over again, and bowing low as they uttered and emphasised the holy name, chanting as they rhythmically raised and bent their bodies, the seemingly ceaseless song, "La illāha ill' Allah Muhammadu rasul Allah."* I could not help, as I watched them, thinking of those apocalyptic worshippers who ceased not day and night. After a time, incense was brought, and the fragrant fumes went up—symbolical, I suppose, of prayer. I did not wait until the end, for I did not know whether it would have any end in reasonable time. The religion of Islam is beautiful and æsthetic, and did the inner life correspond with the outer ordinances, it would doubtless be beneficial. The holy professors of any religion are necessarily few, and perhaps one should not be disappointed at not meeting them among slave-raiding Arabs and their servile following.

In conclusion I can only briefly allude to burial

* "God is God, and Mahomet is His prophet."

customs. I have already described the method in the case of a chief: the poor and slaves are cast out to wild beasts. Mahometans always place the dead in a sort of niche or cave in the earth; the shaft is sunk, and then men stand at the bottom and at one side hollow out the earth, and the body is placed in the recess and a board is placed at the side as a door; the grave is then filled up. Wailing for the dead is common among all the tribes. Baganda women sit and rock themselves and apostrophise the corpse, crying out some such words as these, " Owe! owe! Munange! ogenze, ogenze!" (" Alas, alas! my friend, thou art gone, thou art gone.") " Owe, owe," &c. Also a shrill, sharp, shaking cry is uttered, the palm of the hand being rapidly struck upon the mouth to produce the shake. This is also used as a cry for help and is termed " striking the ' endulu.' " As a death wail, it is called " Kiwobe." At Kwa Mazengo, in Useguha, a man died while I was there, and all the female friends of the family gathered in the house, sobbing and wailing. The cry was a set and ordered arrangement like a part-song, most musical and most melancholy. The next day the dead man was carried out of the village and buried, and a cooking pot was placed over the grave. Every day for some time afterwards at midday the women collected in the house where he had died and uttered with melodious reiteration their cry of despairing sweetness.

In the next chapter I shall say something of the Bahuma or Bayima.

CHAPTER XXIV.

The Bahuma Wahuma or Bayima.

That delightful old geographer, Pomponius Mela,[*] is never more interesting than when he speaks of the marvels which travellers had related of the interior of Africa. When he ventures to repeat what others have told of the strange races and objects of wonder which are hidden in the heart of these dim regions of twilight and mystery, he does so with an air of caution but with a reverence too for statements which had reached him, which the more modern professors of his science would have summarily disposed of as nonsense, as they disposed of Mela's Fons Nili, Nichul (or Nyanza), erasing it from the latest maps before Rebman and Krapf. For my own part, I do not doubt that even his most astounding statements rest upon some actual habit or custom of the peoples of whom he speaks, though perhaps the story has been wrongly reported.

---

* A Latin geographer, who lived in the early part of the first century of our era; he was a native of Spain. His valuable work, entitled " De Situ Orbis," is divided into three parts, and contains a succinct description of the world as known to the Romans at that time. By some authorities he is supposed to have been related to Seneca and Lucan, both of whom were natives of Corduba (Cordova).

For example, the existence of pigmies or dwarfs is now beyond dispute. Dr. Junker in his travels came across these diminutive people, though indeed they were not quite so tiny as a lover of the marvellous might desire; he will no doubt give interesting particulars on this point in his book now appearing. The great traveller Stanley also speaks of being attacked by these minute though valorous warriors.

Again the saying current among the surrounding tribes, that in Buganda there are no men, which has arisen doubtless from the custom of wearing the long bark cloth robes common to both sexes might give rise to a story similar to that related by Mela, of a people whose women were so prolific that they bore children spontaneously, *sua sponte fæcundæ*, pretty much the same statement as that there were no men. Another custom of the Baganda, that of drinking the banana cider through tubes, might have given rise to the story of the people whose lips were stuck together, and who, instead of a mouth, had only a duct beneath their noses through which they drank with straws, and who when hungry could only absorb a single grain at a time of some growing fruit, soft enough I suppose to be easily drawn through the tube.

Mela, in his short general description of Africa, describes it as being bounded on the east by the Nile. And the region inhabited by the Æthiopians on the west of the Nile is reckoned by him as belonging to Asia; and both sides of the Red Sea are called Arabia, a fact which might be urged in favour of the likelihood of the Semitic descent of many of the tribes in Africa. Mela in describing particularly Asia, begins with Egypt, from whence there came a tribe of people called *Automolæ, pulchri forma,* a description applicable to the light-coloured peoples represented by the Gallas and Bahuma. But Mela also mentions "Leucoæthiopes," or white Ethiopians, so that in very early times there may have been an incursion from Arabia or Palestine of fair Semitic people into Africa, from whom, with the indigenous negroes, the Bahuma race may have sprung. Whether Africa is the original cradle of the negro race, or whether in the more remote and distant past the descendants of the accursed Canaan passed into that continent and there became developed into negroes, is an interesting if insoluble question.[*]

Speke, in his remarkable book on the discovery of the sources of the Nile, devotes part of a chapter to the history of the Wahuma, a tribe known in Unyamwezi as Watusi or Batushi, and in Buganda as Bawitu (?) There are also some interesting though brief notices of them in the letters of Emin Pasha lately published. According to Speke, the Wahuma are a branch of the Abyssinian or Galla nation who fought in the Somali country, then passed on southward to Mombasa, and from thence

---

[*] It is a curious circumstance that negro babies when born are many shades lighter than when a few weeks older. They possess also a kind of long silky hair, which they lose later on and exchange for wool.

westward to the shores of the Victoria Lake, where they settled. The attention of every one who spends a few days or even hours in Aden must be attracted by the handsome faces and wavy, not woolly, hair of the Somalis from the African coast, who in some respects resemble the Wahuma in the interior. At Mombasa the same type of face will here and there be found among the Waswahili people as well as in other of the coast towns; while in making a journey from the east coast to the Victoria Lake the same phenomenon constantly presents itself to the observer. Moreover, among the people of the ordinary negro type, unmistakable with thick lips and woolly hair, are many faces with clear-cut and well-shaped features, showing that there must have been an admixture of some foreign race with the indigenous negro. There is yet another very fine race, who possess real hair, met with to the east of Unyamwezi, called Watetura, but though as handsome as the Bahima, the type of face is different. But pure Watetura and pure Bahuma are of a very much lighter shade than the chocolate colour of the older peoples of East Africa. The Batushi found in Unyamwezi live, as the Bayima do in Buganda, in distinct and separate communities. They have come down from the neigh-bourhood of the Nyanza in recent years, so that if the immigration from the east coast, spoken of by Speke, ever took place, it must have been many ages back. When questioning the Bahuma in Buganda as to their origin, they have told me that they came from the north-east. Here perhaps I may quote what Emin Pasha says of this most interesting people :—" Unyoro once formed with Usoga, Uganda, Uddu, and Karagwe, one great country, inhabited by the Wichwèze (Bikwezi?). Then people with a white skin came from the far north-east, and crossed the river (Somerset Nile). Their number was very great, and the inhabitants were afraid of them, for the white people were " valiabantu "* (man-eaters). When the strangers had forded the river, they assembled in Matyum, a place still existing to the south-east of Mrūli, and determined to send a column to Unyoro, and another to the south (Uganda, etc.), to take possession of these countries. The intruders called themselves Wawitu, people of Witu, a name still given to the ruling families; but the people called them ' Wahuma,' men of the north; in Uganda also ' Walindi.' They were and are herdsmen, whereas the Wichwèzi were cultivators of the soil. As the Wawitu continually advanced, the Wichwèzi retired before them further to the west, many of them being drowned in the ' Mwuta Nzige ' (slayer of locusts), or Albert Lake, because they possessed no boats. The remainder were enslaved, and from their intermixture with the new-

---

* " Valiabantu." This is really two words—balia bantu, *lit.* they ate men. It is evidently a metaphor, like " kulia ensi," to eat a country ; " kulia ngoma," to eat a drum. Though cannibalism is practised in many districts in Africa, it is impossible to suppose such people as these capable of so degraded a practice.

comers sprang the present light-coloured race. Where
the immigrants have kept their race pure, they are still
quite white, as in T'oru or Gambaragara; where the
Wichwèzi have remained pure—and many of them
still wander over the country as minstrels or magicians
—they are quite black. The immigrants adopted the
language of the aborigines, but to the present day
speak among themselves the language of the Bahuma.
In Unyoro the name Wichwèzi is now synonomous
with bondsman, just as in Uganda the word "Muddu"
(inhabitant of Uddu) now denotes a slave."

There are, however, two points in the foregoing most
interesting account which require special notice and
which present some difficulty. The first is that the
light-coloured newcomers are spoken of as enslaving
the races which they conquered, and as intermarrying
with them. Now, as far as I could learn from my
conversations with the people of this tribe, slavery is
not a recognized institution among them, and as
Wilson observes in his book on Buganda, the Bahuma
are a most exclusive race, and will not marry or inter-
mix with the surrounding peoples. Possibly, like their
prototypes the children of Israel—if they be not in
truth Israelites themselves—they may have disobeyed
some Divine command to exterminate the demi-savages
whom they conquered; and as the Israelites found
their ruin in the Canaanites whom they spared, so
these Bahuma have now become contaminated by the
lower races whom they left, and have so far enriched

z

these races as to give them power in turn to become their oppressors. However this may be, they are free from the two greatest moral blots still recognised in the world—unlimited polygamy and slavery. It is certainly true that their Bakama or chiefs have several wives, and there are found also in some instances slaves among them, but, like the hardy Germans of old who hurled back the all-conquering legions of Rome, they reject slavery and its attendant evils.

Though brighter and more intelligent than the negro peoples, they are of wandering and nomadic habits, moving from place to place in search of pasture for their cattle. Unlike the low type negro they are scrupulously modest, and are clothed in dressed skins. Their huts are built in the roughest manner, and are sometimes enclosed in "zerebas" or palisades, but are more often built outside the stockade of the village to which they have attached themselves. They live apart from the other inhabitants of the country and speak a language of their own. I am inclined to think it may perhaps be the usual language of the people on the west of the Nyanza at Ihangiro and Busongora and Karagwe and Usui or Busubi. I had a lad who had been captured by a Muganda chief at Ihangiro, who could converse fluently with the Batushi herdsmen whom we encountered in Unyamwezi. This language was also used by the Bayima in Buganda, and I give a few specimens of it in the appendix. The Bahuma are essentially herdsmen. The cattle kept are usually the small species

with a hump, though larger straight backed cattle
are also found. The buffalo is never tamed; the
only animals I have seen natives make any attempt to
tame were some pigs which an Unyamwezi chief had
in his village. The Bahuma live entirely upon milk;
those of them of less pure origin eat also potatoes and
vegetables of various kinds, and in this fact one sees
the sign of the gradual change from the purely pastoral
life to the agricultural.

In Ugogo both the pastoral and agricultural manner
of life is carried on by the same people. The
Wagogo are very like the Masai, so much so that
those Masai whom I saw I could not distinguish from
Wagogo; and the former, as Mr. Thomson shows, live
entirely upon milk; the latter depend chiefly for
subsistence on their cultivation, though they keep
enormous herds of cattle. In Unyamwezi and Buganda, the Bahuma alone tend the cattle. These
people never, so far as I am aware, kill their cows
for food; they have a great affection for them; yet
when they die they eat the carcases. They have a
curious custom of bleeding their cattle, which they say
not only does them no harm but tends to fatten them.
The blood drawn is mixed with milk and boiled and
eaten. I have never seen the Bahuma adulterate their
milk in a way which Thomson describes the Wak-
avirondo as doing. Though the same, to European
taste, disagreeable custom is common at Kageye and in
Roma's country. In the latter country Mackay told me

z 2

that the higher the rank of the person, the more of the unpleasant addition was thought necessary. When I used to get milk thus adulterated at Kageye, I put aside the suspicion which passed through my mind as being what I hoped was only an idea arising from a morbid condition of health. Afterwards I found that what I feared was a most common practice. As a good general rule, one may always eat and drink what one sees natives partake of; still the unwary traveller may wake up some day to find that he has unknowingly become a cannibal, or something else nearly as unpleasant.

The Bahuma, however, flavour the milk by holding the vessel before being used over a fire made of sweepings of the cattle krààl or "Lugo." The Wagogo give the milk an even more disagreeable taste by making the fire of a strong unpleasantly-smelling wood. The cattle are always milked by the men, a woman being forbidden to touch the cow's udder. The women, however, churn the milk by holding a great bottle gourd in their lap while they sit on the ground. They rock the gourd to and fro until the butter is formed. They churn all the milk—not skimming off the cream. They do not know anything of making cheese. Bahuma children are given cattle at a very early age— the boys, at any rate—so that all the members of a family have a deep personal interest in the health and welfare of the herd. Bahuma children when quite little are betrothed to one another, and then brought up in the same household. I suppose the little girl is taken to the home of the parents of the little boy she will afterwards be married to. The advantage of this is, that they get to know one another, and are not disappointed after marriage, as is so often the case in the scratch matches in our own quarter of the globe, when the couple sometimes find one another out not to be all that they had hoped or supposed.

The wooden vessel used for milking into is called a "kyanze." It is a long cylindrical utensil, hollowed out by burning with a hot iron. It is rounded at the bottom, and rather narrower at the top than at the base. Outside it has one or two black rings burnt round it, about half an inch wide; the rest of the vessel is whitened by putting on a kind of china clay. Bahuma houses, as I mentioned before, are of a very miserable kind, being simply grass huts. The inmates sleep upon a sort of raised framework which runs round the house, the mattress being a hard cow skin, the covering a soft dressed skin. Both men and women are most scrupulously covered, and the modesty of the former is a striking and pleasing contrast to the absolute lack of it in the men of the Wanyamwezi and Wagogo and Wasukuma tribes. The Bahuma are entirely clad in skins, though they are fond of getting hold of cloth. They are great believers in witchcraft, and load themselves with charms. They plaster themselves with butter, and this gives them a disagreeable odour, which, to do them justice, unlike most Africans, they would not otherwise have. The absence of this rather unpleasant quality may mark them as not belonging to the negro race. Though they have as a rule very handsome faces, their ears are often rather prominent, but they altogether fail in their teeth. Since writing this, I observe that Mr. Thomson makes the same remark about the Masai. I have not learnt anything of the marriage customs of this singular people, but I have been informed that the condition of a Muhuma widow is a very unhappy one, and that it is common for a woman, when deprived of the prop and stay of her life, to commit suicide, hanging being the method employed. Their ideas of a hereafter seem nearly as vague as those of an ordinary dweller— say in Whitechapel, though they have some hazy idea of a deity whom they call "Lugabba," but this word is used also of a chief or any person whom they wish to flatter. They are, like most Africans, easily moved to laughter or to tears. But to my mind they have more lovable qualities than the people of any other tribe which I have encountered during my sojourn in Africa.

APPENDIX.

SOME SPECIMENS OF ONE OR TWO EASTERN AND EQUATORIAL AFRICAN LANGUAGES.

The following specimens consist of a fable and a letter in the Luganda language, and a few words taken from the languages of the Bahuma Wanyamwezi and Waseguha tribes.

The fable is that which I read to Mutesa, and with which he was considerably amused.

It runs as follows :—

WAKAYIMA NE WANGO.

Wakayima ne Wango nebata mu kago, nebabera mu nju emu. Wakayima naagenda abba embuzi, Wango naye naagenda abba embuzi. Wango embuzi naagileta Waka-yima naagenda naalindirira mu kikande. Yali aliawo, naalaba Wango nga aja ne mbuzi, naadira omugo naakuba wansi. Wango naatiya enyo naasula embuzi naaduka Wakayima neyetika embuzi naaja neyo naasanga Wango ngali mu nju. Wakayima bweyasanga Wango, naagamba nti, "ndese embuzi eno. Wango naagambe nti," nze ngenze-yo wala gyenabbye, munange, nze gyenagenzo baankubide emigo mingi. Wakayima naamugamba nti, kale tubage eno, tugirye. Nebamala okulya, nebebaka. Nate obude nebukera enkya Wakayima naagamba nti, nnada lui eno, Wango naagamba nti, nnada lui eno. Wakayima gyeyagambye okugenda naatagendayo. Naalaba nga Wango amaze okuleta embuzi. Wakayima naalindirira mu nsiko. Nate Wango naaja ne mbuzi, Wakayima naadira omugo naakuba wansi, Wango naasula embuzi, naaduka, naatiya enyo. Wakayima neyctika embuzi naagileta. Wango naalindirira mu kikande neyekweka naalaba nga Wakayima naja ne mbuzi. Wango naamukwata naamuleta ku mugwa, naaja naamusula mu bunya, naayita namung'ona naagambi nti, "kuuma omusibe ono, nkime omuliro njije mmuokye." Bweyali amaze okugenda, Wakayima naagamba namung'ona nti, "Kwako enswa," naadira etaka naamufukira mu maso, namung'ona naasangula etaka mu maso. Etaka weriyagwamu mu maso naalaba nga Wakayima aduse. Namung'ona naatiya naagenda anoga entengo naaleta naasaa mu bunya. Awo Wango naaja naagamba nti—"Omusibe aluwa?" Namung'ona naagamba nti, "Mwali ma bunya." Wango naakuma omuliro, naasaako enku. Namung'ona byatade mu bunya nebitulika ba! pu! naagamba wango nti—"Owulira omusibe bwatulika?" Nga namung'ona naaduka. Wango naatakula mu muliro naalaba nga wakayima talimu.

THE HARE AND THE LEOPARD.*

The hare and the leopard made blood brotherhood, and dwelt in one house. The hare went to steal goats, and the leopard also went to steal goats. The leopard brought

---

* Kayima means a hare, and engo a leopard. The prefix "wa" shows that the animal is personified; and so the personal pronominal prefix "a" is used with the verb. Thus, kayima kabba but wakayima abba.

a goat and the hare went and waited in the long-grass. While he was there, he saw the leopard coming with the goat, and he took a stick and beat on the ground. The leopard was terribly frightened, and threw down the goat and ran, and the hare took up the goat, and came with it and met the leopard who was in the house. The hare, when he met the leopard, said, " I have brought this goat." And the leopard said, " For my part, I went far off where I was stealing, and my friend, where I went they beat me with many blows. The hare said, " All right, we'll flay this (goat) and eat it ; " and they finished eating and went to sleep. Again, when the day dawned, the hare said, " I shall go in this direction," and the leopard said, " and I shall go in that." The hare where he said he was going, there he did not go, and he saw the leopard finish bringing a goat ; the hare waited in the thicket, and again the leopard came with a goat. The hare took a stick and beat on the ground, and the leopard threw down the goat and ran, and was terribly frightened. And the hare took up the goat and brought it. The leopard waited in the long-grass and hid himself, and saw the hare coming with the goat. And the leopard seized him and brought him with a cord (*lit.* on a cord), and he came and threw him into a pit and called a raven and said, " Guard this prisoner that I may go and fetch fire and come and burn him." When he was gone (*lit.* had finished to go), the hare said to the raven, " Receive the ants," * and he took earth and scattered it into her eyes ; the raven wiped the earth from her eyes, and when the earth was cleared away she saw that the hare had escaped. The raven was now afraid, and went

* White ants in Buganda are a great luxury. They are caught when in a winged state, and are roasted. The hare pretends that he has found some in the hole, which was an old ant's nest.

and gathered some " entengo," * and brought them and put them in the hole. Presently the leopard came and said, " Where is the prisoner ? " The raven said, " He is in the hole." The leopard then kindled a fire and put on fire-wood, and the things which the raven had put into the hole exploded " ba pu ! " and she said to the leopard, " Do you hear the prisoner, how he is exploding ? " Whereupon the raven escaped. The leopard now scraped away the fire and he found the hare was not inside.

I next give a letter written to me by Kizito, one of the members of the Buganda Native Church Council; it will give some idea of the way these people express themselves.

This unfortunately is the only letter which I have by me ; and so I have no choice, though it is by no means the best that I have received.

Natete, Buganda,
Jun 22, 1888.

SEBO kitange Bwana Ashe otyano munafe tulumibwa omoyo nga obubalagaze bwe kiwundu kyo fumu mu kutu. Jukira nga otwagala enyo nyini abanabo bozala mu dini ya Isa Masiya, nze omwanawo omuganze enyo asinga, nze Zakariya Kizito, nze mpandise ebaruwa eno.

Otyano? Gwe omubili gwange, amagumba gange omusayi gwange, amagumba gange, amagezi gange. Nkulamusidza, otyano baba, sebo, kitange. Nkubulire omwanawo omuganze, Bajalirwa Yonatani yafwa. Kaum-puli yamutta, yalwalira enaku satu naafwa.

Ne Mwemba alye Kasubi yafwa. Mugema gwebawa ekasubi yaliyo, ne wafwo nkyaliyo tebangoba. Sebo ne Mwemba omulamu asoma bulungi nokwagala abantu.

---

* Entengo is a wild and poisonous fruit, perhaps the colocinth. It is very like the things which grow upon ripe potato plants.

Nange nagendayo okumulaba nokumutwalira ekitabu "Agano jipya" nanjagala nyo nyini nampa ne kitibwa okyesagala ekitansanide, nampa ekita kyo mwenge, nendeku emu. Nebareta emere ne bibya bye nva bisatu nadira ebibya bye nva byona ature nampa ye omwami omukulu adilira Mukwenda asinga ne bakulungi (nabo kulungi) obunene nakoleza kundagala nganze nkoleza mu bibya nga ne nsonyi zingwata, nampayo nente eyo bubaka Bwana. Bwana Gordon yeyantuma okumutwalira ekitabu ne "Enjatula" zewatuletera Munafwe.

Oluvanyuma yali amuwereza Bwana ente nga eliko ne nyana. Ababaka nebagyamuko nga bajireta mu kubo nga jigya mu kyaro naye yalimu mu kyaro. Ababaka bali babatumye ewuwe kumutwalira Bugabe nga bamugambye okutabala ebunyoro. Ye mugabe kakano, bali Bunyoro Mwezi guno June mwebagendera.

Baba sebo nate ne Katonda tumutendereze nyo nyini dala kyenvude ng'amba bwentyo ndabye ekigambo kino ekinene. Kauta eyaturopanga bulijo, lero enaku zino asoma kyama alifu. Yohana Bunjo yamusomesa amwagala nyo nyini yamugana okumwanjula ewuwe nti nowonsa— nganga nga nebase omalanga kulaba nga nebakide dala nalyoka odayo.

Sebo ebyo byenkubulide ebifa ewafwe sebo, bino bye bino ebigambo bya salamu nze muno akwagala enyo akusabira bulijo mu maso ga, Katonda bulijo, kuku jukira mu kusaba kwange ninkusabira bulijo kuba buli baluwa gyempandika kano ke kabonero okuwakana ne banange bona bwetukwagala. Ndowoza nti nze nsinga, wabula okulekayo abakade abaakuzala bombi ebulaya be bansinga abo, kuba oli musayi gwabwe. Nkulamusidza. Katonda akukume akuwe no mukisa ne milembe ne kisa no kawagala kwa mukama wafe Isa Masiya wamu no Moyo Mutukuvu. Banange mwalaba ekitalo banange, banafwe okufwa bombine naku ezimu, nabasaasira nyo. Mbala-musidza.

Nze Zakariya Kizito.

Natete, Buganda,
June 22, 1888.

Sir, my father, Mister Ashe, how are you? Our friend, we are cut to the heart with pain, as of the wound of a spear in the ear (*i.e.* we are grieved at bad news). Remember that you love us very much, your children whom you have begotten in the religion of Jesus Christ. I am your child, your greatest favourite—I am Zakariah Kizito, I have written this letter.

How are you? You are my body, my bones, my blood, my bones, my reason. I greet you! How are you, mister, sir, my father? Let me inform you that your child, the favourite, Bajalirwa Yonatani is dead; Kaumpuli (the plague) killed him, he was ill three days and died.

And Muwemba who was at Kasubi is dead. Mugema, whom they gave Kasubi, is still living. I am still at our place, they have not driven me away. Sir, Muwemba is alive and reads well, and is a good man (one who loves men). I went there to see him, and to take him a book—the New Testament. He was very well disposed towards me, and gave me honour which I did not desire, and of which I am unworthy. He gave me a "kita" bottle gourd of "Mwenge" (banana cider), and one cup; they also brought mashed plantains and three dishes of vege-tables, and he took all the dishes of vegetables that he might sit and serve me himself, even he, the chief, the highest next to Mukwenda. And he dipped his morsel in the leaf as I dipped mine in the dishes, while shamo possessed me. And he gave me a cow as Mr. Gordon's messenger, who had sent me to take him a book

and the "Enjatula," * which you, our friend, brought
for us. Afterwards he sent Mister (Gordon) a cow with
a calf; the messengers took it and brought it on the way,
having got it from the country place.

And he is now at his country place. They have sent
messengers to him to take him his commission as commander-in-chief, and have ordered him to raid Bunyoro;
and so he is by this time commander-in-chief, and they
are in Bunyoro, whither they have gone this month, June.

Mister sir, again let us praise God exceedingly much.
I must thus tell you that I have seen an important matter.
Kawuta (chief cook), who used to inform on us every day,
now these days is learning the letters in secret. John
Bunjo is teaching him—he likes him exceedingly, and
does not allow him to open his door to any one (saying)
" You find me sleeping, you see me sleeping soundly," that
he (the intruder) may go away again.

Sir, these things which I have told you have taken
place here where we are. Sir, these are words of salutation—I am your friend who loves you exceedingly, who
prays for you daily in the presence of God. Daily do
I remember you in my prayers, and I pray for you always,
for every letter which I write this is a sign. There is a
dispute with all my companions how much we love you.
I consider that I do most, excepting and leaving out of
the question both your parents in Europe, who were the
authors of your existence; † they excel me, indeed, because
they are your blood. I greet you, God guard you and
give you blessing and peace and mercy, and the love of

* "Enjatula," I confess, first word in a book of prayers which
the Church Missionary Society had sent out by me.

† "Authors of existence," a "vile phrase;" but in Luganda the
word "kuzala" (to bear) is used of both parents, and I do not
know any equivalent in English.

our Lord Jesus Christ together with the Holy Ghost. My friends,* you have had a terrible blow, the death of both our friends,† and it is a cause of grief; I sympathise much with you. I greet you both. I am,

ZAKARIYA KIZITO.

THE LANGUAGE OF THE BAHUMA AND BAGANDA COMPARED.

BAHUMA.	ENGLISH.	BAGANDA.
Kujeyenda	to go	kugenda
Kuwheta	to call	kuita
Kuiruka	to run	kuduka. But I run = nziruka
Kwanga	to hate	kukyawa
Kutehemba	to climb	kulinya
Muhanga	God or sun	muhanga = mwanga
Kazoba	sun	enjuba
Kusthama	to sit	kutula
Kugamba	to say	kugamba
Kulamushya	to salute	kulamusa
Kuirira	to cry	kukaaba
Kusheka	to laugh	kuseka
Kuwaga	to hunt	kuyiga; but the word for the dead game is buswago
Entama	a sheep	endiga
Lugayo	come	jangu
Kugaruha	to return	kukomao
Kuruwana	to fight	kuruwana
Kunwana	to make friends	kukwana
Lukwhera	white man	mweru
Lukwiragura	black man	mudugavu
Ishoki	hair	mviri

* Mackay and myself.
† Bishop Parker and Rev. J. Blackburn.

BAHUMA.	ENGLISH.	BAGANDA.
Maisho	eyes	maso
Rurimi	tongue	lulimi
Ebyara	nails	enjala
Ekirezhu	chin	ekirevu
Kutekereza	to consider—think	kulowoza
Kuroka	to dream	kulota
Kubyama	to sleep	kwebaka
Kugarama	to stretch oneself	
Lugalama	proper name	
Kitabo	bedstead	kiriri
Muriro	fire	muliro
Kuzuwara	to dress (oneself)	kuyambala
Kubinga	to drive	kugoba
Kuzumbuka	stampede of wild beasts	kufubutuka
Kukina	to gallop (of cow)	
Kuzuga	to low	
Entale	a lion	emporogoma
Kusinda	to roar	
Kuwoga	to wash	kunaba
Kuzina	to sing	kuyimba
Kubina	to dance	kuzina
Kwiza	to come	kuja
Kutera	to beat	kukuba
Kuiba	to steal	kubba
Kusuwera	to be married of woman	kufumbirwa
Kwesengereza	to beseech	kwegairira
Kuwombeha	to build	kuzimba
Buta	arrows	
Kulesa?	to smoke	kunyuwa
Mwika	smoke	muka
Muwozo	lad	mulenzi
Kutora tora	to choose	kulonda
Bikya	throat	bulago
Kutanaka	to vomit	kusesima
Ruhu	a skin	diba
Kusura orairote?	How do you do?	Kulungi wasuzotya?
Osibirotai?		Oliawo?
Ogendege?	Are you going?	Ogenda?

BAHUMA.	ENGLISH:	BAGANDA.
Mwikalege !	Sit awhile !	Tulawo !
Ija hanu	Come here	Jangu wano ?
Kanyije	I'm coming	Kanjije.
Ikalaha !	Sit here !	Tula wano !
Norugankai ?	Where have you come from ?	Ovwa wa ?
Ndugire hale	I have come from far.	Mvude wala.
Noyenda ki hanu ?	What do you want here ?	Oyagala ki wano ?
Nyenda kunwana na ingwe	I want to make friends with you.	Njagala kukwana namwe.
Nyenda kubagambira bigambo birungi	I want to tell you good words.	Njagala kubagamba bigambo birungi.
Bigambo ki ?	What words ?	Bigambo ki ?
Ingwe mulisa ente?	Do you herd cows ?	Mwe mulunda ente ?
Tulisa nyingi	We herd many.	Tulunda nyingi.
Ebiro byona mukama kangahe ?	How often do you milk, every day ?	Bulijo mirundi meka mulamula ?
Tukama ebiro byona kabiri	We milk twice every day.	Tulamula bulijo mirundi biri.
Mu nsi yenyu ziriho entale ?	Are there lions in your country ?	Munsi yenu ziriwo emporogoma ?
Zikwata ente zenyu ?	Do they seize your cattle ?	Zikwata ente zamwe ?
Mu nsi yenu bashaja bakira bakazi ?	In your country do the men exceed in numbers the women ?	Mu nsi yamwe basaja bakira bakazi ?
Ekintu kino nenki ?	What is this thing ?	Ekintu kino ki ?
Abaana bojua	boys	abaana balenzi
Mwishki	girl	muwala
Baba nyenda awo kubyama	Mother, I want a place to sleep	Nyabo njagala wensule.
Ija obyame hanu	Come and sleep here.	Jangu osule wano.
Tata ninkwenda muno	My friend, I love you much.	Baba nkwagala enyo.

The word "baba" means father in Swahili. In Buganda it is a sexless word of respect, meaning friend. The Bahuma use it for mother.

"Kwenda" is to love in the Luhuma language; but in the Luganda it means to commit fornication.

And there are not a few words which in one language are perfectly proper, but which in another are exceedingly the reverse.

THE LANGUAGES OF UNYAMWEZI AND USEGUHA COMPARED.

I give a few words from these two languages,—

WANYAMWEZI.	ENGLISH.	WASEGUHA.
Kutwe	ear	gutwe
Nindo	nose	pula
Liso	eye	giso
Hawushu	forehead	kihanga
Bere	breast	tombo
pl. Mabere	breasts	*pl.* matombo
Kikuba	chest	kifuwa
Munda	stomach	ifu
Mutwe	head	itwe
Ikundi	navel	duo
Muhingo	throat	kongomero
Mulundi	shin	
Igumbiso	eyebrow	kumbito
Matango	thighs	mawambo
Isaku	calf of leg	kijumbulo
Engohye	eyelash	engohye
Hingo	back of neck	shingo
Isumbi	stool	fumbi
Lushu	knife	ngora
Budidi	bed	usazi
Igolo	to-morrow	mutondo
Bunduchi	gun	futi
Holo	sheep	ngoro
Mugosha	man (male)	mugasu
Mukima	woman	muvele
Kayanda	lad	kibangeki
Mwanike	girl	kindere
Kulala	to sleep	kugona
Kut'hula	to beat	kufidula

2 A

WANYAMWEZI.	ENGLISH.	WASEGUHA.
Ligi	door	bakwa
Kupera	to run	ku guluka
Kutogwa	to love	kukunda
Kulema	to refuse	(ku)sibera
Kupeza	to drive away	kulima
Kukora mirimu	to work	kudamanya
Zugu henaha	come here	so kuno

Salutations.

Wangaluka	good morning	nihede, kirovede
Wazubuku		nikyede
Wapanga ?		ogonire ?
Wadira	good afternoon	mwenda

LONDON: PRINTED BY WILLIAM CLOWES AND SONS, LIMITED,
STAMFORD STREET AND CHARING CROSS.

A Catalogue of American and Foreign Books Published or
Imported by MESSRS. SAMPSON LOW & CO. can
be had on application.

St. Dunstan's House, Fetter Lane, Fleet Street, London,
September, 1888.

A Selection from the List of Books

PUBLISHED BY

SAMPSON LOW, MARSTON, SEARLE, & RIVINGTON,

LIMITED.

ALPHABETICAL LIST.

ABBOTT (C. C.) Poaetquissings Chronicle. 10s. 6d.

———— *Waste Land Wanderings.* Crown 8vo, 7s. 6d.

Abney (W. de W.) and Cunningham. Pioneers of the Alps.
With photogravure portraits of guides. Imp. 8vo, gilt top, 21s.

Adam (G. Mercer) and Wetherald. An Algonquin Maiden.
Crown 8vo, 5s.

Adams (C. K.) Manual of Historical Literature. Cr. 8vo, 12s. 6d.

Agassiz (A.) Three Cruises of the Blake. Illustrated. 2 vols.,
8vo, 42s.

Alcott. Works of the late Miss Louisa May Alcott :—
Eight Cousins. Illustrated, 2s.; cloth gilt, 3s. 6d.
Jack and Jill. Illustrated, 2s.; cloth gilt, 3s. 6d.
Jo's Boys. 5s.
Jimmy's Cruise in the Pinafore, &c. Illustrated, cloth, 2s.; gilt edges,
3s. 6d.
Little Men. Double vol., 2s.; cloth, gilt edges, 3s. 6d.
Little Women. 1s. ⎫ 1 vol., cloth, 2s. ; larger ed., gilt
Little Women Wedded. 1s. ⎬ edges, 3s. 6d.
Old-fashioned Girl. 2s.; cloth, gilt edges, 3s. 6d.
Rose in Bloom. 2s.; cloth gilt, 3s. 6d.
Silver Pitchers. Cloth, gilt edges, 3s. 6d.
Under the Lilacs. Illustrated, 2s.; cloth gilt, 5s.
Work: a Story of Experience. 1s. ⎫ 1 vol., cloth, gilt
———— Its Sequel, "Beginning Again." 1s. ⎬ edges, 3s. 6d.

Alden (W. L.) Adventures of Jimmy Brown, written by himself.
Illustrated. Small crown 8vo, cloth, 2s.

Aldrich (T. B.) Friar Jerome's Beautiful Book, &c. 3s. 6d.

Alford (Lady Marian) Needlework as Art. With over 100
Woodcuts, Photogravures, &c. Royal 8vo, 21s. ; large paper, 84s.

Amateur Angler's Days in Dove Dale : Three Weeks' Holiday
in 1884. By E. M. 1s. 6d. ; boards, 1s. ; large paper, 5s.

Andersen. Fairy Tales. An entirely new Translation. With over 500 Illustrations by Scandinavian Artists. Small 4to, 6s.

Anderson (W.) Pictorial Arts of Japan. With 80 full-page and other Plates, 16 of them in Colours. Large imp. 4to, £8 8s. (in four folio parts, £2 2s. each); Artists' Proofs, £12 12s.

Angler's Strange Experiences (An). By COTSWOLD ISYS. With numerous Illustrations, 4to, 5s. New Edition, 3s. 6d.

Angling. See Amateur, "British," "Cutcliffe," "Fennell," "Halford," "Hamilton," "Martin," "Orvis," "Pennell," "Pritt," "Senior," "Stevens," "Theakston," "Walton," "Wells," and "Willis-Bund."

*Annals of the Life of Shakespeare, from the most recent authori-*ties. Fancy boards, 2s.

Annesley (C.) Standard Opera Glass. Detailed Plots of 80 Operas. Small 8vo, sewed, 1s. 6d.

Antipodean Notes, collected on a Nine Months' Tour round the World. By Wanderer, Author of "Fair Diana." Crown 8vo, 7s. 6d.

Appleton. European Guide. 2 Parts, 8vo, 10s. each.

Armytage (Hon. Mrs.) Wars of Victoria's Reign. 5s.

Art Education. See "Biographies," "D'Anvers," "Illustrated Text Books," "Mollett's Dictionary."

Artistic Japan. Illustrated with Coloured Plates. Monthly. Royal 4to, 2s.

Attwell (Prof.) The Italian Masters. Crown 8vo, 3s. 6d.

Audsley (G. A.) Handbook of the Organ. Top edge gilt, 42s.; large paper, 84s.

—— *Ornamental Arts of Japan.* 90 Plates, 74 in Colours and Gold, with General and Descriptive Text. 2 vols., folio, £15 15s.; in specially designed leather, £23 2s.

—— *The Art of Chromo-Lithography.* Coloured Plates and Text. Folio, 63s.

—— *and Tomkinson. Ivory and Wood Carvings of Japan.* 84s. Artists' proofs (100), 168s.

Auerbach (B.) Brigitta. (B. Tauchnitz Collection.) 2s.

—— *On the Heights.* 3 vols., 6s.

—— *Spinoza.* 2 vols., 18mo, 4s.

BADDELEY (S.) Tchay and Chianti. Small 8vo, 5s.

Baldwin (James) Story of Siegfried. 6s

—— *Story of the Golden Age.* Illustrated by HOWARD PYLE. Crown 8vo, 6s.

Baldwin (James) Story of Roland. Crown 8vo, 6s.

Bamford (A. J.) Turbans and Tails. Sketches in the Unromantic East. Crown 8vo, 7s. 6d.

Barlow (Alfred) Weaving by Hand and by Power. With several hundred Illustrations. Third Edition, royal 8vo, £1 5s.

Barlow (P. W.) Kaipara, Experiences of a Settler in N. New Zealand. Illust., crown 8vo, 6s.

Barrow (J.) Mountain Ascents in Cumberland and Westmore- land. Crown 8vo, 7s. 6d.; new edition, 5s.

Bassett (F. S.) Legends and Superstitions of the Sea. 7s. 6d.

THE BAYARD SERIES.

Edited by the late J. HAIN FRISWELL.

Comprising Pleasure Books of Literature produced in the Choicest Style.

"We can hardly imagine better books for boys to read or for men to ponder over."—*Times.*

Price 2s. 6d. each Volume, complete in itself, flexible cloth extra, gilt edges, with silk Headbands and Registers.

The Story of the Chevalier Bayard.
Joinville's St. Louis of France.
The Essays of Abraham Cowley.
Abdallah. By Edouard Laboullaye.
Napoleon, Table-Talk and Opinions.
Words of Wellington.
Johnson's Rasselas. With Notes.
Hazlitt's Round Table.
The Religio Medici, Hydriotaphia, &c. By Sir Thomas Browne, Knt.
Coleridge's Christabel, &c. With Preface by Algernon C. Swinburne.
Ballad Poetry of the Affections. By Robert Buchanan.
Lord Chesterfield's Letters, Sentences, and Maxims. With Essay by Sainte-Beuve.
The King and the Commons. Cavalier and Puritan Songs.
Vathek. By William Beckford.
Essays in Mosaic. By Ballantyne.
My Uncle Toby; his Story and his Friends. By P. Fitzgerald.
Reflections of Rochefoucauld.
Socrates: Memoirs for English Readers from Xenophon's Memorabilia. By Edw. Levien.
Prince Albert's Golden Precepts.

A Case containing 12 Volumes, price 31s. 6d ; or the Case separately, price 3s. 6d.

Baynes (Canon) Hymns and other Verses. Crown 8vo, sewed, 1s.; cloth, 1s. 6d.

Beaugrand (C.) Walks Abroad of Two Young Naturalists. By D. SHARP. Illust., 8vo, 7s. 6d.

Beecher (H. W.) Authentic Biography, and Diary. [*Preparing*

Behnke and Browne. Child's Voice : its Treatment with regard to After Development, Small 8vo, 3s. 6d.

Beyschlag. Female Costume Figures of various Centuries. 12 reproductions of pastel designs in portfolio, imperial. 21s.

Bickersteth (Bishop E. H.) Clergyman in his Home. 1s.

—— *Evangelical Churchmanship.* 1s.

A 2

Bickersteth (Bishop E. H.) From Year to Year: Original Poetical Pieces. Small post 8vo, 3s. 6d. ; roan, 6s. and 5s.; calf or morocco, 10s. 6d.

———— *The Master's Home-Call.* 20th Thous. 32mo, cloth gilt, 1s.

———— *The Master's Will.* A Funeral Sermon preached on the Death of Mrs. S. Gurney Buxton. Sewn, 6d. ; cloth gilt, 1s.

———— *The Reef, and other Parables.* Crown 8vo, 2s. 6d.

———— *Shadow of the Rock.* Select Religious Poetry. 2s. 6d.

———— *The Shadowed Home and the Light Beyond.* 5s.

*Bigelow (John) France and the Confederate Navy. An Inter-*national Episode. 7s. 6d.

Biographies of the Great Artists (Illustrated). Crown 8vo, emblematical binding, 3s. 6d. per volume, except where the price is given.

Claude le Lorrain, by Owen J. Dullea.	Mantegna and Francia.
Correggio, by M. E. Heaton. 2s. 6d.	Meissonier, by J. W. Mollett. 2s. 6d.
Della Robbia and Cellini. 2s. 6d.	Michelangelo Buonarotti, by Clément.
Albrecht Dürer, by R. F. Heath.	Murillo, by Ellen E. Minor. 2s. 6d.
Figure Painters of Holland.	Overbeck, by J. B. Atkinson.
Fra Angelico, Masaccio, and Botticelli.	Raphael, by N. D'Anvers.
Fra Bartolommeo, Albertinelli, and Andrea del Sarto.	Rembrandt, by J. W. Mollett.
Gainsborough and Constable.	Reynolds, by F. S. Pulling.
Ghiberti and Donatello. 2s. 6d.	Rubens, by C. W. Kett.
Giotto, by Harry Quilter.	Tintoretto, by W. R. Osler.
Hans Holbein, by Joseph Cundall.	Titian, by R. F. Heath.
Hogarth, by Austin Dobson.	Turner, by Cosmo Monkhouse.
Landseer, by F. G. Stevens.	Vandyck and Hals, by P. R. Head.
Lawrence and Romney, by Lord Ronald Gower. 2s. 6d.	Velasquez, by E. Stowe.
Leonardo da Vinci.	Vernet and Delaroche, by J. Rees.
Little Masters of Germany, by W. B. Scott.	Watteau, by J. W. Mollett. 2s. 6d.
	Wilkie, by J. W. Mollett.

Bird (F. J.) American Practical Dyer's Companion. 8vo, 42s.

———— *(H. E.) Chess Practice.* 8vo, 2s. 6d.

Black (Robert) Horse Racing in France : a History. 8vo, 14s.

Black (Wm.) Novels. See " Low's Standard Library."

———— *Strange Adventures of a House-Boat.* 3 vols., 31s. 6d.

———— *In Far Lochaber.* 3 vols., crown 8vo., 31s. 6d.

Blackburn (Charles F.) Hints on Catalogue Titles and Index Entries, with a Vocabulary of Terms and Abbreviations, chiefly from Foreign Catalogues. Royal 8vo, 14s.

Blackburn (Henry) Breton Folk. With 171 Illust. by RANDOLPH CALDECOTT. Imperial 8vo, gilt edges, 21s.; plainer binding, 10s. 6d.

———— *Pyrenees.* Illustrated by GUSTAVE DORÉ, corrected to 1881. Crown 8vo, 7s. 6d. See also CALDECOTT.

Blackmore (R. D.) Lorna Doone. *Édition de luxe.* **Crown 4to,** very numerous Illustrations, cloth, gilt edges, 31*s.* 6*d.*; parchment, uncut, top gilt, 35*s.*; new issue, plainer, 21*s.*; small post 8vo, 6*s.*

—————— *Novels.* See "Low's Standard Library."

—————— *Springhaven.* Illust. by PARSONS and BARNARD. Sq. 8vo, 12*s.*

Blaikie (William) How to get Strong and how to Stay so. Rational, Physical, Gymnastic, &c., Exercises. Illust., sm. post 8vo, 5*s.*

—————— *Sound Bodies for our Boys and Girls.* 16mo, 2*s.* 6*d.*

Bonwick. British Colonies. Asia, 1*s.*; Africa, 1*s.*; America, 1*s.*; Australasia, 1*s.* One vol., cloth, 5*s.*

Bosanquet (Rev. C.) Blossoms from the King's Garden : Sermons for Children. 2nd Edition, small post 8vo, cloth extra, 6*s.*

—————— *Jehoshaphat ; or, Sunlight and Clouds.* 1*s.*

Boussenard (L.) Crusoes of Guiana. Gilt, 2*s.* 6*d.*; gilt ed , 3*s.* 6*d.*

—————— *Gold-seekers.* Sequel to the above. Illust. 16mo, 5*s.*

Boyesen (F.) Story of Norway. Illustrated, sm. 8vo, 7*s.* 6*d.*

Boyesen (H. H.) Modern Vikings : Stories of Life and Sport in Norseland. Cr. 8vo, 6*s.*

Boy's Froissart. King Arthur. Knightly Legends of Wales. Percy. See LANIER.

Bradshaw (J.) New Zealand of To-doy, 1884-87. 8vo.

Brannt (W. T.) Animal and Vegetable Fats and Oils. 244 Illust., 8vo, 35*s.*

—————— *Manufacture of Soap and Candles, with many Formulas.* Illust., 8vo, 35*s.*

—————— *Metallic Alloys. Chiefly from the German of Krupp* and Wilberger. Crown 8vo, 12*s.* 6*d.*

Bright (John) Public Letters. **Crown 8vo,** 7*s.* 6*d.*

Brisse (Baron) Ménus (366). A *ménu,* in French and English, for every Day in the Year. 2nd Edition. Crown 8vo, 5*s.*

British Fisheries Directory. Small 8vo, 2*s.* 6*d.*

Brittany. See BLACKBURN.

Browne (G. Lennox) Voice Use and Stimulants. Sm. 8vo, 3*s.* 6*d.*

—————— *and Behnke (Emil) Voice, Song, and Speech.* N. ed., 5*s.*

Bryant (W. C.) and Gay (S. H.) History of the United States. 4 vols., royal 8vo, profusely Illustrated, 60*s.*

Bryce (Rev. Professor) Manitoba. Illust. **Crown 8vo,** 7*s.* 6*d.*

—————— *Short History of the Canadian People.* 7*s.* 6*d.*

Burnaby (Capt.) On Horseback through Asia Minor. **2 vols.,** 8vo, 38*s.* Cheaper Edition, 1 vol., crown 8vo, 10*s.* 6*d.*

Burnaby (Mrs. F.) High Alps in Winter; or, Mountaineering in Search of Health. With Illustrations, &c., 14*s*. See also MAIN.

Burnley (J.) History of Wool and Woolcombing. Illust. 8vo, 21*s*.

Burton (Sir R. F.) Early, Public, and Private Life. Edited by F. HITCHMAN. 2 vols., 8vo, 36*s*.

Butler (Sir W. F.) Campaign of the Cataracts. Illust., 8vo, 18*s*.

—————— *Invasion of England, told twenty years after.* 2*s*. 6*d*.

—————— *Red Cloud; or, the Solitary Sioux.* Imperial 16mo, numerous illustrations, gilt edges, 3*s*. 6*d*.; plainer binding, 2*s*. 6*d*.

—————— *The Great Lone Land; Red River Expedition.* 7*s*. 6*d*.

—————— *The Wild North Land; the Story of a Winter Journey* with Dogs across Northern North America. 8vo, 18*s*. Cr. 8vo, 7*s*. 6*d*.

CABLE (G. W.) Bonaventure: A Prose Pastoral of Acadian Louisiana. Sm. post 8vo, 5*s*.

Cadogan (Lady A.) Illustrated Games of Patience. Twenty-four Diagrams in Colours, with Text. Fcap. 4to, 12*s*. 6*d*.

—————— *New Games of Patience.* Coloured Diagrams, 4to, 12*s*.6*d*.

Caldecott (Randolph) Memoir. By HENRY BLACKBURN. With 170 Examples of the Artist's Work. 14*s*.; large paper, 21*s*.

California. See NORDHOFF.

Callan (H.) Wanderings on Wheel and on Foot. Cr. 8vo, 1*s*. 6*d*.

Campbell (Lady Colin) Book of the Running Brook: and of Still Waters. 5*s*.

Canadian People: Short History. Crown 8vo, 7*s*. 6*d*.

Carleton (Will) Farm Ballads, Farm Festivals, and Farm Legends. Paper boards, 1*s*. each; 1 vol., small post 8vo, 3*s*. 6*d*.

—————— *City Ballads.* Illustrated, 12*s*. 6*d*. New Ed. (Rose Library), 16mo, 1*s*.

Carnegie (A.) American Four-in-Hand in Britain. Small 4to, Illustrated, 10*s*. 6*d*. Popular Edition, paper, 1*s*.

—————— *Round the World.* 8vo, 10*s*. 6*d*.

—————— *Triumphant Democracy.* 6*s*.; also 1*s*. 6*d*. and 1*s*.

Chairman's Handbook. By R. F. D. PALGRAVE. 5th Edit., 2*s*.

Changed Cross, &c. Religious Poems. 16mo, 2*s*. 6*d*.; calf, 6*s*.

Chaplin (J. G.) Three Principles of Book-keeping. 2*s*. 6*d*.

Charities of London. See Low's.

Chattock (R. S.) Practical Notes on Etching. New Ed. 8vo, 10*s*. 6*d*.

Chess. See BIRD (H. E.).

Children's Praises. Hymns for Sunday-Schools and Services. Compiled by LOUISA H. H. TRISTRAM. 4*d*.

Choice Editions of Choice Books. 2*s*. 6*d*. each. Illustrated by C. W. COPE, R.A., T. CRESWICK, R.A., E. DUNCAN, BIRKET FOSTER, J. C. HORSLEY, A.R.A., G. HICKS, R. REDGRAVE, R.A., C. STONEHOUSE, F. TAYLER, G. THOMAS, H. J. TOWNSHEND, E. H. WEHNERT, HARRISON WEIR, &c.

Bloomfield's Farmer's Boy.	Milton's L'Allegro.
Campbell's Pleasures of Hope.	Poetry of Nature. Harrison Weir.
Coleridge's Ancient Mariner.	Rogers' (Sam.) Pleasures of Memory.
Goldsmith's Deserted Village.	Shakespeare's Songs and Sonnets.
Goldsmith's Vicar of Wakefield.	Tennyson's May Queen.
Gray's Elegy in a Churchyard.	Elizabethan Poets.
Keat's Eve of St. Agnes.	Wordsworth's Pastoral Poems.

"Such works are a glorious beatification for a poet."—*Athenæum*.

Chreiman (Miss) Physical Culture of Women.   A Lecture at the Parkes Museum.   Small 8vo, 1*s*.

Christ in Song.   By PHILIP SCHAFF.   New Ed., gilt edges, 6*s*.

Chromo-Lithography.   See AUDSLEY.

Cochran (W.) Pen and Pencil in Asia Minor.   Illust., 8vo, 21*s*.

Collingwood (Harry) Under the Meteor Flag.   The Log of a Midshipman.   Illustrated, small post 8vo, gilt, 3*s*. 6*d*.; plainer, 2*s*. 6*d*.

———— *Voyage of the " Aurora."*   Gilt, 3*s*. 6*d*. ; plainer, 2*s*. 6*d*.

Cook (Dutton) Book of the Play.   New Edition.   1 vol., 3*s*. 6*d*.

———— *On the Stage : Studies.*   2 vols., 8vo, cloth, 24*s*.

Cowen (Jos., M.P.) Life and Speeches.   8vo, 14*s*.

Cowper (W.) Poetical Works : A Concordance.   Roy. 8vo, 21*s*.

Cozzens (F.) American Yachts.   27 Plates, 22 × 28 inches. Proofs, £21 ; Artist's Proofs, £31 10*s*.

Crew (B. J.) Practical Treatise on Petroleum.   Illust., 8vo, 28*s*.

Crouch (A. P.) On a Surf-bound Coast.   Crown 8vo, 7*s*. 6*d*.

Crown Prince of Germany : a Diary.   2*s*. 6*d*.

Cudworth (W.) Life and Correspondence of Abraham Sharp. Illustrated from Drawings.   (To Subscribers, 21*s*.) 26*s*.

Cumberland (Stuart) Thought Reader's Thoughts.   Cr. 8vo., 10*s*. 6*d*.

———— *Queen's Highway from Ocean to Ocean.*   Ill., 8vo, 18*s*. ; new ed., 7*s*. 6*d*.

Cundall (Joseph) Annals of the Life and Work of Shakespeare. With a List of Early Editions.   3*s*. 6*d*. ; large paper, 5*s*.; also 2*s*.

———— *Remarkable Bindings in the British Museum.*

Curtis (W. E.) Capitals of Spanish America..   Illust., roy. 8vo.

Cushing (W.) Initials and Pseudonyms.   Large 8vo, 25*s*. ; second series, large 8vo, 21*s*.

Custer (Eliz. B.) Tenting on the Plains; Gen. Custer in Kansas and Texas. Royal 8vo, 18s.

Cutcliffe (H. C.) Trout Fishing in Rapid Streams. Cr. 8vo, 3s. 6d.

DALY (Mrs. D.) Digging, Squatting, and Pioneering in Northern South Australia. 8vo, 12s.

D'Anvers. Elementary History of Art. New ed., 360 illus., cr. 8vo, 2 vols. (5s. each), gilt, 10s. 6d.

—— *Elementary History of Music.* Crown 8vo, 2s. 6d.

Davidson (H. C.) Old Adam; Tale of an Army Crammer. 3 vols. crown 8vo, 31s. 6d.

Davis (Clement) Modern Whist. 4s.

Davis (C. T.) Bricks, Tiles, Terra-Cotta, &c. Ill. 8vo, 25s.

—— *Manufacture of Leather.* With many Illustrations. 52s. 6d.

—— *Manufacture of Paper.* 28s.

Davis (G. B.) Outlines of International Law. 8vo. 10s. 6d.

Dawidowsky. Glue, Gelatine, Isinglass, Cements, &c. 8vo, 12s. 6d.

Day of My Life at Eton. By an ETON BOY. 16mo. 2s. 6d.

Day's Collacon: an Encyclopædia of Prose Quotations. Imperial 8vo, cloth, 31s. 6d.

De Leon (E.) Under the Stars and under the Crescent. N. ed., 6s.

Dethroning Shakspere. Letters to the Daily Telegraph; and Editorial Papers. Crown 8vo, 2s. 6d.

Dictionary. See TOLHAUSEN, " Technological."

Dogs in Disease. By ASHMONT. Crown 8vo, 7s. 6d.

Donnelly (Ignatius) Atlantis; or, the Antediluvian World. 7th Edition, crown 8vo, 12s. 6d.

—— *Ragnarok: The Age of Fire and Gravel.* Illustrated, crown 8vo, 12s. 6d.

—— *The Great Cryptogram: Francis Bacon's Cipher in the* so-called Shakspere Plays. With facsimiles. 2 vols., 30s.

Doré (Gustave) Life and Reminiscences. By BLANCHE ROOSEVELT. Illust. from the Artist's Drawings. Medium 8vo, 24s.

Dougall (James Dalziel) Shooting: its Appliances, Practice, and Purpose. New Edition, revised with additions. Crown 8vo, 7s. 6d.
" The book is admirable in every way. . . . . We wish it every success."—*Globe.*
" A very complete treatise. . . . . Likely to take high rank as an authority on shooting."—*Daily News.*

Dupré (Giovanni). By FRIEZE. With Dialogues on Art. 7s. 6d.

EDMONDS (C.) Poetry of the Anti-Jacobin. With additional matter. New ed. Illust., crown 8vo.

Educational List and Directory for 1887-88. 5s.

Educational Works published in Great Britain. A Classified Catalogue. Third Edition, 8vo, cloth extra, 6s.

Edwards (E.) American Steam Engineer. Illust., 12mo, 12s. 6d.

Eight Months on the Argentine Gran Chaco. 8vo, 8s. 6d.

Elliott (H. W.) An Arctic Province: Alaska and the Seal Islands. Illustrated from Drawings; also with Maps. 16s.

Emerson (Dr. P. H.) Pictures of East Anglian Life. Ordinary ed., 105s.; édit. de luxe, 17 × 13½, vellum, morocco back, 147s.

—— *Naturalistic Photography for Art Students.* Crown 8vo.

—— *and Goodall. Life and Landscape on the Norfolk* Broads. Plates 12 × 8 inches, 126s.; large paper, 210s.

English Catalogue of Books. Vol. III., 1872—1880. Royal 8vo, half-morocco, 42s. See also "Index."

English Etchings. Published Quarterly. 3s. 6d. Vol. VI., 25s.

English Philosophers. Edited by E. B. IVAN MÜLLER, M.A. Crown 8vo volumes of 180 or 200 pp., price 3s. 6d. each.

Francis Bacon, by Thomas Fowler.	Shaftesbury and Hutcheson.
Hamilton, by W. H. S. Monck.	Adam Smith, by J. A. Farrer.
Hartley and James Mill.	

Esmarch (F.) Handbook of Surgery. Translation from the last German Edition. With 647 new Illustrations. 8vo, leather, 24s.

Etching. See CHATTOCK, and ENGLISH ETCHINGS.

Etchings (Modern) of Celebrated Paintings. 4to, 31s. 6d.

Evans (E. A.) Songs of the Birds. Analogies of Spiritual Life. New Ed. Illust., 6s.

Evelyn. Life of Mrs. Godolphin. By WILLIAM HARCOURT, of Nuneham. Steel Portrait. Extra binding, gilt top, 7s. 6d.

FARINI (G. A.) Through the Kalahari Desert. 8vo, 21s.

Farm Ballads, Festivals, and Legends. See CARLETON.

Fawcett (Edgar) A Gentleman of Leisure. 1s.

Fenn (G. Manville) Off to the Wilds: A Story for Boys. Profusely Illustrated. Crown 8vo, gilt edges, 3s. 6d.; plainer, 2s. 6d.

—— *Silver Cañon.* Illust., gilt ed., 3s. 6d.; plainer, 2s. 6d.

Fennell (Greville) Book of the Roach. New Edition, 12mo, 2s.

Ferns. See HEATH.

Field (H. M.) Greek Islands and Turkey after the War. 8s. 6d.

Field (Mrs. Horace) Anchorage. 2 vols., crown 8vo, 12s.

Fields (J. T.) Yesterdays with Authors. New Ed., 8vo, 10s. 6d.

Fitzgerald (P.) Book Fancier. Cr. 8vo. 5s.; large pap. 12s. 6d.

Fleming (Sandford) England and Canada : a Tour. Cr. 8vo, 6s.

Florence. See YRIARTE.

Folkard (R., Jun.) Plant Lore, Legends, and Lyrics. 8vo, 16s.

Forbes (H. O.) Naturalist in the Eastern Archipelago. 8vo. 21s.

Foreign Countries and British Colonies. Cr. 8vo, 3s. 6d. each

Australia, by J. F. Vesey Fitzgerald.	Japan, by S. Mossman.
Austria, by D. Kay, F.R.G.S.	Peru, by Clements R. Markham.
Denmark and Iceland, by E. C. Otté.	Russia, by W. R. Morfill, M.A.
Egypt, by S. Lane Poole, B.A.	Spain, by Rev. Wentworth Webster.
France, by Miss M. Roberts.	Sweden and Norway, by Woods.
Germany, by S. Baring-Gould.	West Indies, by C. H. Eden,
Greece, by L. Sergeant, B.A.	F.R.G.S.

Foreign Etchings. From Paintings by Rembrandt, &c., 63s.; india proofs, 147s.

Fortunes made in Business. Vols. I., II., III. 16s. each.

Frampton (Mary) Journal, Letters, and Anecdotes. 8vo, 14s.

Franc (Maud Jeanne). Small post 8vo, uniform, gilt edges :—

Emily's Choice. 5s.	Vermont Vale. 5s.
Hall's Vineyard. 4s.	Minnie's Mission. 4s.
John's Wife : A Story of Life in South Australia. 4s.	Little Mercy. 4s.
	Beatrice Melton's Discipline. 4s.
Marian ; or, The Light of Some One's Home. 5s.	No Longer a Child. 4s.
	Golden Gifts. 4s.
Silken Cords and Iron Fetters. 4s.	Two Sides to Every Question. 4s.
Into the Light. 4s.	Master of Ralston. 4s.

Also a Cheap Edition, in cloth extra, 2s. 6d. each.

Frank's Ranche ; or, My Holiday in the Rockies. A Contribution to the Inquiry into What we are to Do with our Boys. 5s.

Freeman (J.) Lights and Shadows of Melbourne Life. Cr. 8vo. 6s.

French. See JULIEN and PORCHER.

Fresh Woods and Pastures New. By the Author of " An Amateur Angler's Days." 1s. 6d.; large paper, 5s. ; new ed., 1s.

Froissart. See LANIER.

Fuller (Edward) Fellow Travellers. 3s. 6d.

—— *Dramatic Year* 1887-88 *in the United States.* With the London Season, by W. ARCHER. Crown 8vo.

GANE (D. N.) New South Wales and Victoria in 1885. 5s.

Gasparin (Countess A. de) Sunny Fields and Shady Woods. 6s.

Geary (Grattan) Burma after the Conquest. 7s. 6d.

Gentle Life (Queen Edition). 2 vols. in 1, small 4to, 6s.

THE GENTLE LIFE SERIES.

Price 6s. each ; or in calf extra, price 10s. 6d. ; Smaller Edition, cloth
extra, 2s. 6d., except where price is named.

The Gentle Life. Essays in aid of the Formation of Character.

About in the World. Essays by Author of " The Gentle Life."

Like unto Christ. New Translation of Thomas à Kempis.

Familiar Words. A Quotation Handbook. 6s.

Essays by Montaigne. Edited by the Author of " The Gentle
Life."

The Gentle Life. 2nd Series.

The Silent Hour: Essays, Original and Selected.

Half-Length Portraits. Short Studies of Notable Persons.
By J. HAIN FRISWELL.

Essays on English Writers, for Students in English Literature.

Other People's Windows. By J. HAIN FRISWELL. 6s.

A Man's Thoughts. By J. HAIN FRISWELL.

The Countess of Pembroke's Arcadia. By Sir PHILIP SIDNEY. 6s.

Germany. By S. BARING-GOULD. Crown 8vo, 3s. 6d.

Gibbon (C.) Beyond Compare : a Story. 3 vols., cr. 8vo, 31s. 6d.

——— *Yarmouth Coast.*

Gisborne (W.) New Zealand Rulers and Statesmen. With
Portraits. Crown 8vo, 7s. 6d.

Goldsmith. She Stoops to Conquer. Introduction by AUSTIN
DOBSON ; the designs by E. A. ABBEY. Imperial 4to, 48s.

Goode (G. Brown) American Fishes. A Popular Treatise.
Royal 8vo, 24s.

Gordon (J. E. H., B.A. Cantab.) Four Lectures on Electric
Induction at the Royal Institution, 1878-9. Illust., square 16mo, 3s.

——— *Electric Lighting.* Illustrated, 8vo, 18s.

——— *Physical Treatise on Electricity and Magnetism.* 2nd
Edition, enlarged, with coloured, full-page, &c., Illust. 2 vols., 8vo, 42s.

——— *Electricity for Schools.* Illustrated. Crown 8vo, 5s.

Gouffé (Jules) Royal Cookery Book. New Edition, with plates
in colours, Woodcuts, &c., 8vo, gilt edges, 42s.

——— Domestic Edition, half-bound, 10s. 6d.

Grant (General, U.S.) Personal Memoirs. 2 vols., 8vo, 28s.
Illustrations, Maps, &c. 2 vols., 8vo, 28s.

Great Artists. See " Biographies."

Great Musicians. Edited by F. HUEFFER. A Series of
Biographies, crown 8vo, 3s. each :—

Bach.	Mendelssohn.	Schubert.
English Church Com-	Mozart.	Schumann.
posers. By BARRETT.	Purcell.	Richard Wagner.
Handel.	Rossini.	Weber.
Haydn.		

Groves (J. Percy) Charmouth Grange. Gilt, 5s.; plainer, 2s. 6d.

Guizot's History of France. Translated by R. BLACK. In
8 vols., super-royal 8vo, cloth extra, gilt, each 24s. In cheaper
binding, 8 vols., at 10s. 6d. each.

"It supplies a want which has long been felt, and ought to be in the hands of all
students of history."—*Times.*

———————————— *Masson's School Edition.* Abridged
from the Translation by Robert Black, with Chronological Index, Historical and Genealogical Tables, &c. By Professor GUSTAVE MASSON,
B.A. With Portraits, Illustrations, &c. 1 vol., 8vo, 600 pp., 5s.

Guyon (Mde.) Life. By UPHAM. 6th Edition, crown 8vo, 6s.

HALFORD (F. M.) Floating Flies, and how to Dress them.
Coloured plates. 8vo, 15s.; large paper, 30s.

———— *Dry Fly-Fishing in Theory and Practice.* Col. Plates.

Hall (W. W.) How to Live Long; or, 1408 Maxims. 2s.

Hamilton (E.) Recollections of Fly-fishing for Salmon, Trout,
and Grayling. With their Habits, Haunts, and History. Illust., 6s.;
large paper, 10s. 6d.

Hands (T.) Numerical Exercises in Chemistry. Cr. 8vo, 2s. 6d.
and 2s.; Answers separately, 6d.

Hardy (Thomas). See Low's STANDARD NOVELS.

Hare (J. S. Clark) Law of Contracts. 8vo, 26s.

Harley (T.) Southward Ho! to the State of Georgia. 5s.

Harper's Magazine. Published Monthly. 160 pages, fully
Illustrated, 1s. Vols., half yearly, I.—XVI., super-royal 8vo, 8s. 6d.
each.

"'Harper's Magazine' is so thickly sown with excellent illustrations that to count
them would be a work of time; not that it is a picture magazine, for the engravings
illustrate the text after the manner seen in some of our choicest *éditions de luxe.*"—
St. James's Gazette.

"It is so pretty, so big, and so cheap. . . . An extraordinary shillingsworth—
160 large octavo pages, with over a score of articles, and more than three times as
many illustrations."—*Edinburgh Daily Review.*

"An amazing shillingsworth . . . combining choice literature of both nations."—
Nonconformist.

Harper's Young People. Vols. I.-IV., profusely Illustrated
with woodcuts and coloured plates. Royal 4to, extra binding, each
7s. 6d.; gilt edges, 8s. Published Weekly, in wrapper, 1d.; Annual
Subscription, post free, 6s. 6d.; Monthly, in wrapper, with coloured
plate, 6d.; Annual Subscription, post free, 7s. 6d.

Harrison (Mary) Skilful Cook. New edition, crown 8vo, 5*s.*

Hartshorne (H.) Household Medicine, Surgery, &c. 8vo. 21*s.*

Hatton (Frank) North Borneo. Map and Illust., &c. 18*s.*

Hatton (Joseph) Journalistic London: with Engravings and Portraits of Distinguished Writers of the Day. Fcap. 4to, 12*s.* 6*d.*

———— See also Low's STANDARD NOVELS.

Hawthorne (Nathaniel) Life. By JOHN R. LOWELL.

Heath (Francis George) Fern World With Nature-printed Coloured Plates. Crown 8vo, gilt edges, 12*s.* 6*d.* Cheap Edition, 6*s.*

*Heath (Gertrude). Tell us Why? The Customs and Ceremo-*nies of the Church of England explained for Children. Cr. 8vo, 2*s.* 6*d.*

Heldmann (B.) Mutiny of the Ship " Leander." Gilt edges, 3*s.* 6*d.*; plainer, 2*s.* 6*d.*

Henty. Winning his Spurs. Cr. 8vo, 3*s.* 6*d.*; plainer, 2*s.* 6*d.*

———— *Cornet of Horse.* Cr. 8vo, 3*s.* 6*d.*; plainer, 2*s.* 6*d.*

———— *Jack Archer.* Illust. 3*s.* 6*d.*; plainer, 2*s.* 6*d.*

Henty (Richmond) Australiana : My Early Life. 5*s.*

Herrick (Robert) Poetry. Preface by AUSTIN DOBSON. With numerous Illustrations by E. A. ABBEY. 4to, gilt edges, 42*s.*

Hetley (Mrs. E.) Native Flowers of New Zealand. Chromos from Drawings. Three Parts, to Subscribers, 63*s.*

Hewitt (James A.) Church History in South Africa, 1795-1848, 12mo, 5*s.*

Hicks (E. S.) Our Boys: How to Enter the Merchant Service. 5*s.*

———— *Yachts, Boats and Canoes.* Illustrated. 8vo, 10*s.* 6*d.*

Hitchman. Public Life of the Earl of Beaconsfield. 3*s.* 6*d.*

Hoey (Mrs. Cashel) See Low's STANDARD NOVELS.

Hofmann. Scenes from the Life of our Saviour. 12 mounted plates, 12 × 9 inches, 21*s.*

Holder (C. F.) Marvels of Animal Life. Illustrated. 8*s.* 6*d.*

———— *Ivory King: Elephant and Allies.* Illustrated. 8*s.* 6*d.*

———— *Living Lights : Phosphorescent Animals and Vegetables.* Illustrated. 8vo, 8*s.* 6*d.*

Holmes (O. W.) Before the Curfew, &c. Occasional Poems. 5*s.*

———— *Last Leaf : a Holiday Volume.* 42*s.*

———— *Mortal Antipathy,* 8*s.* 6*d.*; also 2*s.*; paper, 1*s.*

———— *Our Hundred Days in Europe.* 6*s.* Large Paper, 15*s.*

———— *Poetical Works.* 2 vols., 18mo, gilt tops, 10*s.* 6*d.*

Homer, Iliad I.-XII., done into English Verse. By ARTHUR S. WAY. 9*s.*

———— *Odyssey, done into English Verse.* By A. S. WAY. Fcap 4to, 7*s.* 6*d.*

Hopkins (Manley) Treatise on the Cardinal Numbers. 2s. 6d.

Hore (Mrs.) To Lake Tanganyika in a Bath Chair. Cr. 8vo, 7s. 6d.

Howard (Blanche W.) Tony the Maid; a Novelette. Illust., 12mo, 3s. 6d.

Howorth (H. H.) Mammoth and the Flood. 8vo, 18s.

Huet (C. B.) Land of Rubens. For Visitors to Belgium. By VAN DAM. Crown 8vo, 3s. 6d.

Hugo (V.) Notre Dame. With coloured etchings and 150 engravings. 2 vols., 8vo, vellum cloth, 30s.

Hundred Greatest Men (The). 8 portfolios, 21s. each, or 4 vols., half-morocco, gilt edges, 10 guineas. New Ed., 1 vol., royal 8vo, 21s.

Hutchinson (T.) Diary and Letters. Vol. I., 16s.; Vol. II., 16s.

Hygiene and Public Health. Edited by A. H. BUCK, M.D. Illustrated. 2 vols., royal 8vo, 42s.

Hymnal Companion to the Book of Common Prayer. By BISHOP BICKERSTETH. In various styles and bindings from 1d. to 31s. 6d. *Price List and Prospectus will be forwarded on application.*

Hymns and Tunes at St. Thomas', New York. Music by G. W. FARREN. Royal 8vo, 5s.

ILLUSTRATED Text-Books of Art-Education. Edited by EDWARD J. POYNTER, R.A. Illustrated, and strongly bound, 5s. Now ready :—

PAINTING.
Classic and Italian. By HEAD. | French and Spanish.
German, Flemish, and Dutch. | English and American.

ARCHITECTURE.
Classic and Early Christian.
Gothic and Renaissance. By T. ROGER SMITH.

SCULPTURE.
Antique: Egyptian and Greek.
Renaissance and Modern. By LEADER SCOTT.

Inderwick (F. A.; Q.C.) Side Lights on the Stuarts. Essays. Illustrated, 8vo.

Index to the English Catalogue, Jan., 1874, to Dec., 1880. Royal 8vo, half-morocco, 18s.

Inglis (Hon. James; "Maori") Our New Zealand Cousins. Small post 8vo, 6s.

—— *Tent Life in Tiger Land: Twelve Years a Pioneer* Planter. Col. plates, roy. 8vo, 18s.

Irving (Henry) Impressions of America. 2 vols., 21s.; 1 vol., 6s.

Irving (Washington). Library Edition of his Works in 27 vols., Copyright, with the Author's Latest Revisions. "Geoffrey Crayon" Edition, large square 8vo. 12s. 6d. per vol. *See also* "Little Britain."

JAMES (C.) Curiosities of Law and Lawyers. 8vo, 7s. 6d.

Japan. See ANDERSON, ARTISTIC, AUDSLEY, also MORSE.

Jefferies (Richard) Amaryllis at the Fair. Small 8vo, 7s. 6d.

Jerdon (Gertrude) Key-hole Country. Illustrated. Crown 8vo, cloth, 2s.

Johnston (H. H.) River Congo, from its Mouth to Bolobo. New Edition, 8vo, 21s.

Johnstone (D. Lawson) Land of the Mountain Kingdom. Illust., crown 8vo.

Jones (Major) Heroes of Industry. Biographies with Portraits. 7s. 6d.

———— *Emigrants' Friend.* Guide to the U.S. N. Ed. 2s. 6d.

Julien (F.) English Student's French Examiner. 16mo, 2s.

———— *Conversational French Reader.* 16mo, cloth, 2s. 6d.

————*French at Home and at School.* Book I., Accidence. 2s.

———— *First Lessons in Conversational French Grammar.* 1s.

———— *Petites Leçons de Conversation et de Grammaire.* 3s.

———— *Phrases of Daily Use.* Limp cloth, 6d.

———— *"Petites Leçons" and "Phrases" in one.* 3s. 6d.

KARR (H. W. Seton) Shores and Alps of Alaska. 8vo, 16s.

Keats. Endymion. Illust. by W. ST. JOHN HARPER. Imp. 4to, gilt top, 42s.

Kempis (Thomas à) Daily Text-Book. Square 16mo, 2s. 6d.; interleaved as a Birthday Book, 3s. 6d.

Kent's Commentaries: an Abridgment for Students of American Law. By EDEN F. THOMPSON. 10s. 6d.

Kerr (W. M.) Far Interior: Cape of Good Hope, across the Zambesi, to the Lake Regions. Illustrated from Sketches, 2 vols. 8vo, 32s.

Kershaw (S. W.) Protestants from France in their English Home. Crown 8vo, 6s.

King (Henry) Savage London; Riverside Characters, &c. Crown 8vo, 6s.

Kingston (W. H. G.) Works. Illustrated, 16mo, gilt edges, 3s. 6d.; plainer binding, plain edges, 2s. 6d. each.

Captain Mugford, or, Our Salt and Fresh Water Tutors.
Dick Cheveley.
Heir of Kilfinnan.

Snow-Shoes and Canoes.
Two Supercargoes.
With Axe and Rifle.

Kingsley (Rose) Children of Westminster Abbey: Studies in English History. 5s.
Knight (E. J.) Cruise of the "Falcon." New Ed. Cr. 8vo, 7s. 6d.
Knox (Col.) Boy Travellers on the Congo. Illus. Cr. 8vo, 7s. 6d.
Kunhardt (C. B.) Small Yachts: Design and Construction. 35s.
———— *Steam Yachts and Launches.* Illustrated. 4to, 16s.

LAMB (Charles) Essays of Elia. Illustrated by C. O. MURRAY. 6s.
Lanier's Works. Illustrated, crown 8vo, gilt edges, 7s. 6d. each.

Boy's King Arthur.
Boy's Froissart.
Boy's Knightly Legends of Wales.
Boy's Percy: Ballads of Love and Adventure, selected from the "Reliques."

Lansdell (H.) Through Siberia. 2 vols., 8vo, 30s.; 1 vol., 10s. 6d.
———— *Russia in Central Asia.* Illustrated. 2 vols., 42s.
———— *Through Central Asia ; Russo-Afghan Frontier, &c.* 8vo, 12s.
Larden (W.) School Course on Heat. Second Ed., Illust. 5s.
Laurie (André) Selene Company, Limited. Crown 8vo, 7s. 6d.
Layard (Mrs. Granville) Through the West Indies. Small post 8vo, 2s. 6d.
Lea (H. C.). History of the Inquisition of the Middle Ages. 3 vols., 8vo, 42s.
Lemon (M.) Small House over the Water, and Stories. Illust. by Cruikshank, &c. Crown 8vo, 6s.
Leo XIII.: Life. By BERNARD O'REILLY. With Steel Portrait from Photograph, &c. Large 8vo, 18s.; *édit. de luxe*, 63s.
Leonardo da Vinci's Literary Works. Edited by Dr. JEAN PAUL RICHTER. Containing his Writings on Painting, Sculpture, and Architecture, his Philosophical Maxims, Humorous Writings, and Miscellaneous Notes on Personal Events, on his Contemporaries, on Literature, &c. ; published from Manuscripts. 2 vols., imperial 8vo, containing about 200 Drawings in Autotype Reproductions, and numerous other Illustrations. Twelve Guineas.
Library of Religious Poetry. Best Poems of all Ages. Edited by SCHAFF and GILMAN. Royal 8vo, 21s.; cheaper binding, 10s. 6d.
Lindsay (W. S.) History of Merchant Shipping. Over 150 Illustrations, Maps, and Charts. In 4 vols., demy 8vo, cloth extra. Vols. 1 and 2, 11s. each; vols. 3 and 4, 14s. each. 4 vols., 50s.
Little (Archibald J.) Through the Yang-tse Gorges: Trade and Travel in Western China. New Edition. 8vo, 10s. 6d.

Little Britain, The Spectre Bridegroom, and *Legend of Sleepy* Hollow. By WASHINGTON IRVING. An entirely New *Édition de luxe*. Illustrated by 120 very fine Engravings on Wood, by Mr. J. D. COOPER. Designed by Mr. CHARLES O. MURRAY. Re-issue, square crown 8vo, cloth, 6*s*.

Longfellow. Maidenhood. With Coloured Plates. Oblong 4to, 2*s*. 6*d*.; gilt edges, 3*s*. 6*d*.

—— *Courtship of Miles Standish.* Illust. by BROUGHTON, &c. Imp. 4to, 21*s*.

—— *Nuremberg.* 28 Photogravures. Illum. by M. and A. COMEGYS. 4to, 31*s*. 6*d*.

Lowell (J. R.) Vision of Sir Launfal. Illustrated, royal 4to, 63*s*.

—— *Life of Nathaniel Hawthorne.* Small post 8vo, .

Low's Standard Library of Travel and Adventure. Crown 8vo, uniform in cloth extra, 7*s*. 6*d*., except where price is given.

1. The Great Lone Land. By Major W. F. BUTLER, C.B.
2. The Wild North Land. By Major W. F. BUTLER, C.B.
3. How I found Livingstone. By H. M. STANLEY.
4. Through the Dark Continent. By H. M. STANLEY. 12*s*. 6*d*.
5. The Threshold of the Unknown Region. By C. R. MARK-HAM. (4th Edition, with Additional Chapters, 10*s*. 6*d*.)
6. Cruise of the Challenger. By W. J. J. SPRY, R.N.
7. Burnaby's On Horseback through Asia Minor. 10*s*. 6*d*.
8. Schweinfurth's Heart of Africa. 2 vols., 15*s*.
9. Through America. By W. G. MARSHALL.
10. Through Siberia. Il. and unabridged, 10*s*.6*d*. By H. LANSDELL.
11. From Home to Home. By STAVELEY HILL.
12. Cruise of the Falcon. By E. J. KNIGHT.
13. Through Masai Land. By JOSEPH THOMSON.
14. To the Central African Lakes. By JOSEPH THOMSON.
15. Queen's Highway. By STUART CUMBERLAND.

Low's Standard Novels. Small post 8vo, cloth extra, 6*s*. each, unless otherwise stated.

A Daughter of Heth. By W. BLACK.
In Silk Attire. By W. BLACK.
Kilmeny. A Novel. By W. BLACK.
Lady Silverdale's Sweetheart. By W. BLACK.
Sunrise. By W. BLACK. -
Three Feathers. By WILLIAM BLACK.
Alice Lorraine. By R. D. BLACKMORE.
Christowell, a Dartmoor Tale. By R. D. BLACKMORE.
Clara Vaughan. By R. D. BLACKMORE.
Cradock Nowell. By R. D. BLACKMORE.
Cripps the Carrier. By R. D. BLACKMORE.
Erema; or, My Father's Sin. By R. D. BLACKMORE.
Lorna Doone. By R. D. BLACKMORE. 25th Edition.
Mary Anerley. By R. D. BLACKMORE.
Tommy Upmore. By R. D. BLACKMORE.

Low's Standard Novels—continued.

Bonaventure. By G. W. CABLE.
An English Squire. By Miss COLERIDGE.
Some One Else. By Mrs. B. M. CROKER.
Under the Stars and Stripes. By E. DE LEON.
Halfway. By Miss BETHAM-EDWARDS.
A Story of the Dragonnades. By Rev. E. GILLIAT, M.A.
A Laodicean. By THOMAS HARDY.
Far from the Madding Crowd. By THOMAS HARDY.
Mayor of Casterbridge. By THOMAS HARDY.
Pair of Blue Eyes. By THOMAS HARDY.
Return of the Native. By THOMAS HARDY.
The Hand of Ethelberta. By THOMAS HARDY.
The Trumpet Major. By THOMAS HARDY.
Two on a Tower. By THOMAS HARDY.
Old House at Sandwich. By JOSEPH HATTON.
Three Recruits. By JOSEPH HATTON.
A Golden Sorrow. By Mrs. CASHEL HOEY. New Edition.
A Stern Chase. By Mrs. CASHEL HOEY.
Out of Court. By Mrs. CASHEL HOEY.
Don John. By JEAN INGELOW.
John Jerome. By JEAN INGELOW. 5s.
Sarah de Berenger. By JEAN INGELOW.
Adela Cathcart. By GEORGE MAC DONALD.
Guild Court. By GEORGE MAC DONALD.
Mary Marston. By GEORGE MAC DONALD.
Stephen Archer. New Ed. of "Gifts." By GEORGE MAC DONALD.
The Vicar's Daughter. By GEORGE MAC DONALD.
Orts. By GEORGE MAC DONALD.
Weighed and Wanting. By GEORGE MAC DONALD.
Diane. By Mrs. MACQUOID.
Elinor Dryden. By Mrs. MACQUOID.
My Lady Greensleeves. By HELEN MATHERS.
Spell of Ashtaroth. By DUFFIELD OSBORNE. 5s.
Alaric Spenceley. By Mrs. J. H. RIDDELL.
Daisies and Buttercups. By Mrs. J. H. RIDDELL.
The Senior Partner. By Mrs. J. H. RIDDELL.
A Struggle for Fame. By Mrs. J. H. RIDDELL.
Frozen Pirate. By W. CLARK RUSSELL.
Jack's Courtship. By W. CLARK RUSSELL.
John Holdsworth. By W. CLARK RUSSELL.
A Sailor's Sweetheart. By W. CLARK RUSSELL.
Sea Queen. By W. CLARK RUSSELL.
Watch Below. By W. CLARK RUSSELL.
Strange Voyage. By W. CLARK RUSSELL.
Wreck of the Grosvenor. By W. CLARK RUSSELL.
The Lady Maud. By W. CLARK RUSSELL.
Little Loo. By W. CLARK RUSSELL.
Bee-man of Orn. By FRANK R. STOCKTON.
My Wife and I. By Mrs. HARRIET B. STOWE.

Low's Standard Novels—continued.

 The Late Mrs. Null. By FRANK R. STOCKTON.
 Hundredth Man. By FRANK R. STOCKTON.
 Old Town Folk. By Mrs. HARRIET B. STOWE.
 We and our Neighbours. By Mrs. HARRIET B. STOWE.
 Poganuc People, their Loves and Lives. By Mrs. STOWE.
 Ulu: an African Romance. By JOSEPH THOMSON.
 Ben Hur: a Tale of the Christ. By LEW. WALLACE.
 Anne. By CONSTANCE FENIMORE WOOLSON.
 East Angels. By CONSTANCE FENIMORE WOOLSON.
 For the Major. By CONSTANCE FENIMORE WOOLSON. 5s.
 French Heiress in her own Chateau.

Low's Series of Standard Books for Boys. With numerous
 Illustrations, 2s. 6d.; gilt edges, 3s. 6d. each.

 Dick Cheveley. By W. H. G. KINGSTON.
 Heir of Kilfinnan. By W. H. G. KINGSTON.
 Off to the Wilds. By G. MANVILLE FENN.
 The Two Supercargoes. By W. H. G. KINGSTON.
 The Silver Cañon. By G. MANVILLE FENN.
 Under the Meteor Flag. By HARRY COLLINGWOOD.
 Jack Archer: a Tale of the Crimea. By G. A. HENTY.
 The Mutiny on Board the Ship Leander. By B. HELDMANN.
 With Axe and Rifle on the Western Prairies. By W. H. G.
  KINGSTON.
 Red Cloud, the Solitary Sioux: a Tale of the Great Prairie.
  By Col. Sir WM. BUTLER, K.C.B.
 The Voyage of the Aurora. By HARRY COLLINGWOOD.
 Charmouth Grange: a Tale of the 17th Century. By J.
  PERCY GROVES.
 Snowshoes and Canoes. By W. H. G. KINGSTON.
 The Son of the Constable of France. By LOUIS ROUSSELET.
 Captain Mugford; or, Our Salt and Fresh Water Tutors.
  Edited by W. H. G. KINGSTON.
 The Cornet of Horse, a Tale of Marlborough's Wars. By
  G. A. HENTY.
 The Adventures of Captain Mago. By LEON CAHUN.
 Noble Words and Noble Needs.
 The King of the Tigers. By ROUSSELET.
 Hans Brinker; or, The Silver Skates. By Mrs. DODGE.
 The Drummer-Boy, a Story of the time of Washington. By
  ROUSSELET.
 Adventures in New Guinea: The Narrative of Louis Tregance.
 The Crusoes of Guiana. By BOUSSENARD.
 The Gold Seekers. A Sequel to the Above. By BOUSSENARD.
 Winning His Spurs, a Tale of the Crusades. By G. A. HENTY.
 The Blue Banner. By LEON CAHUN.

Low's Pocket Encyclopædia: a Compendium of General Know-
 ledge for Ready Reference. Upwards of 25,000 References, with
 Plates. New ed., imp. 32mo, cloth, marbled edges, 3s. 6d.; roan, 4s. 6d.

Low's Handbook to London Charities. Yearly, cloth, 1s. 6d.; paper, 1s.

M^cCORMICK (R.). *Voyages in the Arctic and Antarctic Seas in Search of Sir John Franklin, &c.* With Maps and Lithos. 2 vols., royal 8vo, 52s. 6d.

Mac Donald (George). See Low's STANDARD NOVELS.

Macdowall (Alex. B.) Curve Pictures of London for the Social Reformer. 1s.

McGoun's Commercial Correspondence. Crown 8vo, 5s.

Macgregor (John) "Rob Roy" on the Baltic. 3rd Edition, small post 8vo, 2s. 6d.; cloth, gilt edges, 3s. 6d.

———— *A Thousand Miles in the "Rob Roy" Canoe.* 11th Edition, small post 8vo, 2s. 6d.; cloth, gilt edges, 3s. 6d.

———— *Voyage Alone in the Yawl "Rob Roy."* New Edition, with additions, small post 8vo, 5s.; 3s. 6d. and 2s. 6d.

Mackay (C.) Glossary of Obscure Words in Shakespeare. 21s.

Mackenzie (Sir Morell) Fatal Illness of Frederick the Noble. Crown 8vo, limp cloth, 2s. 6d.

Mackenzie (Rev. John) Austral Africa : Losing it or Ruling it? Illustrations and Maps. 2 vols., 8vo, 32s.

McLellan's Own Story : The War for the Union. Illust. 18s.

McMurdo (Edward) History of Portugal. 8vo, 21s.

Macquoid (Mrs.). See Low's STANDARD NOVELS.

Magazine. See ENGLISH ETCHINGS, HARPER.

Maginn (W.) Miscellanies. Prose and Verse. With Memoir. 2 vols., crown 8vo, 24s.

Main (Mrs.; Mrs. Fred Burnaby) High Life and Towers of Silence. Illustrated, square 8vo, 10s. 6d.

Manitoba. See BRYCE.

Manning (E. F.) Delightful Thames. Illustrated. 4to, fancy boards, 5s.

Markham (Clements R.) The Fighting Veres, Sir F. and Sir H. 8vo, 18s.

———— *War between Peru and Chili,* 1879-1881. Third Ed. Crown 8vo, with Maps, 10s. 6d.

———— See also "Foreign Countries," MAURY, and VERES.

Marshall (W. G.) Through America. New Ed., cr. 8vo, 7s. 6d.

Marston (W.) Eminent Recent Actors, Reminiscences Critical, &c. 2 vols. Crown 8vo, 21s.

Martin (F. W.) Float Fishing and Spinning in the Nottingham Style. New Edition. Crown 8vo, 2s. 6d.

Matthews (J. W., M.D.) Incwadi Yami: Twenty years in South Africa. With many Engravings, royal 8vo, 14s.

Maury (Commander) Physical Geography of the Sea, and its Meteorology. New Edition, with Charts and Diagrams, cr. 8vo, 6s.

—— *Life.* By his Daughter. Edited by Mr. CLEMENTS R. MARKHAM. With portrait of Maury. 8vo, 12s. 6d.

Men of Mark: Portraits of the most Eminent Men of the Day. Complete in 7 Vols., 4to, handsomely bound, gilt edges, 25s. each.

Mendelssohn Family (The), 1729—1847. From Letters and Journals. Translated. New Edition, 2 vols., 8vo, 30s.

Mendelssohn. See also " Great Musicians."

Merrifield's Nautical Astronomy. Crown 8vo, 7s. 6d.

Merrylees (J.) Carlsbad and its Environs. 7s. 6d.; roan, 9s.

Milford (P.) Ned Stafford's Experiences in the United States. 5s.

Mills (J.) Alternative Elementary Chemistry. Illust., cr. 8vo.

—— *Alernative Course in Physics.*

Mitchell (D. G.; Ik. Marvel) Works. Uniform Edition, small 8vo, 5s. each.

Bound together.	Reveries of a Bachelor.
Doctor Johns.	Seven Stories, Basement and Attic.
Dream Life.	Wet Days at Edgewood.
Out-of-Town Places.	

Mitford (Mary Russell) Our Village. With 12 full-page and 157 smaller Cuts. Cr. 4to, cloth, gilt edges, 21s.; cheaper binding, 10s. 6d.

Moffatt (W.) Land and Work; Depression, Agricultural and Commercial. Crown 8vo, 5s.

Mohammed Benani: A Story of To-day. 8vo, 10s. 6d.

Mollett (J. W.) Illustrated Dictionary of Words used in Art and Archæology. Illustrated, small 4to, 15s.

Moloney (Governor) Forestry of West Africa. 10s. 6d.

Money (E.) The Truth about America. New Edition. 2s. 6d.

Morlands, The. A Tale of Anglo-Indian Life. By Author of " Sleepy Sketches." Crown 8vo, 6s.

Morley (Henry) English Literature in the Reign of Victoria. 2000th volume of the Tauchnitz Collection of Authors. 18mo, 2s. 6d.

Mormonism. See " Stenhouse."

Morse (E. S.) Japanese Homes and their Surroundings. With more than 300 Illustrations. Re-issue, 10s. 6d.

Morten (Honnor) Sketches of Hospital Life. Cr. 8vo, sewed, 1s.

Morwood. Our Gipsies in City, Tent, and Van. 8vo, 18s.

Moxon (Walter) Pilocereus Senilis. Fcap. 8vo, gilt top, 3s. 6d.

Muller (E.) Noble Words and Noble Deeds. Illustrated, gilt edges, 3s. 6d.; plainer binding, 2s. 6d.

Murray (E. C. Grenville) Memoirs. By his widow. 2 vols.

Musgrave (Mrs.) Miriam. Crown 8vo.

Music. See "Great Musicians."

NAPOLEON and Marie Louise: Memoirs. By Madame DURAND. 7s. 6d.

Nethercote (C. B.) Pytchley Hunt. New Ed., cr. 8vo, 8s. 6d.

New Zealand. See BRADSHAW.

New Zealand Rulers and Statesmen. See GISBORNE.

Nicholls (J. H. Kerry) The King Country: Explorations in New Zealand. Many Illustrations and Map. New Edition, 8vo, 21s.

Nisbet (Hume) Life and Nature Studies. With Etching by C. O. MURRAY. Crown 8vo, 6s.

Nordhoff (C.) California, for Health, Pleasure, and Residence. New Edition, 8vo, with Maps and Illustrations, 12s. 6d.

Norman (C. B.) Corsairs of France. With Portraits. 8vo, 18s.

Northbrook Gallery. Edited by LORD RONALD GOWER. 36 Permanent Photographs. Imperial 4to, 63s.; large paper, 105s.

Nott (Major) Wild Animals Photographed and Described. 35s.

Nursery Playmates (Prince of). 217 Coloured Pictures for Children by eminent Artists. Folio, in coloured boards, 6s.

Nursing Record. Yearly, 8s.; half-yearly, 4s. 6d.; quarterly, 2s. 6d.; weekly, 2d.

O'BRIEN (R. B.) Fifty Years of Concessions to Ireland. With a Portrait of T. Drummond. Vol. I., 16s., II., 16s.

Orient Line Guide Book. By W. J. LOFTIE. 5s.

Orvis (C. F.) Fishing with the Fly. Illustrated. 8vo, 12s. 6d.

Osborne (Duffield) Spell of Ashtaroth. Crown 8vo, 5s.

Our Little Ones in Heaven. Edited by the Rev. H. ROBBINS. With Frontispiece after Sir JOSHUA REYNOLDS. New Edition, 5s.

Owen (Douglas) Marine Insurance Notes and Clauses. New Edition, 14s.

PALLISER (Mrs.) A History of Lace. New Edition, with additional cuts and text. 8vo, 21s.

—— *The China Collector's Pocket Companion.* With upwards of 1000 Illustrations of Marks and Monograms. Small 8vo, 5s.

Parkin (J.) Antidotal Treatment of Epidemic Cholera. 3s. 6d.

—— *Epidemiology in the Animal and Vegetable Kingdom.* Part I., crown 8vo, 3s. 6d.; Part II., 3s. 6d.

—— *Volcanic Origin of Epidemics.* Popular Edition, crown 8vo, 2s.

Payne (T. O.) Solomon's Temple and Capitol, Ark of the Flood and Tabernacle (four sections at 24*s.*), extra binding, 105*s.*

Pennell (H. Cholmondeley) Sporting Fish of Great Britain 15*s.* ; large paper, 30*s.*

————— *Modern Improvements in Fishing-tackle.* Crown 8vo, 2*s.*

Perelaer (M. T. H.) Ran Away from the Dutch ; Borneo, &c. Illustrated, square 8vo, 7*s. 6d.*

Pharmacopœia of the United States of America. 8vo, 21*s.*

Philpot (H. J.) Diabetes Mellitus. Crown 8vo, 5*s.*

————— *Diet System.* Tables. I. Diabetes ; II. Gout ; III. Dyspepsia ; IV. Corpulence. In cases, 1*s.* each.

Plunkett (Major G. T.) Primer of Orthographic Projection. Elementary Solid Geometry. With Problems and Exercises. 2*s. 6d.*

Poe (E. A.) The Raven. Illustr. by DORÉ. Imperial folio, 63*s.*

Poems of the Inner Life. Chiefly Modern. Small 8vo, 5*s.*

Polar Expeditions. See MCCORMICK.

Porcher (A.) Juvenile French Plays. With Notes and a Vocabulary. 18mo, 1*s.*

Porter (Admiral David D.) Naval History of Civil War. Portraits, Plans, &c. 4to, 25*s.*

Porter (Noah) Elements of Moral Science. 10*s. 6d.*

Portraits of Celebrated Race-horses of the Past and Present Centuries, with Pedigrees and Performances. 4 vols., 4to, 126*s.*

Powles (L. D.) Land of the Pink Pearl : Life in the Bahamas. 8vo, 10*s. 6d.*

Poynter (Edward J., R.A.). See "Illustrated Text-books."

Pritt (T. E.) North Country Flies. Illustrated from the Author's Drawings. 10*s. 6d.*

Publishers' Circular (The), and General Record of British and Foreign Literature. Published on the 1st and 15th of every Month, 3*d.*

Pyle (Howard) Otto of the Silver Hand. Illustrated by the Author. 8vo, 8*s. 6d.*

RAMBAUD. History of Russia. New Edition, Illustrated. 3 vols., 8vo, 21*s.*

Reber. History of Mediæval Art. Translated by CLARKE. 422 Illustrations and Glossary. 8vo, .

Redford (G.) Ancient Sculpture. New Ed. Crown 8vo, 10*s. 6d.*

Reed (Sir E. J., M.P.) and Simpson. Modern Ships of War. Illust., royal 8vo, 10*s. 6d.*

Richards (W.) Aluminium : its History, Occurrence, &c. Illustrated, crown 8vo, 12*s. 6d.*

Richter (Dr. Jean Paul) Italian Art in the National Gallery. 4to. Illustrated. Cloth gilt, £2 2s.; half-morocco, uncut, £2 12s. 6d.
———— See also LEONARDO DA VINCI.

Riddell (Mrs. J. H.) See Low's STANDARD NOVELS.

Robertson (Anne J.) Myself and my Relatives. New Edition, crown 8vo, 5s.

Robin Hood; Merry Adventures of. Written and illustrated by HOWARD PYLE. Imperial 8vo, 15s.

Robinson (Phil.) In my Indian Garden. New Edition, 16mo, limp cloth, 2s.
———— *Noah's Ark. Unnatural History.* Sm. post 8vo, 12s. 6d.
———— *Sinners and Saints : a Tour across the United States of* America, and Round them. Crown 8vo, 10s. 6d.
———— *Under the Punkah.* New Ed., cr. 8vo, limp cloth, 2s.

Rockstro (W. S.) History of Music. New Edition. 8vo, 14s.

Roland, The Story of. Crown 8vo, illustrated, 6s.

Rolfe (Eustace Neville) Pompeii, Popular and Practical. Cr. 8vo, 7s. 6d.

Rome and the Environs. With plans, 3s.

Rose (J.) Complete Practical Machinist. New Ed., 12mo, 12s. 6d.
———— *Key to Engines and Engine-running.* Crown 8vo, 8s. 6d.
———— *Mechanical Drawing.* Illustrated, small 4to, 16s.
———— *Modern Steam Engines.* Illustrated. 31s. 6d.
———— *Steam Boilers. Boiler Construction and Examination.* Illust., 8vo, 12s. 6d.

Rose Library. Each volume, 1s. Many are illustrated—
Little Women. By LOUISA M. ALCOTT.
Little Women Wedded. Forming a Sequel to " Little Women.
Little Women and Little Women Wedded. 1 vol., cloth gilt, 3s. 6d.
Little Men. By L. M. ALCOTT. Double vol., 2s.; cloth gilt, 3s. 6d.
An Old-Fashioned Girl. By LOUISA M. ALCOTT. 2s.; cloth, 3s. 6d.
Work. A Story of Experience. By L. M. ALCOTT. 3s. 6d.; 2 vols., 1s. each.
Stowe (Mrs. H. B.) The Pearl of Orr's Island.
———— The Minister's Wooing.
———— We and our Neighbours. 2s.; cloth gilt, 6s.
———— My Wife and I. 2s.
Hans Brinker; or, the Silver Skates. By Mrs. DODGE. Also 5s.
My Study Windows. By J. R. LOWELL.
The Guardian Angel. By OLIVER WENDELL HOLMES.
My Summer in a Garden. By C. D. WARNER.
Dred. By Mrs. BEECHER STOWE. 2s.; cloth gilt, 3s. 6d.
City Ballads. New Ed. 16mo. By WILL CARLETON.

Rose Library (*The*)—*continued.*

 Farm Ballads. By WILL CARLETON. ⎫
 Farm Festivals. By WILL CARLETON. ⎬ 1 vol., cl., gilt ed., 3*s.* 6*d.*
 Farm Legends. By WILL CARLETON. ⎭
 The Rose in Bloom. By L. M. ALCOTT. 2*s.*; cloth gilt, 3*s.* 6*d.*
 Eight Cousins. By L. M. ALCOTT. 2*s.*; cloth gilt, 3*s.* 6*d.*
 Under the Lilacs. By L. M. ALCOTT. 2*s.*; also 3*s.* 6*d.*
 Undiscovered Country. By W. D. HOWELLS.
 Clients of Dr. Bernagius. By L. BIART. 2 parts.
 Silver Pitchers. By LOUISA M. ALCOTT. Cloth, 3*s.* 6*d.*
 Jimmy's Cruise in the "Pinafore," and other Tales. By
  LOUISA M. ALCOTT. 2*s.*; cloth gilt, 3*s.* 6*d.*
 Jack and Jill. By LOUISA M. ALCOTT. 2*s.*; Illustrated, 5*s.*
 Hitherto. By the Author of the "Gayworthys." 2 vols., 1*s.* each;
  1 vol., cloth gilt, 3*s.* 6*d.*
 A Gentleman of Leisure. A Novel. By EDGAR FAWCETT. 1*s.*

Ross (*Mars*) *and Stonehewer Cooper. Highlands of Cantabria;*
 or, Three Days from England. Illustrations and Map, 8vo, 21*s.*

Rothschilds, the Financial Rulers of Nations. By JOHN
 REEVES. Crown 8vo, 7*s.* 6*d.*

Rousselet (*Louis*) *Son of the Constable of France.* Small post
 8vo, numerous Illustrations, gilt edges, 3*s.* 6*d.*; plainer, 2*s.* 6*d.*

—— *King of the Tigers: a Story of Central India.* Illustrated. Small post 8vo, gilt, 3*s.* 6*d.*; plainer, 2*s.* 6*d.*

—— *Drummer Boy.* Illustrated. Small post 8vo, gilt
 edges, 3*s.* 6*d.*; plainer, 2*s.* 6*d.*

Russell (*Dora*) *Strange Message.* 3 vols., crown 8vo, 31*s.* 6*d.*

Russell (*W. Clark*) *Jack's Courtship.* New Ed., small post
 8vo, 6*s.*

—— *English Channel Ports and the Estate of the East*
 and West India Dock Company. Crown 8vo, 1*s.*

—— *Frozen Pirate.* New Ed., Illust., small post 8vo, 6*s.*

—— *Sailor's Language.* Illustrated. Crown 8vo, 3*s.* 6*d.*

—— *Sea Queen.* New Ed., small post 8vo, 6*s.*

—— *Strange Voyage.* New Ed., small post 8vo, 6*s.*

—— *The Lady Maud.* New Ed., small post 8vo, 6*s.*

—— *Wreck of the Grosvenor.* Small post 8vo, 6*s.* 4to,
 sewed, 6*d.*

*S*AINTS *and their Symbols: A Companion in the Churches*
 and Picture Galleries of Europe. Illustrated. Royal 16mo, 3*s.* 6*d.*

Samuels (*Capt. J. S.*) *From Forecastle to Cabin: Autobiography.*
 Illustrated. Crown 8vo, 8*s.* 6*d.*; also with fewer Illustrations, cloth.
 2*s.*; paper, 1*s.*

Sandlands (*J. P.*) *How to Develop Vocal Power.* 1*s.*

Saunders (A.) Our Domestic Birds: Poultry in England and New Zealand. Crown 8vo, 6s.

—— *Our Horses: the Best Muscles controlled by the Best* Brains. 6s.

Scherr (Prof. J.) History of English Literature. Cr. 8vo, 8s. 6d.

Schley. Rescue of Greely. Maps and Illustrations, 8vo, 12s. 6d.

Schuyler (Eugène) American Diplomacy and the Furtherance of Commerce. 12s. 6d.

—— *The Life of Peter the Great.* 2 vols., 8vo, 32s.

Schweinfurth (Georg) Heart of Africa. 2 vols., crown 8vo, 15s.

Scott (Leader) Renaissance of Art in Italy. 4to, 31s. 6d.

—— *Sculpture, Renaissance and Modern.* 5s.

Semmes (Adm. Raphael) Service Afloat: The " Sumter " and the " Alabama." Illustrated. Royal 8vo, 16s.

Senior (W.) Near and Far: an Angler's Sketches of Home Sport and Colonial Life. Crown 8vo, 6s.

—— *Waterside Sketches.* Imp. 32mo, 1s. 6d.; boards, 1s.

Shakespeare. Edited by R. GRANT WHITE. 3 vols., crown 8vo, gilt top, 36s.; *édition de luxe,* 6 vols., 8vo, cloth extra, 63s.

—— See also CUNDALL, DETHRONING, DONNELLY, MACKAY, and WHITE (R. GRANT).

Shakespeare's Heroines: Studies by Living English Painters. 105s.; artists' proofs, 630s.

—— *Songs and Sonnets.* Illust. by Sir JOHN GILBERT, R.A. 4to, boards, 5s.

Sharpe (R. Bowdler) Birds in Nature. 39 coloured plates and text. 4to, 63s.

Sidney (Sir Philip) Arcadia. New Edition, 6s.

Siegfried, The Story of. Illustrated, crown 8vo, cloth, 6s.

Simon. China: its Social Life. Crown 8vo, 6s.

Simson (A.) Wilds of Ecuador and Exploration of the Putumayor River. Crown 8vo, 8s. 6d.

Sinclair (Mrs.) Indigenous Flowers of the Hawaiian Islands. 44 Plates in Colour. Imp. folio, extra binding, gilt edges, 31s. 6d.

Sloane (T. O.) Home Experiments in Science for Old and Young. Crown 8vo, 6s.

Smith (G.) Assyrian Explorations. Illust. New Ed , 8vo, 18s.

—— *The Chaldean Account of Genesis.* With many Illustrations. 16s. New Ed. By PROFESSOR SAYCE. 8vo, 18s.

Smith (G. Barnett) William I. and the German Empire. New Ed., 8vo, 3s. 6d.

Smith (J. Moyr) Wooing of Æthra. Illustrated. 32mo, 1s.

Smith (Sydney) Life and Times. By STUART J. REID. Illustrated. 8vo, 21*s.*

Smith (W. R.) Laws concerning Public Health. 8vo, 31*s.* 6*d.*

Spiers' French Dictionary. 29th Edition, remodelled. 2 vols., 8vo, 18*s.*; half bound, 21*s.*

Spry (W. J. J., R.N., F.R.G.S.) Cruise of H.M.S. " Challenger." With Illustrations. 8vo, 18*s.* Cheap Edit., crown 8vo, 7*s.* 6*d.*

Spyri (Joh.) Heidi's Early Experiences : a Story for Children and those who love Children. Illustrated, small post 8vo, 4*s.* 6*d.*

———— *Heidi's Further Experiences.* Illust., sm. post 8vo, 4*s.* 6*d.*

Stanley (H. M.) Congo, and Founding its Free State. Illustrated, 2 vols., 8vo, 42*s.* ; re-issue, 2 vols. 8vo, 21*s.*

———— *How I Found Livingstone.* 8vo, 10*s.* 6*d.* ; cr. 8vo, 7*s.* 6*d.*

———— *Through the Dark Continent.* Crown 8vo, 12*s.* 6*d.*

Start (J. W. K.) Junior Mensuration Exercises. 8*d.*

Stenhouse (Mrs.) Tyranny of Mormonism. An Englishwoman in Utah. New ed., cr. 8vo, cloth elegant, 3*s.* 6*d.*

Sterry (J. Ashby) Cucumber Chronicles. 5*s.*

Stevens (E. W.) Fly-Fishing in Maine Lakes. 8*s.* 6*d.*

Stevens (T.) Around the World on a Bicycle. Vol. II. 8vo. 16*s.*

Stockton (Frank R.) Rudder Grange. 3*s.* 6*d.*

———— *Bee-Man of Orn, and other Fanciful Tales.* Cr. 8vo, 5*s.*

———— *The Casting Away of Mrs. Lecks and Mrs. Aleshine.* 1*s.*

———— *The Dusantes.* Sequel to the above. Sewed, 1*s.*; this and the preceding book in one volume, cloth, 2*s.* 6*d.*

———— *The Hundredth Man.* Small post 8vo, 6*s.*

———— *The Late Mrs. Null.* Small post 8vo, 6*s.*

———— *The Story of Viteau.* Illust. Cr. 8vo, 5*s.*

———— See also Low's STANDARD NOVELS.

Stoker (Bram) Under the Sunset. Crown 8vo, 6*s.*

Storer (Professor F. H.) Agriculture in its Relations to Chemistry. 2 vols., 8vo, 25*s.*

Stowe (Mrs. Beecher) Dred. Cloth, gilt edges, 3*s.* 6*d.*; cloth, 2*s.*

———— *Flowers and Fruit from her Writings.* Sm. post 8vo, 3*s.* 6*d*.

———— *Little Foxes.* Cheap Ed., 1*s.*; Library Edition, 4*s.* 6*d.*

———— *My Wife and I.* Cloth, 2*s.*

Stowe (Mrs. Beecher) Old Town Folk.   **6s.**

———— *We and our Neighbours.*   **2s.**

———— *Poganuc People.*   **6s.**

———— See also ROSE LIBRARY.

Strachan (J.) Explorations and Adventures in New Guinea.
Illust., crown 8vo, 12s.

Stuttfield (Hugh E. M.) El Maghreb : 1200 Miles' Ride through
Marocco. 8s. 6d.

Sullivan (A. M.) Nutshell History of Ireland. Paper boards, 6d.

TAINE (H. A.) " Origines." Translated by JOHN DURAND.
    I.   **The Ancient Regime.** Demy 8vo, cloth, 16s.
    II. **The French Revolution.** Vol. **1.**   do.
    III.   **Do.**   do.   **Vol. 2.**   do.
    IV.   **Do.**   do.   **Vol. 3.**   do.

Tauchnitz's English Editions of German Authors. Each
volume, cloth flexible, 2s. ; or sewed, 1s. 6d. (Catalogues post free.)

Tauchnitz (B.) German Dictionary.   2s.; paper, 1s. 6d.; roan,
2s. 6d.

———— *French Dictionary.*   2s.; paper, 1s. 6d.; roan, 2s. 6d.

———— *Italian Dictionary.*   2s.; paper, 1s. 6d.; roan, 2s. 6d.

———— *Latin Dictionary.*   2s.; paper, 1s. 6d.; roan, 2s. 6d.

———— *Spanish and English.*   2s.; paper, 1s. 6d.; roan, 2s. 6d.

———— *Spanish and French.*   2s.; paper, 1s. 6d.; roan, 2s. 6d.

Taylor (R. L.) Chemical Analysis Tables.   1s.

———— *Chemistry for Beginners.* Small 8vo, 1s. 6d.

Techno-Chemical Receipt Book.   With additions by BRANNT
and WAHL. 10s. 6d.

Technological Dictionary.   See TOLHAUSEN.

Thausing (Prof.) Malt and the Fabrication of Beer. 8vo, 45s.

Theakston (M.) British Angling Flies. Illustrated. Cr. 8vo, 5s.

Thomson (Jos.) Central African Lakes. New edition, 2 vols.
in one, crown 8vo, 7s. 6d.

———— *Through Masai Land.* Illust. **21s.**; new edition, 7s. 6d.

———— *and Miss Harris-Smith.* *Ulu: an African Romance.*
crown 8vo, 6s.

Thomson (W.) Algebra for Colleges and Schools. With Answers, 5*s.* ; without, 4*s.* 6*d.* ; Answers separate, 1*s.* 6*d*

Tolhausen. Technological German, English, and French Dictionary. Vols. I., II., with Supplement, 12*s.* 6*d.* each ; III., 9*s.* ; Supplement, cr. 8vo, 3*s.* 6*d.*

Tromholt (S.) Under the Rays of the Aurora Borealis. By C. SIEWERS. Photographs and Portraits. 2 vols., 8vo, 30*s.*

Tucker (W. J.) Life and Society in Eastern Europe. 15*s.*

Tupper (Martin Farquhar) My Life as an Author. 14*s.*

Turner (Edward) Studies in Russian Literature. Cr. 8vo, 8*s.* 6*d.*

*U*PTON *(H.) Manual of Practical Dairy Farming.* Cr. 8vo, 2*s.*

*V*AN DAM. *Land of Rubens ; a companion for visitors to* Belgium. See HUET.

Vane (Denzil) From the Dead. A Romance. 2 vols., cr. 8vo, 12*s.*

Vane (Sir Harry Young). By Prof. JAMES K. HOSMER. 8vo, 18*s.*

Veres. Biography of Sir Francis Vere and Lord Vere, leading Generals in the Netherlands. By CLEMENTS R. MARKHAM. 8vo, 18*s.*

Victoria (Queen) Life of. By GRACE GREENWOOD. Illust. 6*s.*

Vincent (Mrs. Howard) Forty Thousand Miles over Land and Water. With Illustrations. New Edit., 3*s.* 6*d.*

Viollet-le-Duc (E.) Lectures on Architecture. Translated by BENJAMIN BUCKNALL, Architect. 2 vols., super-royal 8vo, £3 3*s.*

*W*AKEFIELD. *Aix-les-Bains : Bathing and Attractions.* 2*s.* 6*d.*

Walford (Mrs. L. B.) Her Great Idea, and other Stories. Cr. 8vo, 10*s.* 6*d.*

Wallace (L.) Ben Hur : A Tale of the Christ. New Edition, crown 8vo, 6*s.* ; cheaper edition, 2*s.*

Waller (Rev. C. H.) The Names on the Gates of Pearl, and other Studies. New Edition. Crown 8vo, cloth extra, 3*s.* 6*d.*

—— *Words in the Greek Testament.* Part I. Grammar. Small post 8vo, cloth, 2*s.* 6*d.* Part II. Vocabulary, 2*s.* 6*d.*

WORKS.	Containing 350 to 600 pp. and from 50 to 100 full-page illustrations.		Containing the whole of the text with some illustrations.	
	In very handsome cloth binding, gilt edges.	In plainer binding, plain edges.	In cloth binding, gilt edges, smaller type.	Coloured boards.
	s. d.	s. d.	s. d.	
20,000 Leagues under the Sea. Parts I. and II.	10 6	5 0	3 6	2 vols., 1s. each.
Hector Servadac	10 6	5 0	3 6	2 vols., 1s. each.
The Fur Country	10 6	5 0	3 6	2 vols., 1s. each.
The Earth to the Moon and a Trip round it	10 6	5 0	2 vols., 2s. ea.	2 vols., 1s. each.
Michael Strogoff	10 6	5 0	3 6	2 vols., 1s. each.
Dick Sands, the Boy Captain	10 6	5 0	3 6	2 vols., 1s. each.
Five Weeks in a Balloon	7 6	3 6	2 0	1s. 0d.
Adventures of Three Englishmen and Three Russians	7 6	3 6	2 0	1 0
Round the World in Eighty Days	7 6	3 6	2 0	1 0
A Floating City	7 6	3 6	2 0	1 0
The Blockade Runners			2 0	1 0
Dr. Ox's Experiment	—	—	2 0	1 0
A Winter amid the Ice	—	—	2 0	1 0
Survivors of the "Chancellor"	7 6	3 6	3 6	2 vols., 1s. each.
Martin Paz			2 0	1s. 0d.
The Mysterious Island, 3 vols.:—	22 6	10 6	6 0	3 0
I. Dropped from the Clouds	7 6	3 6	2 0	1 0
II. Abandoned	7 6	3 6	2 0	1 0
III. Secret of the Island	7 6	3 6	2 0	1 0
The Child of the Cavern	7 6	3 6	2 0	1 0
The Begum's Fortune	7 6	3 6	2 0	1 0
The Tribulations of a Chinaman	7 6	3 6	2 0	1 0
The Steam House, 2 vols.:—				
I. Demon of Cawnpore	7 6	3 6	2 0	1 0
II. Tigers and Traitors	7 6	3 6	2 0	1 0
The Giant Raft, 2 vols.:—				
I. 800 Leagues on the Amazon	7 6	3 6	2 0	1 0
II. The Cryptogram	7 6	3 6	2 0	1 0
The Green Ray	6 0	5 0	—	1 0
Godfrey Morgan	7 6	3 6	2 0	1 0
Kéraban the Inflexible:—				
I. Captain of the "Guidara"	7 6	3 6	2 0	1 0
II. Scarpante the Spy	7 6	3 6	2 0	1 0
The Archipelago on Fire	7 6	3 6	2 0	1 0
The Vanished Diamond	7 6	3 6	2 0	1 0
Mathias Sandorf	10 6	5 0		
The Lottery Ticket	7 6			
Clipper of the Clouds	7 6			
North against South	7 6			
Adrift in the Pacific	7 6			
Flight to France	7 6			

CELEBRATED TRAVELS AND TRAVELLERS. 3 vols., 8vo, 600 pp., 100 full-page illustrations, 12s. 6d.; gilt edges, 14s. each :—(1) THE EXPLORATION OF THE WORLD. (2) THE GREAT NAVIGATORS OF THE EIGHTEENTH CENTURY. (3) THE GREAT EXPLORERS OF THE NINETEENTH CENTURY.

Waller (*Rev. C.H.*) *Adoption and the Covenant.* On Confirmation. 2s. 6d.

—————— *Silver Sockets ; and other Shadows of Redemption.* Sermons at Christ Church, Hampstead. Small post 8vo, 6s.

Walsh (*A.S.*) *Mary, Queen of the House of David.* 8vo, 3s. 6d.

Walton (*Iz.*) *Wallet Book*, CIƆIƆLXXXV. Crown 8vo, half vellum, 21s. ; large paper, 42s.

—————— *Compleat Angler.* Lea and Dove Edition. Ed. by R. B. MARSTON. With full-page Photogravures on India paper, and the Woodcuts on India paper from blocks. 4to, half-morocco, 105s.; large paper, royal 4to, full dark green morocco, gilt top, 210s.

Walton (*T. H.*) *Coal Mining.* With Illustrations. 4to, 25s.

Wardrop (*O.*) *Kingdom of Georgia.* Illust. and map. 8vo. 14s.

Warner (*C. D.*) *My Summer in a Garden.* Boards, 1s. ; leatherette, 1s. 6d. ; cloth, 2s.

—————— *Their Pilgrimage.* Illustrated by C. S. REINHART. 8vo, 7s. 6d.

Warren (*W. F.*) *Paradise Found; the North Pole the Cradle* of the Human Race. Illustrated. Crown 8vo, 12s. 6d.

Washington Irving's Little Britain. Square crown 8vo, 6s.

Wells (*H. P.*) *American Salmon Fisherman.* 6s.

—————— *Fly Rods and Fly Tackle.* Illustrated. 10s. 6d.

Wells (*J. W.*) *Three Thousand Miles through Brazil.* Illustrated from Original Sketches. 2 vols. 8vo, 32s.

Wenzel (*O.*) *Directory of Chemical Products of the German* Empire. 8vo, 25s.

White (*R. Grant*) *England Without and Within.* Crown 8vo, 10s. 6d.

—————— *Every-day English.* 10s. 6d.

—————— *Fate of Mansfield Humphreys, &c.* Crown 8vo, 6s.

—————— *Studies in Shakespeare.* 10s. 6d.

—————— *Words and their Uses.* New Edit., crown 8vo, 5s.

Whitney (*Mrs.*) *The Other Girls.* A Sequel to "We Girls." New ed. 12mo, 2s.

—————— *We Girls.* New Edition. 2s.

Whittier (*J. G.*) *The King's Missive, and later Poems.* 18mo, choice parchment cover, 3s. 6d.

—————— *St. Gregory's Guest, &c.* Recent Poems. 5s.

Wilcox (*Marrion*) *Real People.* Sm. post 8vo, 3s. 6d.

—————— *Señora Villena ; and Gray, an Oldhaven Romance.* 2 vols. in one, 6s.

William I. and the German Empire. By G. BARNETT SMITH. New Edition, 3s. 6d.

Willis-Bund (J.) Salmon Problems. 3s. 6d.; boards, 2s. 6d.

Wills (Dr. C. J.) Persia as it is. Crown 8vo, 8s. 6d.

Wills, A Few Hints on Proving, without Professional Assistance. By a PROBATE COURT OFFICIAL. 8th Edition, revised, with Forms of Wills, Residuary Accounts, &c. Fcap. 8vo, cloth limp, 1s.

Wilmot (A.) Poetry of South Africa. Collected and arranged. 8vo, 6s.

Wilson (Dr. Andrew) Health for the People. Cr. 8vo, 7s. 6d.

Winsor (Justin) Narrative and Critical History of America. 8 vols., 30s. each; large paper, per vol., 63s.

Woolsey. Introduction to International Law. 5th Ed., 18s.

Woolson (Constance F.) See "Low's Standard Novels."

Wright (H.) Friendship of God. Portrait, &c. Crown 8vo, 6s.

Wright (T.) Town of Cowper, Olney, &c. 6s.

Written to Order; the Journeyings of an Irresponsible Egotist. By the Author of "A Day of my Life at Eton." Crown 8vo, 6s.

YRIARTE (Charles) Florence: its History. Translated by C. B. PITMAN. Illustrated with 500 Engravings. Large imperial 4to, extra binding, gilt edges, 63s.; or 12 Parts, 5s. each.
History; the Medici; the Humanists; letters; arts; the Renaissance; illustrious Florentines; Etruscan art; monuments; sculpture; painting.

London:

SAMPSON LOW, MARSTON, SEARLE, & RIVINGTON, Ld.,

St. Dunstan's House,

FETTER LANE, FLEET STREET, E.C.

Gilbert and Rivington, Ld., St. John's House, Clerkenwell Road E.C.

CPSIA information can be obtained at www.ICGtesting.com
Printed in the USA
LVOW092326080512

280882LV00015B/151/P